The Torture Letters

The Torture Letters

Reckoning with Police Violence

LAURENCE RALPH

The University of Chicago Press

Chicago and London

The University of Chicago Press, Chicago 60637
The University of Chicago Press, Ltd., London
© 2020 by Laurence Ralph
Published 2020
Printed in the United States of America

29 28 27 26 25 24 23 22 21 20   1 2 3 4 5

ISBN-13: 978-0-226-49053-3 (cloth)
ISBN-13: 978-0-226-65009-8 (paper)
ISBN-13: 978-0-226-72980-0 (e-book)
DOI: https://doi.org/10.7208/chicago/9780226729800.001.0001

Library of Congress Cataloging-in-Publication Data

Names: Ralph, Laurence, author.
Title: The torture letters : reckoning with police violence / Laurence
    Ralph.
Description: Chicago ; London : The University of Chicago Press, 2020. |
    Includes bibliographical references and index.
Identifiers: LCCN 2019005353 | ISBN 9780226490533 (cloth : alk. paper) |
    ISBN 9780226650098 (pbk : alk. paper) | ISBN 9780226729800 (e-book)
Subjects: LCSH: Police brutality—Illinois—Chicago. | African
    Americans—Violence against—United States. | Torture—United States.
Classification: LCC HV8148.C52 R35 2019 | DDC 363.25/4—dc23
LC record available at https://lccn.loc.gov/2019005353

♾ This paper meets the requirements of ANSI/NISO Z39.48-1992
(Permanence of Paper).

Contents

Southern trees bear strange fruit
Blood on the leaves and blood at the root
Black bodies swinging in the southern breeze
Strange fruit hanging from the poplar trees

WRITTEN BY ABEL MEERPOOL (1937),
SUNG BY BILLIE HOLIDAY (1939)

Once the classic method of lynching was the rope.
Now it is the policeman's bullet.

WILLIAM PATTERSON, *CIVIL RIGHTS
CONGRESS* (1951)

Prologue:
A Half Century of Torture

Here are the facts: between 1972 and 1991, approximately 125 African American suspects were tortured by police officers in Chicago.[1] The means of torture were numerous, but they all were conducted at Chicago's Area 2 detective headquarters, which used to be located at 91st Street and Cottage Grove Avenue.[2] Beyond these verified instances, in 2003 journalists documented other episodes of torture before and after these dates, and elsewhere in the city, placing the total number of survivors of police torture in Chicago at roughly two hundred.

The numbers themselves are astounding enough, but they offer only the surface of this horror. Even now, after researching the topic of police torture for fourteen years, the reality is hard to grasp but impossible to doubt: For almost a half century, over and over and over again, police officers who took an oath to protect and serve the residents of Chicago have instead done the opposite. They have beaten residents of Chicago. They have electrocuted residents of Chicago. They have tied residents of Chicago to radiators and left them there for hours. They have suffocated them with typewriter covers and plastic bags. They have raped them.

The scope of the problem is so vast that, after decades of denial and avoidance, in 2009, the state government created the Illinois Torture Inquiry and Relief Commission. Although it was founded in the hopes of bringing to a close this aspect of Chicago's past, the commission has done the opposite. Today it investigates the claims of anyone in Chicago convicted by confessions allegedly coerced through torture. So far, more than four hundred cases are pending investigation. But the commission has the resources to investigate only sixteen cases per year. At this rate, Duaa Eldeib, of the *Chicago Tribune*, calculated in October 2016 that "the Commission would need more than 23 years to make it through the cases currently before them."[3] That figure does not take into account the three to five new torture claims the commission still receives each week.

• • •

Despite the ongoing nature of the problem, this book takes the criminal suspects who were systematically subject to sadism in the 1980s and 1990s as its point of departure. They ignited what is widely known today as the Chicago police torture scandal. With some rare exceptions, all the torture survivors were men, and Black men in particular.[4] Overwhelming evidence suggests that multiple generations of police have systematically targeted Black men, making this the story not just of police brutality but also—as excessive policing so often is—of institutional racism. The reality of institutional racism and the circumstances that led to police torture all those years ago remain largely unchanged. As a result, police torture is very much an ongoing problem, as relevant today as it was when the first allegations of torture surfaced in 1982, prompting lawyers to dig deeper and find out that systematic torture in Chicago's precincts had begun at least a decade earlier.

As we'll see, police torture in Chicago is built on a contradiction: the existence of torture is, of course, a secret, and yet it is a secret that everyone seems to know about. Thus, we can understand police torture—and hope to change the circumstances that allowed it to happen—only if we understand it as the "open secret" that it is.

"It goes beyond just the police department," said Flint Taylor, the lawyer who has tried many of the police torture cases in Chicago.

When I interviewed him in the summer of 2017, Taylor said that the open secret extends to judges as well, because many of them were former prosecutors who "worked hand in glove with the cops" for convictions. They were in those station houses when the confessions were being taken, Taylor said. What's more, some of the prosecutors were former police officers themselves. "There's a web that starts with suspected criminals on the streets and it ends with some of the most powerful people in the city," Taylor said. He uttered these words at the end of an hour-long conversation in which he described the complex network that connected cops to judges to prosecutors to politicians. "That web," he said, "is a major roadblock to the truth in these cases."

I have spent more than a decade trying to figure out what this truth consists of. What is police torture? Why do certain officers commit horrific acts in the name of justice? And what can we do about it? In pursuit of the truth about police torture, this book explores the "web" that Taylor describes. I show that many people who work for the city of Chicago—whether serving on the police force, or in the legal system, or in the city and state government—have chosen to remain silent about torture because of this delicate tangle of connections. They have wanted to avoid risking their careers, their safety, and, in some cases, their lives. Those who stayed quiet also became masters at looking the other way.

The open secret is what people in power know but refuse to say about police torture. And it is why in writing this book, I have often felt discouraged. If justice had been denied torture survivors for so many decades, if so many powerful people were in on the secret, I have often worried that nothing I wrote would be meaningful. Eventually, I came to understand that the true goal of my research was less about exposing police torture than investigating the openness of the secret. Why have so many powerful and influential people in Chicago been unwilling to publicly acknowledge acts of extrajudicial police force such as torture?[5]

Torture is a practice that people in power have long done against "the other"—and that "other" has been defined in various ways throughout US history. For most of US history, Black people have been the most obvious "other" in what Michelle Alexander has called a "racial caste system." Within this system, those at the bottom tend to be Black, and they are the farthest away from the privileges and protections that the country gives to the white people at the top. Because Blacks, brought to this country as enslaved people, have occupied the lower rung of this social order for so long, torture has always been an essential element of the African American experience. This is why racial violence is another major focus of this book. The open secret of police torture reveals important lessons about the relationship between torture and racism in this country.

In *The Condemnation of Blackness*, for instance, historian Khalil Gibran Muhammad notes that, since the 1600s, and the dawn of American slavery, Black people have been viewed as potential criminal threats to US society.[6] As enslaved people were considered legal property, to run away was, by definition, a criminal act. From there, it wasn't much of a leap to link Blackness to criminality. Unlike other racial, religious, or ethnic groups, whose crime rates were commonly attributed to social conditions and structures, Black people were (and are) considered inherently prone to criminality. For many years, this link was thought to be biological; now, it is considered a cultural eventuality. But however one explains the link, Muhammad argues that equating Blackness and criminality is part of America's cultural DNA.

The tendency of white Americans to view Blacks as criminals helps us better understand the phenomenon of police torture. To paraphrase one police officer discussing the Black people he arrested on suspicion of crimes, even if the suspects had done nothing wrong at that particular time, you could be sure that they either had done something for which they *should* have been arrested in the past or would do something wrong in the future. They were always guilty of some crime because they were Black.[7]

If these assumptions are encoded in our cultural DNA, as Muhammad suggests—and I agree with him—then the City of Chicago's preferred method of dealing with police torture (i.e., compensating

torture survivors with million-dollar payouts) will not solve the problem of police violence.[8] At the very least, addressing this concern will
require a willingness to interrogate why this country's commitment
to the principle that a person is innocent until proven guilty, one of
the fundamental ideals of the US justice system, has never been fully
extended to Blacks. Chicago is my case study to explore a broader
national and transnational problem that should concern us all. This
global concern is that, as agents of the state, police officers and military personnel kill and debilitate vulnerable people in ways that are
systematic and thus predictable. And yet, precisely because they are
agents of the state, they rarely face repercussions for the crimes they
commit and the generational trauma they inflict.[9]

The history of Chicago police torture that I tell begins with the
Black men who were suffocated and shocked and violated and humiliated at Area 2. Sometimes the officers at Area 2 tortured suspects
after they confessed to crimes as a form of punishment. Other times,
they tortured them to elicit a confession, as happened to Andrew
Wilson, who became the first person to file a civil suit against the
City of Chicago for the crime of torture. These men endured beatings,
"baggings" (in which police officers suffocate criminal suspects with
plastic bags), and sometimes much worse.

Many of these torture survivors were eventually exonerated. Some
received monetary settlements as recompense for their torture and
confinement. But their exoneration should not reaffirm our faith in the
law—quite the contrary. Instead, we might wonder how many others
have been wrongly imprisoned because of confessions extracted by
torture. How many will never achieve the redemption that a few lucky
exceptions did?

Judge Joan Lefkow, who presided over the trial of the disgraced
and recently deceased police commander Jon Burge, one of Chicago's
most infamous torturers, argued that "when a confession is coerced,
the truth of the confession is called into question. When this becomes
widespread, as one can infer from the accounts that have been presented here in this court, the administration of justice is undermined
irreparably."[10] But how can torture undermine the basis of the legal

system when this system has always allowed police officers to kill and torture vulnerable people without sanction?

Of course, the vulnerable populations that are susceptible to torture are not exclusively Black. Even though race is a favored way of establishing "the other" in the United States, in recent decades religion has been another prominent way of creating a threat that is necessary to justify torture, particularly after the war on terror.

In the winter of 2016, while I was in the throes of this research project, Donald Trump, the forty-fifth president of the United States, clarified his position on torture. He did so during his first interview after being elected. Speaking of the group known as the Islamic State in Iraq and Syria (ISIS), Trump said: "When they're shooting—when they're chopping off the heads of our people and other people, when they're chopping off the heads of people because they happen to be a Christian in the Middle East, when ISIS is doing things that nobody has ever heard of since medieval times, would I feel strongly about waterboarding? As far as I'm concerned, we have to fight fire with fire."

Trump followed this comment with the claim that he had recently "spoken . . . with people at the highest level of intelligence," by which, I assume, he meant high-ranking US military officials. According to Trump, these military officials told him that techniques of torture, such as waterboarding, do, in fact, "work."

Trump's statements on torture may strike us as banal, especially given the sheer exhaustion of the twenty-four-hour news cycle in the United States. We have become so used to this president making one racist, Islamophobic, and otherwise-xenophobic statement after another that his comments on torture may barely even register. But it is important to realize that the idea of torture as a necessary evil in an increasingly dangerous world is consistent with George W. Bush's CIA torture program, and even with the way Muslims were targeted for detention and unjustly detained at black sites like Guantánamo Bay during Barack Obama's time in office.

The recent history of torture during the war on terror tells us a great deal about what this country views as a threat, who our society fears, and how much society is willing to compromise its ideals to defend itself against that threat. Being considered the enemy, and then being purposefully tormented because of that—this is what connects all the survivors of torture in my book, from the Black Chicagoans I discuss to a Guantánamo detainee named Mohamedou Ould Slahi.

Slahi's interrogators stripped him, blindfolded him, and diapered him, before subjecting him to extreme isolation; physical, psychological, and sexual humiliation; death threats and threats to his family; and mock kidnapping and rendition, by which I am referring to the practice of sending terrorist suspects to countries that do not have any legal obligations to treat prisoners humanely. In a comparable way, we know that police officers in Chicago bagged a Black man named Andrew Wilson, beat him, and electrocuted him before torturing his brother, Jackie, who was arrested at the same time as he was. And yet it is not so much these techniques of torture that I focus on in this book. It is the justification by police, politicians, and the courts that rationalizes their use.

Time and time again over the course of this book, as police or military officers torture suspects, their racist and Islamophobic assumptions about suspects become self-fulfilling prophecy. Torture produces tainted knowledge that confirms a police or military officer's contempt not just for the criminal but also for the social group to which the supposed criminal belongs. Slahi might seem a strange person to include in a book about torture committed against Black people in Chicago. But as we will see, the torture of a suspected drug dealer in the Midwest is intimately linked to the torture of a suspected terrorist half a world away.

The central themes of this book are twofold: torture persists in Chicago because of the complicity of people in power, and it persists in the United States because of our history of violence against populations we perceive as threatening to us. These twinned ideas come together in the image of the torture tree.

In this book, the *torture tree* references the words Billie Holiday crooned, painfully and deliberately, in "Strange Fruit," a song recorded in the same year that Germany united with the Soviet Union to invade Poland, igniting a world war. Of the "Black bodies swinging in the southern breeze," she sang:

> Here is fruit for the crows to pluck
> For the rain to gather, for the wind to suck
> For the sun to rot, for the trees to drop
> Here is a strange and bitter crop

In this song, the dead Black bodies swaying in the wind seem "strange" when compared to what a healthy tree would sprout. Holiday tells us that soil fertilized with racism and hate naturally yields a rotten and "bitter" harvest. Of course, lynching can be distinguished from torture by the fact that the practice was often perpetrated by vigilante figures or angry mobs who took the law into their own hands when they strung up and hung Black people from trees. By contrast, the severe pain and suffering that defines torture—well, at least by the United Nations definition that I subscribe to in this book—must be "inflicted by or with the consent of a public official," such as a police officer.[11] Still, aside from this important distinction, there are some equally significant similarities. Both lynching and torture are forms of extrajudicial violence that demonstrate the victim's position within society's racial caste system. And thus, whether in the Jim Crow South of the early 1900s or on the South Side of Chicago today, these violent practices of punishment attest to a contempt not merely for the crime a person is accused of committing but also for the criminal. In short, these practices manifest the racism that is still prevalent in US society.

The metaphor of the torture tree also helps me explain several significant themes related to the contempt and the assumed guilt of the supposed criminal. Later in this book, we will see how the torture tree is rooted in our country's investment in fear—an investment that is political, financial, and psychological—which maintains the enduring racial caste system in the United States. Its trunk is the mistreatment, harassment, torture, and death that stems from the current system of law and order, a system that injures and kills Black people at disproportionate rates as compared to white Americans. Just follow the branches to find the police and military officers connected to the aforementioned spectrum of violence that too often starts at mistreatment and ends in death. And finally, through this analogy, I show how and why the torture tree's leaves come to represent everyday acts of police violence.

To be clear, in describing the violence and suffering associated with this tree, I use the word *torture* carefully. In the field of African American studies, there is a huge debate about whether scholars should talk explicitly about this type of violence and pain. The danger is that such descriptions can titillate readers and contribute to what Karen Sánchez-Eppler calls the "pornography of violence."[12] Even when these descriptions are used toward a greater good—as when slave abolitionists used them to demonstrate the horrors of a corrupt system—the way Black people are put on display can make their inferior state seem impossible to overcome. For some important thinkers, describing torture in vivid detail can do more harm than good.

Still, I have decided to describe torture in this book when appropriate. There are many reasons for this choice. First, the torture survivors whom I spoke with wanted the public to know that they were not just "roughed up." They were not just mistreated. What happened to them was horrifying. The suffering they endured was something that no human should be made to experience. Second, that suffering was worsened by the fact that the rest of us didn't see it. For so long—for decades, in fact—the details of their torture were not believed. Had they not testified about torture from the witness stand, under oath, the torture survivors might never have found one another. When these survivors described the particular instruments used on them, what they looked like, how they felt, what kind of marks they left on their flesh, they transformed the morbid details of torture into evidence. This evidence, in turn, made it possible for other torture survivors to say, "I have been tortured too" or "The same thing happened to me."

Indeed, the specificity of detail—horrifying as that detail often is—has been crucial to revealing the extent of torture. Not only has court testimony allowed survivors to find one another; investigative journalists over the past two decades especially have used that testimony to slowly identify the branches of this tree. It was through detailed and specific descriptions that investigative journalists have been able to reveal the truth of police torture. After a long struggle, so has the Illinois judicial system and the Chicago city government. But even among those aware of Chicago's decades-long scandal, there is almost no understanding of how deeply the roots are embedded in the institutions of government. Nor has there been a research study concerned with how Chicago residents are coping with the history and ongoing threat that the torture tree represents. That is, until now.

Research for *The Torture Letters* began in the spring of 2007, and it consisted, at first, of a single obsession. That obsession was poring over transcripts of police torture cases in Chicago. I created a list of anyone who had sued the City of Chicago on the basis of having been tortured, and I was determined to read about how they described torture in their own words. To come up with this list, I looked at old newspaper articles and cross-referenced the names there with reports on police torture that the city had released over the years, the oldest of which was the Goldston Report from 1990. I found that Black people in Chicago had been claiming that they had been tortured long before that report was published. They continued to make these claims in the late 2000s, when I started this research in earnest, and those claims continue until today.

But I did not draw my conclusions only from reports on torture and court testimony. Over the course of my research, I talked to lawyers such as Flint Taylor who have tried torture cases, I went to rallies and heard torture survivors speak about what they endured, and I interviewed activists who have worked to bring attention to the scandal of police torture. I amassed reams of files consisting of court proceedings and interviews I had conducted with lawyers, torture survivors, and activists. Still, I felt that the book was missing something. What it was missing, I eventually realized, was what everyday Chicagoans thought about this history of torture. Did the scandal of police torture relate to their everyday lives?

To answer this question, I organized group discussions (which I called focus groups) that consisted of eight to ten people as well as one-on-one interviews with Chicago residents. My criteria were that participants had to be interested in learning about the history of police torture (if they didn't already know about it), and they had to be willing to share their own experiences with the police, whether good or bad, and even if those encounters seemed unremarkable to them. As it turned out, these criteria were broad enough to attract more than one hundred curious and engaged Chicagoans. They came from all parts of the city—from the South Side to the East Side, and from the North Side to the West Side. They ranged in age from fourteen to fifty-one years old. They were Black, white, Asian, and Latino.

Speaking with such a diverse group of Chicagoans has obvious benefits, but also some disadvantages. One reward is that I had access to multiple perspectives on a complex issue. As a researcher, I am always intrigued by the prospect that people's interpretations can add nuance to the way I have been thinking about a given issue. And as a writer, I am also interested in listening to people voice their concerns. Doing so makes my work more accessible—something that's always been important to me. But there is a significant downside to this approach. Having such a diverse group, with such different experiences, makes it hard to organize a group discussion. Once such an event is organized, it can easily go off the rails.

As a way to address this problem, I came up with an idea. I decided to use some of the material I came across during the course of doing research as starting points—icebreakers, if you will—to structure my focus groups. The first part of a typical focus group began with court testimony from a torture case. By sharing and discussing court testimony and statements from police officers who had knowledge of the scandal, I could usually tell what people already knew about police torture. I organized the next part of the focus-group discussion around a newspaper article that described how criminal suspects were systematically tormented while in police custody. I found that such media reports typically prompted people to discuss how victims of police violence were portrayed, and whether or not they agreed with that portrayal. Finally, I ended the focus groups by sharing one of two letters I had written, which discussed how I became aware of the phenomena of police torture. One draft open letter was to Black youth in Chicago, and the other was to the superintendent of the Chicago Police Department, Eddie Johnson. Both letters had the effect of eliciting discussion about who was responsible for inflicting pain on criminal suspects in the city.

I shared these letters for a particular reason: I wanted Chicago residents to get a sense of my perspective, my voice. Having facilitated these kinds of groups for previous research projects, I knew that most of the discussion would take place between the participants. I inserted myself into the conversation only when the discussion had stalled, or to change topics, or to keep track of time. But I wanted to create space to test my own assumptions about how I was thinking about the issue. And I'm glad I did. Chicagoans injected a much-needed dose of nuance into my thinking about police torture. From them, I learned that I could not talk about police torture in isolation. For Chicagoans, torture was uniquely horrible, but it was never unique. Chicagoans could not talk about torture without talking about all the other things that they experienced at the hands of the police. It was in speaking with Chicago residents that I really understood, for the first time, something that I had read about in the police department's manual but never really had a sense of: the *use-of-force continuum*. This refers to the guidelines that the police are supposed to abide by when determining how much force to deploy during an encounter with a civilian.

Chicago police are required to de-escalate situations, whenever possible, to reduce the need for them to use force. If police officers confront someone who is agitated, they are trained to reason with that person and persuade him or her to calm down. If that person is not harming anyone, then police can allow the person to cool off for a certain period of time. Or if someone has a history of mental illness, the police can call on a crisis-intervention team to assist in making the arrest.

Police officers, in fact, are *required* to make their way through "all reasonable alternatives" before deploying force.[13] According to the Chicago Police Department's 2017 policy on the use of force: "The use of deadly force is a last resort that is permissible only when necessary to protect against an imminent threat to life or to prevent great bodily harm to the member [of the police force] or another person."[14]

But how, you may be wondering, do police officers navigate the terrain between de-escalation techniques and deadly force? Here's where the use-of-force continuum comes in: it defines the types of force that police can use to respond to specific types of resistance. If a civilian is threatening someone verbally, the officer is permitted to physically restrain that person; if the person takes out a knife, the officer is permitted to take out his or her gun. The police think of this continuum as a staircase on which they are permitted to always be one step ahead of the individual in deploying force. In other words, police are permitted to escalate force depending on an offender's behavior as well as the threat the offender poses.

In reality, though, many Black Chicagoans feel that the use-of-force continuum is inherently flawed. They argue that because of their skin color, the police judge them as threats prematurely, and then use that prejudice to ascend the staircase too quickly. To add insult to injury, the police often face no consequences whatsoever for their role in escalating violence. They have to state later only that they felt scared. By doing so, police officers are often given the benefit of the doubt and so do not face consequences for injuring or killing residents. Because of this reality, Chicagoans wanted my work to hold police officers accountable for the violence they inflicted. These residents felt that their city was in the midst of a legitimacy crisis and thought that my book should be written for someone who could effect change. The problem was that there was no consensus on whom exactly that "someone" should be.

Some residents mentioned the mayor, others brought up the police officers who had committed torture, a few thought that the governor should be addressed, and others wanted me to write to activists in the hopes that the protests against police violence would continue. The list that research participants came up with was so varied, in fact, that for a long time I thought it was impossible that a single book would be able to address the different constituencies they mentioned. After all, each of the people they mentioned had different skills and training, different knowledge of the issue, and different tools at their disposal to grapple with the problem. How could a single message adequately address them all?

Nevertheless, I could not help but think long and hard about these residents' concerns. I did not want what they told me to just be beneficial to other scholars who theorized torture for a living. I wanted to honor what I had learned from them by embracing their challenge to speak to multiple audiences. Eventually, I would figure out how to write this book in a way that spoke to the various people who my research participants wanted me to address: those who were complicit in torture and those whom the participants felt needed to know about the issue. My solution was to write this book as a series of open letters.

Something occurred to me shortly after I decided to write this book as a compilation of letters: I noticed that letters had been vital to my research all along.

Over the fourteen years I have been working on this project, my office desk had become a repository of piles of letters—letters from torture survivors that had made their way into case files, letters from prisoners to their families, letters from prisoners to their lawyers and to the judges who would rule on torture claims, letters from family members to prisoners, and letters to the media. Indeed, letters were a significant factor in exposing torture in Chicago. An anonymous police insider, who came to be known as "Deep Badge," wrote the letters that escalated the investigation into police torture in 1989. The information Deep Badge provided to lawyers representing Andrew Wilson in his civil suit against the police department was detailed enough to verify the accuracy of what Wilson said. Deep Badge's letters also helped lawyers identify many of the more than fifty police officers involved in the torture operation at Area 2. They also helped track down other torture survivors who could corroborate Wilson's claims. Without them, the mechanics of this operation might still be nothing more than an open secret.

In taking an epistolary approach to unpacking the truth about what happened in Chicago, I also wanted this book to sit within a larger tradition of meditations on racism in the United States, such as James Baldwin's *The Fire Next Time*, Ta-Nehisi Coates's *Between the World and Me*, and, more recently, Danielle Allen's *Cuz*, which use the intimacy of letters to write profound reflections on personal experiences of race and racism.

But to whom does one write?

First, I decided to write to all the future mayors of Chicago, because they will have to grapple with the impact that police torture still has on this city. Then I wrote to Chicago youth of color, because they are the next generation who has to fear violence from the cops and the people whom the torture survivors I spoke to wanted most desperately to address. From there, I decided to focus on public figures, such as the superintendent of the police department and the mayor, because they have to grapple with this history as part of their job. I also wrote to activists working on this issue and to individual torture survivors—addressing those drawn into the terrible orbit of police torture directly. I felt that personal letters would help readers identify with the people being addressed. Torture would become real, I hoped, not just an abstraction happening years ago to an unfortunate, faceless group.

Through letter writing I develop an important critique of our current moment, one that not only exposes injustice but also goes a step farther to indict those responsible. It is important to note that letter writing has always operated as a call to action. The process of writing letters, and (in some cases) receiving responses to these letters, has made apparent—again and again and again—what lies beneath the surface of everyday life: the suppressed consciousness of a history of secrecy and torture in Chicago.

Of the many lessons I learned while writing these letters, chief among them is this: it is not enough to be aware that torture has been committed against the vulnerable and to throw up your hands in horror, as most people of goodwill do. One must also recognize the racism or Islamophobia that made this torture possible and acknowledge how endemic these social problems are. Only then can there be an honest reckoning with police violence and a genuine attempt to question the extent to which the American public is also complicit in perpetuating police torture, both at home and abroad.

Introduction

An Open Letter to All the Future Mayors of Chicago

I'm a researcher who is writing a book on the history of police torture in your city. The more I learn about this history, the more I feel the need to write to you, even though I cannot be certain who exactly you will be. If history is any guide, you—and all other future mayors of Chicago—are likely a well-connected politician who has a cozy relationship with exactly the instruments of government that I am suggesting are most in need of change. But I must write to you anyway because I believe that change is always possible, however unlikely it may seem in the present.

Indeed, you might already be a career politician, comfortably settled into the state capitol, but you might be, at this very moment, a high school student with lots of big and unrealistic ideas. You may be white or Black, Asian or Latino, or you might not identify with any race at all. You may be gay, straight, or have a fluid gender identity. You may become Chicago's mayor five years from now, or maybe twenty-five years. Regardless of who you are and how you find yourself as the public persona of this city, it is my sincerest hope that you want to change the culture that has allowed torture to scandalize the Chicago Police Department.

You likely have been briefed about police torture. Perhaps you have gotten assurances from the superintendent of the police department. You might have even met with survivors of police torture. But what I have found in studying this issue for more than a decade is that its complexities are endless. And thus, a strict historical approach, or a policy-oriented approach, doesn't actually clarify the full extent of the problem. To do that, we need not facts but a metaphor.

The first thing you must know is that the torture tree is firmly planted in your city. Its roots are deep, its trunk sturdy, its branches spread wide, its leaves cast dark shadows.

The torture tree is rooted in an enduring idea of threat that is foundational to life in the United States. Its trunk is the use-of-force continuum. Its branches are the police officers who personify this continuum. And its leaves are everyday incidents of police violence.

• • •

Let's begin with the roots, as they are, so tragically, steeped in fear. For all of our achievements as humans, we are still a species that is ruled by very basic instincts, instincts developed millions of years ago and ones shared by most animals. The most basic of instincts is the desire to keep ourselves alive; thus, we are incredibly attuned to danger, and fear shapes much of our emotional life. Because we are fearful of threats, what we crave—perhaps even more than food or companionship—is a sense of safety.

The very idea of safety in the United States is rooted in the frontier logic that justified the settlement of this country in the 1700s. For the white settlers, safety was premised on viewing Native Americans as threats and so transforming them into "savages." It has long been said, most notably by the historian Frederick Jackson Turner, that the idea of the frontier—the extreme limit of settled land beyond which lies wilderness and danger—stimulated invention and rugged individualism and was therefore an important factor in helping to cultivate a distinctive character among the citizens of the United States. This "traditional" narrative has long celebrated our frontier spirit, but the unspoken shadow of that narrative is the fact that invention and individualism are inseparable from the other thing that happened on the frontier—namely, destroying the other. The "civilized" world believed that it had to beat the savages into submission in order to ensure the future of the white race.

This frontier logic is still prevalent today. It is foundational, in fact, to modern-day policing. We can see it at work when one court after another acquits cops who gun down African Americans under the pretext that those cops felt threatened. In such cases, the violence enacted against Black people works to turn the police officers who actually committed the violence into the victims of those Black people. This is how the tangled and twisted logic of fear became rooted in the security apparatus of the United States. But those roots would likely erode were it not for the financial, political, and psychological investment in fear.

Today this investment takes the form of public funding that grounds, supports, and nourishes this country's enduring logic of threat. Indeed, a key resource that maintains the racial caste system in the United States is the ever-increasing amount of public funding invested in policing and incarcerating people of color. Public funding is the lifeblood of the torture tree. And yet it remains debatable as to whether this funding has made our society any safer—especially for a person of color at the receiving end of police violence. Of the ten most populous cities in the United States, Chicago has the highest number of fatal shootings involving the police from 2010 to 2014.[1] Given that these shootings are often found to be unwarranted, you may be aware that it is common practice for civilians to sue the city and the police department. I'm sure you know that your constituents absorb the cost of those misconduct payouts. But do you realize just how massive the costs have been?

Police misconduct payouts related to incidents of excessive force have increased substantially since 2004. From 2004 to 2016, Chicago has paid out $662 million in police misconduct settlements, according to city records.[2] Furthermore, there is no reason to believe that these figures will decrease. Hundreds of Chicago Police Department misconduct lawsuit settlements were filed between 2011 and 2016, and they have cost Chicago taxpayers roughly $280 million.[3] When I was writing this letter in July 2018, the city had paid more than $45 million in misconduct settlements thus far, in that year alone. Keep in mind that misconduct payouts are only a fraction of what the city spends on policing. Chicago allocates $1.46 billion annually to policing, or 40 percent of its budget—that's the second-highest share of a city budget that goes to policing in the nation. It trails only Oakland, which allocates 41 percent.[4]

I recently came across a report about the funding for police departments in several US cities. The Center for Popular Democracy, Law for Black Lives, and the Black Youth Project 100 authored it. This report is of interest to you. As I read it, one quote in particular stood out:

> For every dollar spent on the Chicago Police Department (including city, state, and federal funds), the Department of Public Health, which includes mental health services, receives two cents. The Department of Planning and Development, which includes affordable housing development, receives 12 cents. The Department of Family and Support Services, which funds youth development, after school programs, and homeless services, receives five cents.[5]

As mayor, you have the opportunity to shift these priorities. Needless to say, the way you decide to use public funding reflects your values and the values of your constituents. Your job requires you to defend your constituents' wants and needs as you negotiate the budget with city council members each year. I know that it will be tempting to spend huge portions of the city's budget on the police department, especially since that is what the vast majority of cities across the country are doing.

Did you know that our country currently spends $100 billion a year on policing, and $80 billion on incarceration? Well, with this trend, your political advisers might argue that adopting a "tough on crime" stance will be key to your longevity as an elected official. But if you want to address the problem of police violence and make Chicago safer, you must resist the urge to follow the status quo.

The social programs that have been shown to improve people's well-being in the United States center on health care, education, housing, and the ability to earn a living wage—programs that work to stabilize people's lives. Time and time again, the research in my field of study has shown that spending money on policing and prison (what scholars call punitive systems) has little proven benefit.[6] To the contrary, Chicago's spending on policing and incarceration has contributed to a cycle of poverty that has had an impact on generations of people living in low-income communities of color.[7] As you might imagine, the investment in police forces, military-grade weapons, detention centers, jails, and prisons also contributes to an "us versus them" mentality in the police department that justifies police violence.

Although there has been some news coverage on this issue, most of the Chicagoans whom I spoke with for this study were unaware of the financial aspect of policing. When I told them about it, they were upset and disgusted but not particularly surprised.

A Black woman named Monica knew that the city used public funding to finance police violence and to compensate the wrongly convicted. But she thought this approach was shortsighted. "It can't just be money," she said. "Money is not enough."

While speaking about the torture survivors who had spent decades in prison, she elaborated: "Money doesn't fix the time that has been taken from them, nor does it fix the mental strain that has occurred. It doesn't fix their access to education or jobs. It's not enough to just give people money, or to just release them from prison. There needs to be a holistic package."

Monica thought that elected officials like you should work to funnel funding from policing into public resources and social services. Other people I interviewed agreed with her. They hoped that instead of spending this money merely to compensate torture survivors for what they have endured, the city would instead use a larger share of its public funds for mental health services, housing subsidies, youth programs, and food benefits. These residents regretted the fact that they were implicated in defending police torture. They could only hope that the wider public would start to pay attention to the present reality, the reality that every Chicagoan is financing torture, every day.

Case in point: On July 5, 2018, Chicago youth of color staged a die-in at city hall to protest Mayor Rahm Emanuel's plan to spend $95 million to build a cop academy. The young protestors set up cardboard tombstones with the names of people who had been killed by the police written on them with black ink. They also wrote the names of schools and facilities that had shuttered because of a lack of public funding.

Speaking about her reasons for helping to organize the event, twenty-year-old Nita Teenyson, said: "In my neighborhood there are no grocery stores. We live in a food desert. There are a bunch of schools getting shut down. The mental health facilities are shut down too. And that just leaves people with nothing to do. They become a danger to themselves and their community." "But if we had those resources," she continued, referring to the funding earmarked for the police academy, "we wouldn't even need the police to try to stop those people because resources would already be in place to help them."

Nita's description of how the lack of resources in her community contributes to violence was laced with resentment, because a vast expenditure of time and resources was being spent to clean up a problem that should not have existed in the first place. And to make matters worse, the cleanup was taking resources away from larger efforts to make life better in her community.[8]

• • •

While the roots of the torture tree symbolize the collective fear that materializes in public funding for the police, its trunk represents the police use-of-force continuum. If you don't have a law enforcement background, you may not know exactly what this continuum is. It's a set of guidelines, established by the city, for how much force police officers are permitted to use against a criminal suspect in a given situation. The progression of force typically begins merely with the presence of a uniformed officer, who can deter crime simply by parking his squad car on the corner; a step above that is a verbal show of force, such as a cop commanding someone to put his hands above his head; a step above that are the physical tactics an officer might use to establish control of a criminal suspect, like putting him in handcuffs; a step of above that are more aggressive techniques that could inadvertently cause injuries or bruising, such as kicking or punching a criminal suspect to subdue him; a step above that is using weapons that have a high probability of injuring someone but are not designed to kill, such as pepper spray; and the last step is the use of weapons that have a high probability of killing someone or at least causing serious injury.

Scholars of policing have often thought that police officers were obligated to be extremely cautious when determining which level of force to use on a civilian. It was this cautiousness, in fact, that was said to distinguish a police officer from a soldier at war. The rationale was that in wartime, one's cautiousness could be a liability. This is why, when encountering the enemy, soldiers needed to start with the highest level of force and work their way down the continuum. Police officers, however, were supposed to start at the lowest level of the continuum and then work their way up. But most of the Chicagoans I spoke with thought that this distinction no longer exists. Police officers ascend this continuum in the blink of an eye.

In describing this use-of-force continuum, I must make something clear: the protocols that constitute it are human judgments, suffused with assumptions about fear and danger that are too often tied to race. That being said, the way that police officers move up this continuum while deciding how much force to use on a criminal suspect is extremely subjective.

In recent decades, scholars have pointed out that the subjective nature of the use of force among police officers is informed by military thinking. For a long time, soldiers have returned from wars and joined their local police departments. Likewise, police officers have long taken on second jobs—sometimes even second careers—as military personnel. What's more, when soldiers fight wars overseas, it is common for their perception of the enemy to be shaped by the marginalized groups they grew up hearing stereotypes about. And when they return home, it is common for their ideas about those marginalized groups to be newly informed by the enemy they were just fighting against.

The phenomenon referred to as "the militarization of the police" is often used to describe the way that military equipment—including armored personnel carriers, assault rifles, submachine guns, "flash-bang" grenades, and sniper rifles—once used overseas eventually are allocated to local police stations in small and large cities and towns across the United States. But less often discussed is how alongside this military-grade equipment comes a military mind-set wherein the police treat residents as if they were enemy combatants, as if their job were to occupy and patrol a war zone. This is the mind-set of Richard Zuley—a Chicago police officer who became a torturer overseas. But I'll tell you about him later.[9]

For now, I only mean to say that I used to picture the use-of-force continuum as it is described in so many scholarly books: a staircase on which the mere presence of police officers resides at the bottom and death and torture reside at the top. But as I talked to more and more Chicagoans, I realized that the ethos of "justifiable" force that grants police officers permission to mistreat people blends into police torture—the two ends form a circle—until you can't easily distinguish where mistreatment ends and torture begins.

• • •

While the torture tree's trunk is the standard set of protocols that guide a police officer's decision-making process, the branches are the manifestation of those actions, which is to say, they are police officers themselves. Indeed, future mayor, in the anatomy of this tree, police officers are the branches because they are the human outgrowth of the use-of-force continuum.

I know you may be thinking, do all police officers grow out of this terrible tree? Well, the answer is yes and no. No, all police officers are not inherently connected to this structure. But yes, abiding by the use-of-force continuum makes them susceptible to losing their humanity—and to becoming hollowed out, wooden, and one with this tree.

A twenty-six year old Black man named Malik made me realize this when he told me a story about meeting a retired cop in the local pub that he went to after work on Fridays.[10] What sparked Malik's conversation with this retired cop was one of his enduring childhood memories: the delight of going to the police station, where the officers would hand him free football cards. Reflecting on that fond memory one day, Malik sat next to this man. Malik knew he used to be a police officer. He seemed to be at the bar, and plastered, every time Malik went in. But on this particular day, Malik decided to ask him a question: "Hey, man, why do you drink so much?"

He would never forget the officer's response: "If you'd seen the things that I've seen, you'd be drunk all the time, too."

The cop began sharing stories with Malik, "really gruesome, vicious stories" that, Malik now says, he wishes he never heard. "It was like a horror movie, what he had to live through for so many years."

The retired officer told Malik that what he had seen and experienced had changed him. Being a policeman had altered his mentality. When he saw people on the street, especially Black people, he couldn't help but think of the threats they might pose and the ulterior motives they might have. After a while, the cop's cynicism was not relegated to the criminal underworld that he patrolled on his beat. "Now, because he was conditioning himself to think in a certain way," Malik said, "his police work was affecting his loving marriage." He was no longer able to transform himself back into a devoted father when he left the police precinct at nights.

"So he became compromised by the profession," said Malik.

Malik explained that after the policemen "lost it all," he turned to alcohol to cope.

"When the cop told me his story, I started to understand a bit more," Malik said. "That was one of the reasons I agreed to this interview, more so than anything else."

By talking with the retired cop, Malik experienced a shift in his thinking about the police officers he's encountered in his life. He didn't always see them as dehumanized extensions of police force. He remembered that he had recognized kindness and "felt welcomed" in the presence of police officers as a child. But going into his teenage years, he had been harassed by the police so often without cause that, as an adult, he dreaded being around them. He feared them. And it frustrated him that he could never make the police feel as afraid of him as he was of them.

"I'll be honest with you," Malik said to me, "my motto up until a year ago, when I was twenty-five—my motto was, 'The only good cop is a dead cop.' Sadly, sadly, that's what I had been pushed to. But it just hurt so bad going through the encounters and being shamed and embarrassed. I had accrued so much debt from the court cases based on senseless traffic stops. Then, once I came across that individual," Malik continued, speaking about the man at the bar, "things started to shift, and I started to understand their position more. When I came across him, my motto changed. Now, I think, 'The only good cop is a retired cop.'"

Malik laughed dryly.

"It didn't change by much," he admitted, "but at least I'm not wishing death upon them now."

What Chicagoans like Malik underscored for me was that the process of profiling people does not merely have an impact on the person at the wrong end of the gaze. Making such judgments has an impact on the police officers who put the use-of-force continuum into effect. They are liable to become hardened, stiff, and ultimately unable to untether themselves from the larger structure that persecutes and maltreats marginalized groups.

• • •

Last but not least, we have the endpoint of each branch: the leaves. In the metaphor of the torture tree, these leaves are any and every incident of police force. I'm sure you realize that, in Chicago, the high-intensity policing and surveillance of low-income communities shows no signs of letting up, so reducing these incidents will not be easy. But have you considered that, even if you are skilled enough to decrease racial profiling, the relationship between the Black community and the police will likely remain fraught? The rift is so wide that Black Chicagoans may still *feel* that police torture is getting worse for a very long time, even if (hypothetically speaking) conditions were to improve. This is because many of them have faced numerous incidents of police harassment throughout the course of their life.

When you take a step back, as I did, and listen to Chicagoans talk about policing, you will see new incidents of police force sprout before your very eyes. Each leaf is the product of one such instance of abuse.

There was the story that Tate told about being presumed a terrorist, harassed and humiliated in front of his wife and kids—all because his middle name was Jihad.

"I'm more American than apple pie," he said, "but instead of looking for the suspect, you're sitting here talking about my name?"

There was the story about the police telling Rodney to "stop and put your hands where I can see them" when he was walking to work, a command that triggered a lifetime of resentment so that when I interviewed Rodney, I gave him permission to pretend that I was the cop who called him out. I told him to say whatever was on his mind that day, during that encounter.

"Just because I'm Black," he said, "who the fuck are you to tell me I can't move anymore? And I don't have to answer your question. I didn't do shit to you. I'm a taxpayer. I pay your salary. So fuck off, you know? Don't fucking tell me I can't walk no more."

There was the story of the thirty-four-year-old torture survivor named Jamal, who told me that officers from "the same police department had been targeting me all my life." When I interviewed him, he said that he had nightmares so often that he suspected an undiagnosed case of post-traumatic stress disorder.

"Every time I see the police, I'm very frightened," he confessed. "I'm scared out of my mind because I don't know what they're going to do to me. It's like I'm an enemy. I'm a target to them. So yes, every time I see the police, I'm very frightened," he repeated.

The leaves of the torture tree can include incidents of racial and religious profiling, the verbal commands Rodney resented having to obey, or the nightmare of torture Jamal experienced and is now forced to relive every time he sees a cop.

I hope that bearing witness to these incidents of force will spark a sense of urgency in you so that you will be motivated to reckon with the torture tree as a whole.

• • •

But even as I hold onto this hope, future mayor, I wouldn't be surprised if you felt discouraged, or if you second-guessed your desire to be mayor of this city. In fact, I would be worried if you did not. Still, there is a silver lining: the torture tree is an organic, living structure, but it grows because of the actions of people. So if you want to address the problems created by the use-of-force continuum, you cannot just rake up the fallen leaves. You cannot just prune the branches. No, to effect change, a concrete step you must take is to reallocate the public funding that allows your city to transform the populations it has systematically marginalized into threats. You must divest this fear-stained funding from the police and into larger efforts to make life better for all of your constituents.

PART I The Black Box

An Open Letter to the Boy and Girl with
Matching Airbrushed Book Bags on
the Corner of Lawndale Avenue and
Cermak Road

I began to worry—I mean, really worry—about
police violence in Chicago back in the summer of
2004. That's when I saw you—a young man and
young woman, barely teenagers—in your white
shirts and khaki pants, on your knees at the corner
of Lawndale Avenue and Cermak Road. Where I
grew up in Columbia, Maryland, those clothes
would've been private school uniforms. But in
Chicago, I've been told, that lack of hue in your
collared shirt is supposed to mean that you are
public school students and not gang members—
who, at that intersection, supposedly wear red
and black.

I know you are much older now, and yet when
I see Black and Brown teenagers of today's Chicago, bustling down the streets, flirting with each

other, clumped together over someone's cell phone, I always flash back to that scene over a decade ago.

Four police cars were parked along the curb. Six officers frisked you on the sidewalk. The cops smiled at one another as they emptied the contents of your book bags into the gutter. Your bags were both white, each with a different word similarly airbrushed in graffiti letters—your names, I assumed, though I couldn't make them out from where I stood. All I could tell was that one of the names was written in green, and the other was in pink. I remember trying to read those letters so that I could yell your names, pretend that I was a friend or relative, and ask if you were OK.

I know how long your encounter lasted because I clocked it: twenty-six minutes, forty-three seconds. I watched the whole time from across the street, transfixed. Later, I told my brother that I watched you so that I could be a witness in the event the incident went awry. But that was only half-true. I also watched because I was afraid and didn't know what else to do.

I had moved to your city two weeks before this incident. And although I moved there to attend the University of Chicago, and to become a professor, tweed jacket and all the rest, I was afraid that I was witnessing an altercation with the police that I, too, might eventually have.

At the same time, I was afraid because I was seeing the past.

When I was around the same age as you were then, or at least the same size—which is to say, around twelve years old—I found myself in a similar position. My two older brothers and I had just moved from Baltimore to Columbia, Maryland, about a half hour's drive south. We decided to go to the mall. We must have worn our Baltimoreness in our walk, in our lingo, or more likely, on our flesh, because before long a plainclothes police officer was following us from store to store. We knew full well that a strange man was bearing down on us, and we fought the temptation to run. I wouldn't have admitted it to myself then, but I felt scared.

Before long, the man ordered us to stop. He frisked both of my brothers, who were fifteen and sixteen, against a rail on the second floor. I was within arm's reach of my brothers, but the cop ignored me. Maybe because I was so puny he thought I was irrelevant. I have to admit: I was relieved he wasn't touching me. But despite that relief, I could feel myself in my own skin unlike ever before. Adrenaline spiked my senses. All of a sudden I felt hair stand up from the follicles on my forearms. I could catch the sound of people chattering below me. I could smell fried potato wedges from the Boardwalk Café on the floor below, where a crowd of people gathered, eyes upward, watching the commotion against the second-story railing. I had been in that restaurant, eating those thick fries, just a few hours earlier. I wanted desperately to return to that moment.

I looked down at the people looking up at me, and I imagined them to be shaking their heads in contempt. An uneasy feeling settled in my stomach and stayed there. I began to worry that a classmate from my new school might see me, tell others, and someone would make fun of me. And then I would be forced to fight. Or even worse: word would spread about the incident and no one would want to be my friend. Then I felt ashamed of how quickly my embarrassment had taken the place of fear. I should still be afraid, I thought to myself, because my brothers had their arms behind their backs and I could tell *they* were scared.

The cop took my eldest brother, Wolé, through one of those doors that you never notice along the corridors of a mall until all your senses are heightened and you start to notice everything. He didn't say anything to me or my other brother, Michael, so we were at a loss. Eventually, terrified, we called our parents. Four hours later, Wolé was released, but only after my mother and father showed up and threatened legal action. The cop had found no evidence to confirm his suspicion that Wolé had been doing something wrong. Only then did my relief feel justified and right.

When the police released you, West Side Chicago teenagers with matching airbrushed book bags, I felt a similar kind of relief. But I also felt a familiar combination of cowardice, anger, guilt, frustration—and yes, fear.

No doubt living in Chicago has taught you valuable lessons about the police. That early encounter with the mall cop taught me valuable lessons, too. When I related the story of that incident to my friends and their parents, they told me far-worse stories of being followed, frisked, humiliated, and even brutalized, for walking in malls or lingering in amusement parks, or for just going to school or coming home from work.

That was when I first learned that the police do not always live by the code of serving and protecting, or at least that they don't serve and protect all citizens equally. Still, as a preteen, I didn't understand just how far certain officers departed from that code, or the extent to which they were allowed to get away with doing so—much less why. I believe this knowledge is crucial for any young person of color growing up in the United States.

I am writing to you today because when I see kids in Chicago being stopped and frisked by the cops, I always feel guilty for not knowing what to do, just like I still feel guilty for not helping you that day. I'm also writing because we all need to talk—whenever and however we can—about the awful things that we have to deal with as Black people in this country, as well as what we can do about them.

• • •

Even though I still don't know what to do, and I still don't know how to solve this scourge, I *have* done something. I have done, as an academic, the thing I know how to do best: research and study and write. So, I started a research project about the history of police violence in your city. For this project I've interviewed youth of color in Chicago and talked about their experiences with the police. What they said would probably sound familiar to you, given that they are your younger brothers, sisters, nieces, nephews, friends—in a way, your younger selves. Although you two are now adults, and probably already have a general idea of the feelings young people might have toward the police, I want to give you a taste of what they said for a particular reason. Before my interviews and group discussions with Chicago youth, I would always tell them about witnessing your stop-

and-frisk encounter as a way to give them some background on my earliest memory of the Chicago police. What happened to you has been an important point of departure for my research, and it has invited sobering reflections from the people I speak with.

In a discussion at Harold Washington Library in the spring of 2016, for instance, Nekia explained to a group of thirteen teenagers that when her brother was around fifteen (the same age she was then), he got arrested. "The police came in my house one night and grabbed him. I was scared," she said.

Nekia saw the police put handcuffs on her brother, and she didn't understand why they were taking him away. "My mom was there, so of course she was trying to calm me down. But she was distracted because I have older siblings. I'm the youngest of seven," she said. Her brothers and sisters were angry and getting more and more agitated, which put pressure on Nekia's mother to make sure no one else went to jail. "I definitely didn't understand what was happening. There was a lot going on, and I was just like, 'Where is he going?'"

Martin could sympathize. He had faced a similar situation. His father was arrested in his home when he was five years old. "I didn't understand what was happening," he said. All he knew then was that "there were a lot of lights."

After Martin had finished sharing his story, Phillip spoke up. "My first memory of the police is from when I was thirteen," he said, "and there was a shooting on the block." Phillip had been walking in a large group with his brothers and cousins—eight of them in all. An unmarked police car braked right in front of them, and an officer jumped out and told everybody to put their hands above their heads.

"He started groping us in our private parts to look for guns and stuff. I'd say it's a negative memory because I don't want another grown man touching my private area. I was thirteen. What would I be doing with a gun?" said Phillip.

"I remember it like yesterday, and it still bothers me," Phillip continued. "But I'm trying to get over it."

Like Phillip, what happened to you at Lawndale and Cermak is probably something you've worked hard to "get over" and move beyond. But I want you to know that, just as your experience affected me, it is now affecting a younger generation of Chicagoans who are searching for a way to process their feelings about the police.

I plan to write letters based on my research on police violence to all of the youth of color in Chicago. By writing to this larger group, I hope that my silence that day in 2004 will be replaced by a loud voice that insists on my apology to you for not stepping forward back then. Through my letters, I'll also be talking to the big, beautiful community of kids of color who still have to reckon with the same institutional racism that you faced on that day.

I cannot change that day. And I cannot change the pain and frustration and confusion you must have felt, walking home with your heads hung low. But what I hope to do is make something useful from that awful moment. I imagine you now, receiving this letter in the mail. I hope that if you could read this letter, you would give me your blessing, that you would feel the pain of that day—the burdens of that mistreatment—growing into something else, a greater sense of purpose, perhaps. When I think about that possibility, I can't help but smile.

An Open Letter to Chicago's Youth of Color

I am writing this letter to you, the tens of thousands of Black and Brown young men and young women living in Chicago. You don't know me. But I know you; or rather, I know what can happen to you. I am writing to all of you because you are the next generation who has to fear violence from the same people who are tasked with protecting you and serving you.

The police department of your city is full, I am sure, of lots of officers who care about the law and serve the community. But the police department is also full of racism and abuse. I am guessing that many of you have already felt this; some of you have been pulled over for no reason or arrested just for being on a certain street corner at a certain time of night. What I hope none of you has experienced, however, is that the dirty looks and the illegal searches are not the extent of it. They are merely part of a long and frightening spectrum of mistreatment by the police—a spectrum (or what scholars call the use-of-force continuum) that extends all the way to the most egregious acts of torture you can imagine. For as long as you have been alive (and much longer than that), certain members of the Chicago Police Department have been torturing your fellow Chicagoans.

I am writing because you need to be aware of what could happen while you walk in this world. And I am also writing to you on behalf of those men and women who have suffered greatly at the hands of the police. When I talk to torture survivors, you are the group of people that they want most desperately to address. They hope that by learning about torture, you might be able to avoid their fate.

I have spent the last fourteen years of my life trying to understand the history of police torture in this city. How it happened. Why it happened. Whom it could happen to next. It is this last concern that connects you most viscerally to this history. And the reason I know this is from talking with your peers.

For example, one of your peers, a sixteen-year-old named Zach, told me that, just days before our interview, he had met a man who had been wrongfully convicted of a crime. The man said he was convicted because "he got tortured into copping a plea." He had been locked up for twenty years, Zach explained, and got out in 2013.

Zach said that when he read the consent form to participate in my study, which mentioned the Chicago police torture cases, he kept thinking, "Is that what that man was talking about when he said he got tortured?" Then, Zach said he was going to ask me a question that he didn't want to ask the tortured man: "If something like that happens to you, how do you survive?"

I still haven't figured out an adequate response.

When one of your peers would ask me about the likelihood that they would be tortured someday, my stomach would ball into a knot and I would grow stiff. I would open my mouth, but no words would come out. It didn't occur to me at the time to tell them that young people who once attended some of the same schools as them had recently traveled to the United Nations to protest police violence. In hindsight, I think that would've provided some reassurance and tamped down some of their fears. The only thing I could ever think of to do was to talk about the political fight for reparations—the struggle that would bring the history of police torture to their classrooms.

I would like to share that history with you.

In the spring of 2015, the City of Chicago's Finance Committee held a hearing during which politicians considered a piece of legislation, officially called the 2015 Reparations Ordinance. This law was filed on behalf of fifty-seven survivors of police torture and included a number of demands, such as a public apology from the city and a monument to be built to honor the torture survivors. The survivors also filed for a monetary settlement to finance what they referred to in the Ordinance as "the Chicago Police Torture Reparations Commission" and additional funding to pay for health care (including psychological counseling), free tuition at the City Colleges, and job training and placement for survivors and their families. On May 6, 2015, the Chicago City Council agreed to many of these demands, including $5.5 million in reparations for the survivors.

Although this dollar amount is not the largest ever awarded to victims of police violence, the ruling was landmark in the way it framed the issue. Although certain previous settlements did acknowledge that a person was tortured, that acknowledgment always hinged on whether someone had committed a crime. To win a judgment, a person had to prove not only that he or she was tortured but also that the victim was innocent of the crime he or she had confessed to. By contrast, the fifty-seven Black men who were awarded reparations from the City of Chicago were never exonerated of the crimes that they were convicted of. They were compensated for their torture, in other words, not for time they had wrongfully spent in jail.

In this sense, the Reparations Ordinance separated the legal notion of guilt from the issue of torture. This is what made the ordinance unique: it was a concession on the part of the City of Chicago that torture was wrong no matter what, regardless of whether the suspect was innocent or guilty. That concession was unprecedented. Because of the intergenerational, interracial movement that arose to fight for this cause, African American men who were tortured received reparations for the first time in US history.

You may be thinking that there is an obvious connection between reparations for slavery and for the Chicago torture cases. If so, you would be right. In 2014, Ta-Nehisi Coates brought renewed attention to the issue with his *Atlantic* article "The Case for Reparations," in which he argued that the United States should "atone" for stealing Black labor and wealth from African Americans and that, if the country did so, it would be very different from what it is today. While it is yet to be determined whether the torture cases in Chicago will have any bearing on the larger reparations debate, the kind of repayment that torture survivors won makes everyone see the legacy of racism and violence in the United States, as well as the impact of that legacy on police, health care, and education.[1]

This points to another reason I am writing you: to tell you about the important concessions the Reparations Ordinance included. Legal settlements typically compensate individuals only for the hardships they have suffered, but the Reparations Ordinance provided resources that are benefiting your entire city. For instance, it called for the Chicago Public Schools system to incorporate into its junior high and high school curriculum a history lesson about the Chicago police torture cases.

As a professor, I understood the call to educate the public about police torture as my call to action. When I heard about this demand, back in 2015, I had been researching police torture for more than a decade. In fact, I was thinking about giving up my research because I was convinced that nothing would ever change. But the thought of helping to educate you filled me with a renewed sense of purpose. I felt that my contribution could be to help teenagers of color like you rethink the idea of what it means to be guilty and to help explain the damage that judging someone to be guilty can do.

Torture is always wrong, no matter if the person is innocent or not. And thus, this letter also aims to dispel the trope of the wrongfully accused. A "trope," simply put, is an idea that you hear over and over again, to the point that it becomes something that you believe in without even thinking about it. And, especially since the civil rights movement of the 1960s, which brought national attention to legal claims of racial discrimination, the trope of the wrongfully accused has become an extremely common way to make sense of the criminal justice system in the United States. As more and more police torturers are brought to light, this trope has become increasingly familiar: it is the story of an unjustly incarcerated and brutalized person who embarks on an ultimately successful quest to prove his or her innocence and obtain freedom.

Living in the United States, we hear stories of the wrongfully convicted—and eventually exonerated—all the time. We read magazine profiles. We watch documentaries. We listen to interviews with the exonerated and their families on morning talk shows and podcasts. These stories all share key elements. They portray the struggle for exoneration in heart-wrenching detail. We learn of the lost years of imprisonment, often numbering in the decades; the suffering of family members whose lives have been devastated by the absence of their loved ones; and the sacrifices that lawyers make on behalf of their clients. The feel-good conclusions to these harrowing narratives appeal to our longing for happy endings. They reveal that terrible things happen in life but that wrongs can be rectified. They conclude by reassuring us that life is fair. Who doesn't want to believe that?

Sometimes, these narratives push a little further and offer a critique of the criminal justice system. Perhaps they mention the disproportionate sentencing of people who are Brown or Black or poor. But the underlying assumption is always the same: every once in a while, authorities might capture, imprison, or even torture the wrong person. Unlike those who are eventually revealed to be innocent, however, these stories tell us that *most people deserve their fate.*

The trope of the wrongfully accused therefore fails to acknowledge how pervasive these abuses are; it fails to acknowledge the fundamental problems within police departments and courthouses and prisons; it fails to acknowledge that our institutions of justice sustain and legitimize police torture. In fact, because the wronged person is exonerated at the end—nearly always through the dogged determination of lawyers or the progressive rationale of forward-thinking judges—these stories reaffirm our faith in the legal system, even though it is that system that has perpetuated the flaws that led to the person being convicted in the first place.

We must understand the problem with this trope.

That's why in all of my letters I ask you not to think of the innocent person as the quintessential torture victim. Rather, imagine a person who committed a crime that you regard as especially heinous. Imagine that person being bagged and suffocated and beaten within an inch of his life. Ask yourself, can I see enough humanity in him to understand why it is just as wrong to torture him as it is to torture an innocent man?

And that question brings me to the other purpose of this letter: to tell you about Andrew Wilson. He is the first person to file a lawsuit against the City of Chicago for the crime of torture. Wilson was convicted of killing two police officers, and for a long time people in Chicago, your city, believed that the police tortured him in revenge for his deeds. Most Chicagoans did not care about Wilson because they believed him to be guilty. But I think you need to care about him. Why? It is not because Wilson could very well have confessed to something he did not do. Although confessions that are coerced from torture are always questionable, his guilt or innocence must be separated from the issue of his torture. You should care about Wilson despite what you think he did, because what was later done to him reveals something important about the anger and loathing directed against Black criminal suspects—indeed, against entire Black communities.

• • •

Andrew Wilson's story begins in 1982. It was a snowy afternoon on February 9, a biting northeasterly wind coming off the lake. Chicago was in the midst of its coldest freezing spell of the year. That afternoon, according to the police report, two officers flashed their lights on a brown Chevrolet Impala. The occupants of the car, Andrew Wilson and his younger brother, Jackie, were suspected of having recently committed a burglary. One of the officers, William Fahey, instructed the Wilson brothers to step out of the vehicle. Both men obeyed. They got out of the car and, as directed, placed their hands on the Impala's hood. Fahey began to frisk Andrew Wilson while his partner, Officer Richard O'Brien, entered the Impala to search it.

Once he finished patting down Andrew Wilson, Fahey turned his attention to Jackie. Moments later, Andrew Wilson attempted to strip the policeman of his weapon. Wilson grabbed Fahey, and as the two men struggled for his gun, they fell to the ground. Andrew Wilson won the wrestling match, which ended when the gun discharged in the scuffle, critically wounding Fahey.

Richard O'Brien didn't realize that the arrest had gone awry until he heard the gunshot. He was sitting in the Impala's back seat, sifting through Jackie and Andrew's plunder. At the sound of gunfire, O'Brien left the car and pointed his weapon at the first person he saw, Jackie Wilson, wide-eyed, his hands still on the hood.

Unaware that his partner was on the ground, wrestling with Andrew Wilson and bleeding out, O'Brien called for Fahey. When Fahey failed to respond, O'Brien approached the rear of the car. Andrew shot him in the chest.

According to the report, Andrew then climbed on the back of the car and while standing on the roof, shot Fahey again. The Wilsons sped off in the Impala as the two policemen bled out in the snow.

These are the events to which Andrew Wilson eventually confessed.

• • •

For four days, Wilson was the subject of a citywide manhunt, at that time, the largest that Chicago had ever seen. Concentrating their efforts on the Near West Side and on the South Side, police officers parked their squad cars and combed Black neighborhoods block by block.

A dragnet like this is a nightmare not just for the person who is the subject of it but also for everyone in the vicinity. The hatred the police harbored for Wilson led to widespread abuses for Black residents across the entire city, all of which suggest a disregard for Black lives that can be accounted for only by deep-rooted assumptions about Black criminality.

Doris Miller, Andrew Wilson's neighbor and friend, reported that the cops hauled her into the police station, handcuffed her to a pipe, and kept her in custody for twenty hours without food or access to a bathroom. When she denied knowing Wilson's whereabouts, the lieutenant in charge of the Area 2 Violent Crimes Unit, Jon Burge, told Miller, "I'll come back in here and beat your ass."

Patricia and Alvin Smith reported that plainclothes policemen had broken down their door at one in the morning. The cops ransacked the premises and pointed their guns at the Smiths' daughter, who was twelve. The Smiths didn't understand how a little girl could be mistaken for a middle-aged man when the only similarity was that both were Black.[2]

An actual middle-aged Black man, Adolph Thornton, was not mistaken for Wilson but apparently his German shepherd was; police broke down Thornton's door and shot the two-year-old dog in his gut.

Here's another one: William Phillips was arrested for standing on the corner. He tried to explain to police that he was a hardworking firefighter. As he talked, Phillips showed his palms, as Black men of a certain station sometimes do to proactively prove their innocence, the officers told him to shut his trap and then knocked out one of his teeth for not quieting quickly enough.

Those were the people mistaken for having criminal associations. Those who actually had criminal records got much worse. Julia Davis, who would later testify against the police in Wilson's case, explained that her son, Larry Milan, had been a gang member, but she was proud that Larry had served his time and come home a changed man. Even so, Larry's prior conviction justified a raid on Davis's home and destruction of her property. But that wasn't the worst of it. Larry was arrested and held at the police station for three days as officers tried to link him to Wilson. Davis worried for her son's safety—and rightly so. Larry came home with bruises on his back and abrasions on his legs from being brutalized by police officers.

And then there was Roy Wade Brown, who also eventually testified against the city in one of Wilson's suits. I've saved his story for last because his experience mirrored the way the police treated Andrew Wilson when they finally caught him. According to Brown, the officers who interrogated him grew so frustrated when he would not admit to killing their colleagues or to knowing who did that they placed a plastic bag over his head, cutting off his air supply. One of the interrogators then put Brown's index finger in a bolt cutter and threatened to cut it off. Brown was hit repeatedly with a paddle before being taken to the roof of the police station. "We'll throw you off if you don't tell us about the shootings," the officers said.

As you can see, the cops broke their own laws systematically and thoroughly. They violated their own codes. I sometimes think they forgot they were cops at all, but of course, they only got away with this *because* they were cops: their uniforms gave them impunity. This was evident in the way they drew a gun on the Smith girl; their assaults on Doris Miller, William Phillips, and Larry Milan; and the threats they made to Roy Brown's life.

If you find yourself getting angry while reading about how the police terrorized the Black community that is perfectly normal. In fact, it is to be expected. This manhunt reminded your peers of their own experiences with the police.

"Honestly, it's disgusting," Danielle said. "We're supposed to be protected by our legal system. They're there to protect us. But to have someone raid your house without a warrant, that's messed up. Just because you were a past felon," she continued, referencing Larry Milan's story, "what gives you that right? And who's to say that you haven't changed?"

Isaac was taken by William Phillips. "Just by standing on the *corner*? Because of the color of his *skin*?" he said. "He didn't deserve it.

And I know there are more people out there that have gone through the same thing. Trying to make a living for himself and his family, and just to be taken away for something like that. It's messed up." Isaac shook his head.

"It's almost sickening," Sharon said, "to read about everything that they did. OK, they were looking for a criminal, but that doesn't give them the right to do what they did. I just feel like, I feel like that could have been any one of us."

I mention what these teenagers said in case you share their sentiments. It's my experience that it can be comforting to know that other people have the same feelings as you do.

During the manhunt, many people living in Wilson's neighborhood were just as angry as you may be feeling now and just as disgusted as your peers. Wilson's neighbors wanted the police to know that just because someone killed two police officers doesn't mean that an entire community should be treated as if all its members were murderers. This is, of course, understandable.

However, I'm asking you to take another, more difficult stance, and to insist that not even a murderer should be treated the way Andrew Wilson was after he was captured. Adopting this more difficult stance is vital if we truly want to understand how police torture found fertile soil to grow in your beloved city of Chicago, and if we want to prevent it from happening again. After all, the same racist assumptions that made it possible for the police to torture Andrew Wilson made it possible for them to terrorize his entire community.

• • •

While the police held hostage Black residents of the West and South Sides, Wilson was still at large but getting weary. The night of February 13, he was hiding in the home of Garnett Vaughn, an acquaintance who had agreed to shelter Wilson while he fled the police. In Vaughn's apartment, Wilson abandoned his grand scheme of fleeing the country for a remote island in favor of a more attainable goal:

lying on the couch and getting some sleep. He managed to get some rest, briefly. But on his fifth day as a fugitive, Wilson's luck ran out. Around four in the morning on February 14, he was awakened by the sound of Lieutenant Burge and several officers, bursting into Vaughn's apartment.

All the officers, including Burge, were white men in civilian clothes. They ordered Wilson and Vaughn against the wall. Once he was identified as the suspect, Wilson was thrown to the floor, his pockets were searched, and he was fitted with handcuffs.

This, Wilson later said, is when he heard Burge speak for the first time. "Handle him with kid gloves," Burge said. "We'll get him at the station."[3]

The comments seemed innocent enough, if slightly foreboding. But Wilson could not possibly have known what they foreshadowed. When they arrived at Area 2 headquarters, the police took Wilson into a small room for questioning, where they punched him repeatedly in the abdomen and kicked him in the eye, which according to Wilson, tore his retina. One of the officers grabbed a bag out of the garbage can and put it over Wilson's head.[4] Near the end of the beating, Burge entered the small room and chided his officers for leaving bruises on Wilson's face. "I wouldn't have messed him up," Burge said, meaning that the officers should have inflicted their punishments without leaving visible marks. The archive illustrates this mistake. In a postcard-size photograph taken after the beatings—and a hospital visit—when Wilson was finally placed in jail, he is bloodied and heavily bandaged. The photo leaves no doubt that Wilson's abuse would have been visible to anyone who crossed his path. That means a lot of people knew what was happening. And that means that a lot of people stayed silent.

Next, Wilson was taken to another interview room. Detective John Yucaitis arrived carrying a brown shopping bag. In it was a device Wilson would come to know as the black box.

Like so many great inventions, the black box was most likely intended for a very different purpose from the one that made it infamous. In all likelihood, it originally served as a portable telephone for military personnel in the field. Jon Burge would have been familiar with these field telephones from his time in the army.[5] Because Burge would never answer questions about it, we don't know for certain if the black box was in fact a military-grade field telephone or a new hybrid torture machine. However, Wilson's lawyers believed that it was exported from the jungles of Vietnam—where Burge likely knew about and probably witnessed the torture of suspected members of the Viet Cong—and dusted off for the streets of Chicago.

In the interview room, Yucaitis pulled two wires out of the black box and attached them with clamps to Wilson's right ear and nostril. He cranked the handle. Wilson hollered because of the pain. Yucaitis stopped cranking when someone came to the door, at which point the detective put the instrument back in the bag and left.

Yucaitis then took his suspect to another room, where Wilson refused to give a confession to state's attorney Larry Hyman and was promptly returned to the place where the detective had shocked him. Half an hour later, Yucaitis returned with the black box. This time, Jon Burge was with him. The lieutenant announced that it was "fun time."

Burge reattached the box's clamps to Wilson's nostrils and ears and began to crank the handle again, which produced an electric current, shocking Wilson.[6] Still handcuffed to the ring on the wall, Wilson had enough freedom of movement to rip the clips from his ears with his shoulders, but when he did this the clips left marks. Although only a few pictures survived from the interrogation, one shows tiny loop marks on the top of Wilson's ears, the other depicts a scar in the middle of each ear.

Frustrated by Wilson's constant squirming and his inability to endure the punishment the officers felt he deserved, Burge and Yucaitis uncuffed one arm and handcuffed him to another ring, as well. Wilson's body was now stretched out so that he was facing a radiator located against the wall between the two rings.

The radiator, positioned just inches from his chest, burned Wilson's flesh. His skin blistered and began to blacken. But this pain so paled in comparison to that caused by the black box's persistent current that Wilson was not yet aware of the radiator. The heat from the radiator "didn't even exist then," Wilson would later testify. "The box existed." Meanwhile, Burge stuck the clamps on Wilson's fingers, and as Wilson was kneeling, with his legs, chest, and face making contact with the radiator, Burge shocked him. At this point, it seems that Burge just wanted to test how much pain Wilson could tolerate.

When he was finished singeing Wilson's flesh, Burge revealed a second electrical device. Here's how Wilson would later describe it: "It's black and it's round and it had a wire sticking out of it and it had a cord on it. He plugged it into the wall. . . . He took it and he ran it up between my legs, my groin area, just ran it up there very gently . . . up and down, up and down, you know, right between my legs, up and down like this, real gentle with it, but you can feel it, still feel it. Then he jabbed me with the thing."

When Burge "jabbed" Wilson with the instrument, Wilson's body slammed against the window grill near the radiator, and, spitting up blood, he fell to the ground.

The electroshock sessions had ended.

Wilson may have thought the worst was over, that he was now going to be subject to the normal booking process. But that was not to be. When the electroshock was finished, Burge placed his gun in Wilson's mouth and cocked it. "He kept doing it," Wilson would later testify, "he kept clicking it and he had it in my mouth and stuff." Wilson was then taken to another police station and made to stand in several lineups. Around 6:30 p.m., Wilson signed a confession statement, which was taken by assistant state's attorney Larry Hyman. Detective Patrick O'Hara was also present, as well as Burge.

Jon Burge, the lieutenant in charge of the high-profile manhunt, seemed satisfied that Wilson was destined for the electric chair.

"We're gonna fry your Black ass," Burge said to Wilson.

By the end of this thirteen-hour ordeal Wilson had been beaten and broken. The police had transformed him, had made that beaten, broken man into the embodiment of the anger that Burge felt toward Black criminal suspects.

An Open Letter to Chicago's Youth of Color

In my previous letter I told you I was writing to talk with you about something that you have probably already glimpsed in your own lives—the hatred directed toward Black people in your city. I began to tell you the story of a confessed killer for a particular reason. As I alluded to in my last letter, I know, from talking with your peers, that some of you will assume that Andrew Wilson was falsely accused of these terrible crimes and turned out to be innocent. I'm sure you know that there are many such stories. They form the subject of non-fiction books like *Convicting the Innocent*, TV shows like *Rectify*, off-Broadway plays like *The Exonerated*, documentaries like *Murder on a Sunday Morning*, motion pictures like *The Hurricane*, and podcasts like *Serial*. But Wilson's is not one of these stories. All available evidence suggests that Wilson was indeed guilty, that Wilson is a cop killer.

In my previous letter I asked you to take a moment and reflect on this question: If he is guilty, is his story any less valuable? The reason I wanted you to consider this question is because I know that this could change things, at least somewhat. Perhaps you feel a distaste now. Perhaps you find yourself wishing that we could talk about something else, now that you know this story won't have a happy ending. Perhaps your first gut reaction is that if he is a cop killer, then he deserved what he got. All those feelings make sense. Whatever your thoughts, know that I am not here to judge those gut reactions. I am here to challenge them.

I already told you that, after more than a decade studying police torture, I believe Wilson's guilt is irrelevant. In my last letter I tried to convince you that even if he is a cop killer, that does not make his story any less valuable. But in this letter I want to tell you exactly why his story matters so much. It matters because by hating and condemning people, we actually make them more vulnerable for torture. To see this, you only have to consider what happened after Wilson was arrested, tortured, and taken out of the interrogation room.

Around nine o'clock on the day that he was tortured, Wilson was taken out of interrogation, and Burge placed Wilson in the care of two officers, Mario Ferro and William Mulvaney. They were tasked with transporting Wilson to the Chicago Police Department's downtown headquarters. But before leaving Area 2, the officers tormented Wilson some more. They hit Wilson and grabbed him by the genitals. When they left the interview room, they verbally abused him and physically beat him some more. Once finished, they realized they had a problem: Wilson was bleeding. Bruises were forming all over his body. Wilson had several large gashes on his forehead, and blood was dripping from his right eye, which was swollen shut. The officers feared these injuries would raise suspicion when he appeared in court for his booking the next day. Therefore, Ferro and Mulvaney decided to put Wilson in an occupied cell; if anyone asked, they could claim that other prisoners had beaten him up.

For their plan to work, Ferro and Mulvaney had to get Wilson past the intake officer downtown. They didn't think this would be a problem, as Ferro and Mulvaney knew many of the intake officers personally. More than that, they knew what a day in intake was like. When those officers weren't filing papers and processing suspects, they were picking up slack by helping answer emergency calls. They were also charged with breaking up fights between inmates. In other words, intake officers were overworked and perpetually busy, and it was unlikely they would notice another suspect with a few bruises, gashes, and cuts.

But when Ferro and Mulvaney arrived at CPD headquarters and tried to process Wilson, the intake officer refused admittance. He didn't want to be held responsible for Wilson's wounds, a refusal that suggests how grisly they must have been. Out of options, Ferro and Mulvaney decided at last to follow protocol and take Wilson to the hospital. At Mercy Hospital, a few miles away from CPD headquarters, the officers told Wilson that if he knew what was good for him, he would refuse to be treated. This intimidation tactic nearly worked. Wilson later said that he would have declined treatment were it not for a Black ward clerk, Thaddeus Williams, who noticed the signs of torture. Williams also overheard the policemen's threats. When the officers weren't looking, Williams told Wilson that he had the right to be seen by a doctor, and, after this reassurance, Wilson signed a consent form and was seen by Geoffrey Korn.[7] Dr. Korn, the attending physician in the emergency room, would later indicate that as an emergency room doctor working in Chicago, he was accustomed to seeing criminal suspects entering the hospital injured and handcuffed. But Wilson's wounds were unlike any he had ever seen.

Wilson responded hesitantly when Dr. Korn asked about his injuries. He stuttered, looking back and forth between the doctor and police officers before answering. Dr. Korn, like Thaddeus Williams, saw signs indicative of torture. The doctor understood that Wilson was scared, and he assumed that Wilson was checking if the cops were listening in on the conversation, as indeed they were. Eventually, Wilson told Dr. Korn that he had fallen outside the police station. Dr. Korn knew this was a lie. The injuries were so many and so varied that he found them difficult to enumerate. This is what Korn wrote in his report:

> Patient claims that he fell outside the police station and incurred all the injuries in that fashion. The injuries include several small hemorrhages to the right eye, ecchymosis below the right eyelid, a one centimeter laceration above the left eyebrow with fresh blood, two eight-centimeter-long linear abrasions to the right cheek, numerous small abrasions under the right chin, a one centimeter laceration to the left occipital scalp, numerous abrasions and bruises on the anterior chest wall, several abrasions to the right deltoid, fifteen-centimeter-long linear by three centimeter wide freshly denuded area along anterior lateral aspect of right thigh with piled up superficial layers of skin at the edges, and erythema about both wrists.

All that means is that Korn reported that Wilson had several ruptured blood vessels in his right eye; a laceration, fresh with blood, above his left eyebrow; two gashes on his right cheek; numerous cuts under the chin; a laceration on the back of the head; radiator burns on his abdomen; several bruises on his chest and right shoulder; deep bruising along both wrists; and a second-degree burn—six inches long and more than an inch wide—on his right thigh.

As Dr. Korn attempted to suture a wound on Wilson's head, Mulvaney took his gun out of its holster—a clear attempt, it seemed, to intimidate doctor and patient alike. Korn had been a doctor long enough to know that this was far from standard procedure. He refused to treat Wilson while Mulvaney's gun was out of its holster and walked out of the examination room when Mulvaney would not put it away.

Only the three of them know what happened when Wilson was left alone with Ferro and Mulvaney. Did the officers remind him of what had been done to him a few hours previously: the black box, the electroshock? Did they remind him what might still occur in a police precinct behind closed doors? I imagine that for Wilson, the precinct was no longer a precinct; it was a building with dark, hidden passageways that led to places of pain, to secret rooms with unimaginably sinister purposes.

Thirty minutes after signing a paper agreeing to treatment, Wilson refused it. He was released after signing another paper, what's known as an AMA, which confirmed that he was leaving the hospital "against medical advice." Once Wilson declined to be a patient, Ferro and Mulvaney returned to police headquarters. This time, they met little resistance from the intake officer. After all, they had taken Wilson to the hospital and couldn't be blamed if he did not want to stay.

Wilson spent the night in lockup. The following morning, he was transported to Cook County Jail and later to court. While he was at the courthouse, an assistant public defender, Barbara Steinberg noticed his injuries. They would have been hard to miss. His head was wrapped in a white bandage through which blood was seeping, and his face was "messed up," Steinberg later testified. Wilson told Steinberg that he had been beaten and shocked. When she asked if he had other injuries, Wilson showed her dark vertical marks— presumably burn marks from the radiator—on his abdominal area. She spoke to the judge to request medical help for Wilson, which the judge granted, and she also telephoned her office to recommend that a photographer be sent to record his injuries.

Upon Wilson's return to jail, photographs were indeed taken. Ordinarily, jail authorities take only mug shots of an arriving prisoner, but because of Andrew Wilson's injuries, and perhaps because of the look of naked vulnerability he wore after his experience with Burge in the torture room, the Cook County authorities took pictures of Andrew's body so as not to be blamed for his wounds. Wilson was then taken to Cermak Health Services, the Cook County Jail hospital facility, where the emergency room doctor detailed his many serious injuries.

Those details were important. Without that documentation it would have been difficult to prove that what happened to Wilson was, indeed, torture.

From the moment Andrew Wilson left the Area 2 police headquarters, the signs of torture were written on his flesh. They were visible to anyone with eyes in his head.[8]

On February 16, Wilson met Dale Coventry, the public defender appointed to represent him in his murder trial. Wilson told Coventry about the torture, and the public defender arranged to have more pictures taken, instructing the photographer to pay particular attention to Wilson's ears, chest, and thighs, where the abrasions were especially raw.

That evening, the medical director at the Cook County Jail hospital facility, Dr. John Raba, examined Wilson's injuries for two consecutive days. Afterwards, Raba sent a letter to the superintendent of the Chicago Police Department, Richard J. Brzeczek. This is what it said.

February 17

Re: Examination of Andrew Wilson

Dear Mr. Brzeczek:

I examined Mr. Andrew Wilson on February 15 & 16, 1982. He had multiple bruises, swellings, and abrasions on his face and head. His right eye was battered and had a superficial laceration. Andrew Wilson had several linear blisters on his right thigh, right cheek and anterior chest, which were consistent with radiator burns. He stated that he had been cuffed to a radiator and pushed into it.

He also stated that electrical shocks had been administered to his gums, lips and genitals.

All these injuries occurred prior to his arrival at the Jail. There must be a thorough investigation of this alleged brutality.

Sincerely,

John M. Raba, M.D.
Medical Director
Cermak (Prison) Health Services

What Raba documented in his letter would later become Deposition Exhibit 2 in Andrew Wilson's court case. But the fact that it would eventually support his claims of torture did not mean much during Wilson's first nights of imprisonment. For the first time in as long as he could remember, Wilson was scared. All his life, people had been afraid of him. Since he was an adolescent, Wilson's teachers, counselors, and coaches had described him as a menace. But the black box had changed everything; his body was in shock, his spirit broken.

Almost a year after his torture, Wilson was tried and found guilty of the murder of the two policemen in January 1983. He was given a death sentence. That sentence was later thrown out, after the Illinois Supreme Court deemed that his confession had been coerced. Wilson was retried, again convicted of murder, and this time sentenced to double life in prison without parole.

While appealing his second murder conviction, Wilson filed what would be the first of several civil suits. Civil cases are different from criminal cases because they involve private disputes between people and organizations. (Criminal cases involve an act that is considered harmful to the whole society.) For example, you could file a civil suit against a business if you thought the company broke the terms of a contract you both agreed to. In that case, you would ask the court to tell the business to fulfill the duty. In this case, Andrew Wilson sued the Chicago police because he felt the government broke the terms of the social contract that he was guaranteed as a citizen of the United States. His civil suit was tried in a federal court because, he argued, the government (rather than another person or business) had violated his constitutional rights by torturing him.

In 1986, when the civil suit was filed, Judge Brian Duff assigned several different firms to act on Wilson's behalf. Perhaps these firms did not have the resources to match the city's, or perhaps they did not want to make an enemy of the Chicago Police Department. Whatever the reason, they all found excuses to evade their obligation until Flint Taylor, John Stainthorp, and Jeffrey Haas of the People's Law Office entered the case on Wilson's behalf in 1987.

The People's Law Office had represented many unpopular political activists, including the families of Fred Hampton and Mark Clark, two Black Panthers who were killed in a middle-of-the-night raid by the Chicago police in 1969. Still, Wilson was a convicted cop killer. Given that the manhunt for the killer of Officers Fahey and O'Brien had been the largest in the city's history, receiving massive news coverage, the law firm, according to Taylor, had a seemingly impossible task.

Indeed, by this time, Andrew Wilson was well known to the public, who reviled him as a cold-blooded murderer. Much of Chicago had rallied around the Fraternal Order of Police, whose members argued that Wilson's lawsuit had no merit and was no less than an attack on law enforcement itself. The People's Law Office faced an increased level of scrutiny and harassment because of the decision to take Wilson's case, but its lawyers persisted, motivated by a desire for justice that outweighed fears of reprisal.

I interviewed Taylor a few years ago. He told me that, by the time he met Wilson, Taylor was a veteran of cases that seemed impossible — "hopeless litigations," he called them. When this civil suit came along, it was another case that just cried out for justice. It had the same issues of race and police violence and unpopular victims as the People's Law Office's previous case, where lawyers proved that the police had murdered members of the Black Panther Party. Of course, the Black Panthers, particularly in the white community, were demonized, "so we had experience with fighting against racism in the courts and in trying to educate people by getting the evidence out," Taylor said.

Fortunately for his client, such challenges seemed to embolden Taylor. He would need all the confidence he could muster to convince a jury of six that Jon Burge, a "star" in the Chicago Police Department, had tortured Wilson. Beyond that, Taylor had to convince the jury that Wilson had the constitutional right *not* to be tortured.

Taylor had a very challenging task: persuading people that torture is unacceptable in any and all circumstances. On an abstract level, most of us would agree. Indeed, the principle is enshrined in the Eighth Amendment to the US Constitution, which prohibits "cruel and unusual punishment" and applies to both the federal and the state criminal justice systems. Yet in practice, many people find themselves on a slippery slope. They think certain criminals are more dangerous than others, and they concede that police officers must sometimes wield force to extract information or confessions from the most dangerous—force that may, on occasion, turn life threatening or lethal. Unfortunate as extrajudicial force might be, many Americans—perhaps even most of them—agree that there are certain circumstances that justify its use. I hope that this story demonstrates the problem with this belief, because it is this belief that allowed police torture to go unpunished for decades in Chicago, and who knows where else.

An Open Letter to Chicago's Youth of Color

As you have already figured out, I have lots of opinions. But I don't want to tell you what you should believe. Instead, I want to show you the parts of this story that have shaped my own thinking. I want to tell you about the black box.

A "black box" can be multiple things. For one, it references the name of a torture device used to send electronic currents through a person's body for the purpose of punishing a criminal suspect or coercing a confession. We now believe that Burge destroyed this torture device. In any event, the machine he used to torture Wilson no longer exists; nor do we have pictures of it. The only image we have of the device is the replica that Taylor built, based on descriptions from Wilson. So the best I can do is try to describe it: the black box was cube shaped and had a handle attached to it like an antique music box. A generator inside the box produced electric current. Electrical wires extended from the generator to alligator clamps. When the handle was cranked, between ninety and one hundred volts of electricity passed through the clamps.

Perhaps the most popular idea of a black box in US culture is the device on an airplane that stores information in the event of a flight accident. But another, lesser-known meaning of black box is the tacit agreement, among a group of police officers, to stop trying to understand how and why torture is taking place in their very own precinct.

An analogy from the social science scholarship should make these twinned meanings clear. In his essay "What is an Instinct," an anthropologist named Gregory Bateson uses the concept of the black box to explain the idea of gravity to his daughter:

> "I can tell you what gravity is supposed to do," Bateson says, "pull objects and things towards the ground. But I can't explain exactly how it does it. It's like a Black Box."
>
> "Oh," his daughter says. "Daddy, what's a Black Box?"
>
> "A Black Box is a conventional agreement between scientists to stop trying to explain things at a certain point. I guess it's usually a temporary agreement."
>
> "But that doesn't sound like a Black Box," she replies.
>
> "No, but that's what it's called," he says. "Things often don't sound like their names."
>
> "No. They don't."
>
> "It's a word that comes from the engineers. When they draw a diagram of a complicated machine, they use a sort of shorthand. Instead of drawing all the details, they make a box to stand for a whole bunch of parts and label the box with what that bunch of parts is supposed to do."

"So, a Black Box is a label for what a bunch of things are supposed to do . . ."

"That's right," Bateson says. "But it's not an explanation of how the bunch works."

"And gravity?" she inquires.

"Is a label for what gravity is supposed to do. It's not an explanation of how it does it."[9]

I mention Bateson's discussion because it fits so nicely with the standard definition of a black box, which *Merriam-Webster's Dictionary* defines as "a complicated electronic device whose internal mechanism is typically hidden from or mysterious to the user."[10]

Throughout Wilson's ordeal, Burge and his henchmen agreed that their torturous activity should remain concealed. That is, in attempting to hide the grisly details of their torture operation, these officers together constructed a conceptual black box. Inside of it were sweeping, unexamined stereotypes about what's good and what's bad, about where and how "the bad" people live, about the skin color of those bad guys, and about what it is permissible to do to them. *That* black box is the racism that keeps torture hidden. It is the contempt for the criminal suspect that allows even those police officers not directly involved in torture to become complicit in their grim silence. They will look the other way when confronted with those who have been suffocated, beaten, and electrocuted, because those people "deserved" what they got. Would that same black box allow a jury of Wilson's peers to condone torture?

I will answer that question throughout the course of this letter. To do so, I must pick up our story in 1987, when the People's Law Office began preparing for Wilson's first civil trial, which would take place two years later. The law office knew it needed to convince the jury of three things: Andrew Wilson's constitutional rights had been violated after his arrest for the murders of Officers Fahey and O'Brien; the Chicago Police Department had a habit of abusing criminal suspects accused of killing cops; and Wilson's abuse fell in line with that habit. If the jury agreed, the City of Chicago would be held financially responsible for torturing Wilson.

The odds were stacked against Andrew Wilson from the start. Indeed, his lawyers knew that many public officials in the police department chose to ignore evidence of torture. Consider, for instance, the fact that people in the state's attorney's and mayor's offices had seen Wilson's injuries during the twenty-four hours after he was beaten and tortured. Additionally, Dr. John Raba had never received a reply to his letter to Police Superintendent Brzeczek describing Wilson's injuries and demanding a full investigation. For his part, Brzeczek did deliver Dr. Raba's letter directly to State's Attorney Richard M. Daley, albeit with a cover letter stating that he (Brzeczek) would not investigate Wilson's alleged torture unless Daley directed him to do so. After consulting with his first assistant, Richard Devine, and another top-level assistant in the State's Attorney's Office, William Kunkle, Daley neglected to respond to Brzeczek and passed the inquiry along to the Special Prosecutions Unit, where, three years later, the investigation was "not sustained." In the meantime, Daley and Brzeczek publicly commended Burge for the capture of Andrew Wilson. Worse, William Kunkle went on to serve as the prosecutor at Andrew Wilson's trial.

By the time Andrew Wilson's civil suit against the city and Burge was filed, Daley had become the mayor. And Chicago City Council's Finance Committee retained the man who had prosecuted Wilson, William Kunkle, then a member of a prestigious law firm where the aforementioned Richard Devine was a partner, to represent Burge and his fellow officers. Clearly, Burge's ties to the mayor's office were so strong that city officials at the highest levels of the government, from Daley on down, were deeply invested in exonerating the police and discrediting Wilson.

A week before the civil trial was to begin, though, something miraculous occurred. A series of letters began arriving at the People's Law Office. The author of those letters was a police insider, a source that Wilson's lawyers dubbed "Deep Badge." This is the first letter:

Mr. Flint Taylor:

I understand you all are representing Andrew Wilson in his civil action against several police officers for brutality.

Check the following:

Several witnesses including the White's were severely beaten at 1121 S State St in front of the Chief of Detectives, the Superintendent of Police and the State's Attorneys. Mayor Byrne and States Attorney Daley were aware of the actions of the detectives. ASA Angarola told both of them and condoned the actions. Several of the officers named in the suit had been previously accused of using torture machines at complaints given to Office of Professional Standards (OPS) and in motions filed in Criminal trial.

The device was destroyed by throwing it off of Lt. Burge's boat. Mayor Byrne and States Attorney Daley ordered that the numerous complaints filed against the police as a result of this crime not be investigated. This order was carried out by an OPS investigator named Buckley who is close to Alderman Burke. You should interview everyone assigned to Area 2's Violent Crime unit at that time because some of them were disgusted and will tell all. The torture was not necessary. Russ Ewing of Channel 7 was investigating this matter and you should talk to him.

DO NOT SHOW THIS TO ANYONE. IF YOU WANT MORE PUT AN AD IN THE SOUTHTOWN ECONOMIST. YOU DO NOT HAVE PERMISSION TO SHOW THIS TO ANYONE. IT IS PRIVILEGED.

They all knew, Deep Badge wrote in another of the four letters he eventually sent to Taylor. "They" included not just the chief of detectives, the superintendent of police, the mayor at the time Jane Byrne, and the state's attorney Richard M. Daley, but also, as emerged in subsequent letters, many other lawyers from the state's attorney's office, as well as judges and lawyers in private practice. The insider said that "they" knew not just about Burge but also about the actions of the officers and detectives in his charge.

In other letters, Deep Badge suggested that Flint Taylor "check the taverns at the intersection of 92nd Street and Western" to locate people Burge had bragged to in the bars where he drank. Burge apparently felt so untouchable, so unassailable, and so above the law that he liked to boast about his harsh interrogation methods, and many citizens in the taverns liked to listen, all of which indicates the shameful fact that Burge's torture of prisoners was an open secret not just in Chicago city government but also on the streets of the city.

Deep Badge named numerous of Burge's "ass kickers" and also identified another torture victim, Melvin Jones. According to Deep Badge, nine days before torturing Wilson, Burge had tortured Jones with electric shock. Taylor found Melvin Jones. It turns out that while torturing him, Burge told Jones that he had also tortured "Satan" (Anthony Holmes) and "Cochise" (Roger Collins), two inmates who Wilson's lawyers subsequently found in prison. Burge would have him "crawling on the floor" like them, he promised Jones. Taylor also met Donald White. In his interview with Taylor, Donald White claimed that Burge and other detectives had beaten him for several hours, suffocated, and shocked him. But if at first the letters Deep Badge provided seemed hard to believe, a stroke of fortune that could have broken open the case, when Taylor attempted to enter Jones's and White's affidavits into evidence, Judge Duff excluded their testimonies on the grounds that "evidence of a prior bad act" was inadmissible.

Judge Duff's ruling provided a stark relief to the optimism Taylor felt upon receiving the letters, dashing his hopes and demonstrating how the institutions of city government would continue to protect those who were guilty of torture. No one can say whether this information would have influenced the jury's decision. Clearly, however, Duff denied the jury information pertaining to the breadth of the unlawful actions that took place under Burge's watch. This information would have established that what happened to Andrew Wilson was not particular to him. Rather, it happened to many other suspects, almost all of them Black men, who were unfortunate enough to have been brought into custody at Area 2.

As soon as the opening statements began, on February 13, 1989, it became clear that Burge's legal team, predictably, wanted to make it as hard as possible for the jury to identify with Wilson. Throughout the case, Kunkle denied repeatedly that Wilson had been tortured, insisting that he had invented the entire scenario. Kunkle, known for eccentricity, put his showmanship on full display in the courtroom. He forced Wilson to show the jury a tattoo on his arm of a rose, two shovels, and a noose. A person willing to be mutilated in this fashion might also inflict a radiator burn on himself, or so Kunkle tried to imply.

Of course, Kunkle reminded the jurors that Fahey and O'Brien had each suffered multiple gunshot wounds, and that Fahey had been killed at close range with a bullet from his own revolver. Kunkle said Wilson had laughed about the murders. Additionally, Kunkle told the jurors that the Wilson brothers had stolen the dead officers' guns and hidden them, along with a sawed-off shotgun used in the murder of yet another Chicago police officer, in a beauty shop.

Was it the brothers' sawed-off shotgun? Did Wilson kill other police officers besides Fahey and O'Brien? Perhaps Wilson's lawyers did not know. Perhaps they did. Or perhaps they held firm to the legal principle that his guilt or innocence was irrelevant to this particular case. Whatever their stance, they knew that if the state had sufficient evidence that Wilson had committed another murder, he certainly would have been charged, but if Wilson's legal team tried explaining that to the jury or refuting any of these allegations, it risked opening the door to a review of Wilson's entire criminal record, which was considerable.

Andrew Wilson took the stand seven days into the trial. His lawyers began by asking Wilson about his formal education, establishing that he had not graduated from elementary school. The goal of Wilson's legal team, it seemed, was to depict their client as someone who had been failed by society at every turn. Only after this theme was established did they ask Wilson about the events of February 14, 1982, when he was arrested, taken into police custody, and tortured.

According to reporters like John Conroy, Wilson's portrayal of the events was as painful to hear as it was convincing.

Then the cross-examination began. The first thing that the city's defense lawyer William Kunkle did was to make it known to the court that Wilson had long made a living by committing crimes. By way of contrast he told the jury that Burge was a US Army veteran who served tours in South Korea and Vietnam. He also informed them that he had earned a Purple Heart, a Bronze Star, and multiple Commendation medals for bravery in war. After returning to the South Side of Chicago in 1970, Kunkle told the jury, Burge began his career as a police officer, rising rapidly through the ranks and eventually becoming a commanding officer at Area 2.

With these biographical details, Kunkle painted an opposition between the criminal and the hero, implicitly asking the jury, Who do you believe? Then, after creating this contrast, he questioned Wilson about the day he was pulled over and his arresting officers were shot.

As Kunkle baited Wilson to respond to questions about his altercation with Fahey and O'Brien, Wilson did as his lawyers advised: he pled the Fifth. On the stand, Wilson did not talk about what he had or had not done before being arrested. Rather, he spoke about what happened to him afterward. Not without hesitation, he described the experience of being electrocuted with the black box.

"He put it on my fingers," Wilson said. "One of the clamps on one finger and one on the other finger. And then he kept cranking it and cranking it, and I was hollering and screaming. I was calling for help. My teeth was grinding. Flickering in my head. Pain . . ."

This last word, *pain*, was a fading whisper. Wilson's voice grew softer as he spoke. He paused for several seconds and, after reflecting on the horrifying spectacle of his torture, returned to his testimony.

"It hurts," Wilson continued. "But it stays in your head, OK? It stays in your head and it grinds your teeth . . . it grinds, constantly grinds, constantly. The pain just stays in your head. And your teeth constantly grinds, and grinds, and grinds, and grinds, and grinds and grinds."

Seven years after he was tortured, Andrew Wilson was still unable to recount what had happened at Area 2 without choking up. When describing the black box, Wilson grew so upset that he wanted to leave the courtroom. The judge declared a short recess to grant him relief. Once the court proceedings resumed, Wilson came close to breaking down again. John Conroy, a reporter who wrote about Wilson's testimony that day, said that his lawyer urged him to "take a minute to compose himself."

"It's just like this light here like when it flickers, it flickers," Wilson said before reminding the jury again of how the current from the black box made him grind his teeth. "All my bottom teeth was loose behind that. These four or five . . . and I tried to get the doctor to pull them. He said he wouldn't pull them because they would tighten back up."

In his closing arguments, Taylor reminded the jury that the case was not about the murder of two policemen. Nor was it about the quality of Andrew Wilson's character. Instead, the trial was premised on an ethical question: was Andrew Wilson beaten, tortured, and deprived of his constitutional rights after his arrest?

Taylor argued that the city had done nothing to investigate Wilson's allegations of torture. "Just because [a policeman] thinks that Andrew Wilson should get the death penalty," Taylor said, "doesn't mean that you can electroshock him and start the process."

The stories Burge and Wilson told must have seemed worlds apart to the jurors. And in the end, the jury had trouble reconciling the different accounts. Wilson's lawyers presented convincing evidence of Wilson's torture. At the same time, the fact that he likely killed two police officers might have tempted the jury to disregard the brutality used to extract Wilson's confession. Burge was swept away by an understandable desire to avenge the deaths of his fellow officers, or so the jury might have reasoned, and grief and rage got the best of him.

After days of deliberation, the jurors were not able to reach consensus. Four times they sent a message to Judge Duff indicating that they were deadlocked. Judge Duff declared a mistrial on March 30, 1989, and the ethical issue of Andrew Wilson's alleged torture and the denial of his constitutional rights remained unresolved.

An Open Letter to Chicago's Youth of Color

Now that you've learned about the circumstances of Andrew Wilson's torture as well as his first civil trial, in this letter I'm going to give you a test—less like a quiz, though, and more like a challenge. In the pages to come, I will present the details of Wilson's second civil trial and the circumstances that led up to it as well as what happened afterward. I'm discussing this new trial and its aftermath because I want to challenge you to see that a person can be convicted of a crime and still have a right not to be tortured. You should understand that many before you have failed this test—including the jurors and judge who presided over Wilson's first civil trial.

My last letter ended at the point at which the jury could not decide whether Wilson had been tortured. The three people of color on the six-person jury believed that he had. The three white jurors believed that he had not. The result was a mistrial. But the mistrial did not end Andrew Wilson's legal journey. He decided to go back to court and continue to fight. Doing so meant he would have to endure the excruciating trial process all over again. It is important to note that verdicts in civil cases have nothing to do with convictions in criminal cases. Wilson's civil case would have no bearing on the crime for which he had already been convicted. Whatever the outcome of the new trial, Wilson would serve out his sentence, spending the rest of his days in prison.

What is more, our legal system has ways of making sure that convicted criminals do not profit from their crimes. For example, if someone is found guilty of a murder and then tries to enrich himself by writing a book about the person he killed, the family of the slain person can sue the convicted murderer for wrongful death, which means that they are attempting to hold him legally responsible for that death. That way, the family would receive the profits from the book—not the convicted murderer.

By the time Andrew Wilson was considering a second trial against the City of Chicago and the police department, the families of Fahey and O'Brien had already won a wrongful death lawsuit, meaning that they had a legal right to garnish any wages Wilson earned, including money awarded to him in a settlement. Wilson knew that any potential compensation he received would go to them because of that previous judgment. Given that he had no economic incentive to carry on, I've always wondered about Wilson's motivations for continuing to fight. While it might have been the right thing to do, returning to court after the first ruling stood to cause Andrew Wilson more pain with no clear benefit to him, not even if he won.

When I first researched this case, I imagined Taylor and his associates persuading Wilson to testify again. *This wasn't some sick fairy tale that you dreamed up to evade responsibility for your crimes*, I imagined them saying. *This is your reality. And who knows how many other people have suffered the same fate?* I assumed that they must have convinced Wilson that another trial could bring him a measure of the justice that had eluded him for so long and could help save other people and keep them from suffering what Wilson had.

Knowing what I did of Wilson's mind-set from reading the courtroom testimony of his criminal trial, I assumed that he would have been weighing the potential for a largely symbolic victory against the inevitable legal ordeal he would again be subjected to, and that he would probably be hesitant to go back to court.

One of Wilson's lawyers, John Stainthorp, was struck by the fact that when Wilson discussed being tortured, he always ended up crying. "He would be absolutely furious with himself," Stainthorp said, "that it affected him that way." And agreeing to another trial meant that Wilson would have to retell the experience of being suffocated, electrocuted, and beaten. He would have to *again* relive the horrors of that day in 1982. The black box was a psychological weight in Wilson's life. In prison, miles and years away from Area 2, he still felt that electricity running through his veins.

Wilson felt these emotional aftershocks throughout his first civil trial, most noticeably when enumerating for the jury the gruesome events following his arrest. Now, Taylor and his legal team were asking him to once again dredge up dark memories—memories, I assumed, that Wilson would be desperately trying to forget. Why relive the grinding pain when the outcome was no more likely to be successful than it had been the first time?

But when I asked Taylor how Wilson felt about a second trial, he told me that my assumptions were wrong. Wilson wanted to go to court again, and seeing Wilson's passion, Taylor would help advocate on his client's behalf.

Taylor reminded me that Wilson had a first-grade education and was the most unpopular guy in the city on account of his being the subject of the biggest manhunt the city had ever seen. Yet, even before the People's Law Office agreed to take his case, back when every other firm in Chicago refused to represent him, Wilson kept insisting that Chicago police officers tortured him. "No, Wilson wanted the second trial," Taylor said. "We were the hesitant ones." Taylor explained that the People's Law Office was small and its more experienced lawyers had been pulled from all the other litigation going on to work on Wilson's case. The office needed to make enough money to keep the doors open. To go on trial again, another eight weeks, "while I was getting held in contempt by a racist judge every other day," Taylor said, was not appealing to him. He did not want to do it. Plus he knew the chances of winning were slim.

All of the lawyers in the firm had serious discussions where they asked themselves: Can we do this again financially and emotionally and in terms of our family? According to Taylor, "At the end of the day, we . . . decided to do it again. I'm glad we did. But we certainly paid a psychic price for it."

Perhaps the "psychic price" that Taylor was referring to was the ridicule that supporters of the police levied against his firm for taking Wilson's case. Perhaps it was just stress from working around the clock. I never got clarification on the matter. What I do know is that the toll the case took on Taylor was not evident from the vigor and effort he put into the case. Indeed, I've always been in awe of how Taylor maintained his resolve in the face of so many setbacks. Eventually, he came up with a way to use testimony from the other victims Burge had tortured: judges could exclude testimonies from Jones and

White, but they could not prevent Taylor from gleaning insight from those testimonies. That is, instead of trying to prove that Wilson, Jones, and White were telling the truth, Taylor would simply believe them. And he would use what they said to find further evidence that Jon Burge had tortured before.

Letters play an important role in this story. The words of Deep Badge, the police insider informant, prompted Taylor to look at the evidence anew. After reading Deep Badge's letters, Taylor remembered Burge saying during Andrew Wilson's arrest that he would "get" him at the station. He remembered Burge complaining to the arresting officers that they should have injured Wilson without leaving marks, and Ferro and Mulvaney trying to place Wilson in an occupied cell so that Burge and his officers could not be held responsible for his wounds. Combined, these actions suggested forethought and routine.

Burge was not a man blinded by rage or driven by a self-destructive compulsion to torture. What the letters helped Taylor understand was that far from being a rogue cop, Burge had developed a set of procedures that all but codified the stages of a successful torture session. The procedures had become so commonplace in Chicago that many police officers knew the drill. Beyond that, many lawyers, judges, and politicians had developed, through prolonged exposure, tried-and-true ways of sweeping torture claims under the rug.

Wilson's second civil trial began on June 19, 1989, and lasted almost eight weeks. For seven of those weeks, the jury heard from witnesses. Most of the witnesses had previously testified in Wilson's first trial, but two were new and of material importance. Wilson's lawyers called Willie Porch, who was serving thirty years in prison for armed robbery and attempted murder. As Porch explained to the jury, remorse for those crimes had not brought him in to testify. Rather, he wanted to document his torture in a US court of law. For Taylor, though, Porch's testimony was critical in proving that Wilson was only one among a host of torture survivors. And this was not merely because he had been subjected to violence while in police custody. It had to do with the way he had been tortured.

Porch said that the police had handcuffed his arms behind his back and that one of the officers stood on his testicles. He said they hit him with a gun on his head. Then one of the officers tried to hang him by his handcuffs to a hook on the door.

But if Taylor's new theory hinged on proving Burge had tortured many other men, Burge's lawyer, once again William Kunkle, wanted the jury to believe that they could not be certain about whether Burge ever tortured anyone at all. After Porch's testimony, Kunkle called William Coleman to the stand. Clearly, Coleman's role was to support Kunkle's claim that Wilson had fabricated his tales of torture.

Coleman and Andrew Wilson had crossed paths in 1987, at Cook County Jail. At the time, Wilson was awaiting his retrial for murder. According to Coleman, Wilson told him that he had killed the two police officers and that he burned himself on the radiator in the interview room.

"He wanted to make it look like his confession was forced out of him," Coleman said from the stand.

Judge Duff did not allow Wilson's lawyers to tell the jury the full extent of Coleman's record, which included convictions going back ten years. Had he been allowed to do so, Jeffrey Haas, who cross-examined him, would have revealed that Mr. "Coleman" had actually gone by ten different aliases, served prison time in seven different countries, and been convicted of eight different crimes in his lifetime. Fortunately, Duff did permit Haas to tell the jury about some of Coleman's criminal offenses. They included blackmail, theft, fraud, cocaine possession, making a false statement to obtain a passport, and a jail escape. In other words, Coleman was a practiced liar. Besides the crimes Coleman had been convicted of, he was also a "jail informant," which suggests that he had an incentive to cooperate with them.

In light of his background, the jury must've found Coleman's claim that Wilson had invented his tales of torture less than convincing: on August 8, 1989, eight weeks after the trial began, and after three days of deliberation, the jury issued its verdict.

The verdict form read: "Do you find that Plaintiff's constitutional rights were violated while he was in police custody,"

"Yes," the jury foreman, Allen Gall, said.

"Do you find that in 1982 the city of Chicago had a de facto policy, practice, or custom whereby the police were allowed to abuse those suspected of injuring or killing another police officer?"

"Yes," Gall said again.

"Do you find that plaintiff was subjected to excessive force as a direct and proximate result of this de facto policy, practice or custom?"

"No," Gall said.

This last answer was perhaps the most important: because the jury found that Wilson's "abuse" occurred outside of the police's de facto policy, they felt that Burge should not be held responsible. He and his colleagues were cleared of all charges. The jury's verdict acknowledged that Wilson's constitutional rights were violated, that criminal suspects accused of killing cops had been systematically abused, and yet still categorized Wilson as an exception to this policy, therefore denying him any damages.

Shortly after the verdict, reporter John Conroy interviewed the foreman of the second six-person jury about their reasoning. This is what Gall said:

> If anything, I believe it was an emotional outburst by them, and that was the reason why he suffered his injuries. I don't think it necessarily had to be done under this policy. . . . We believe that he did sustain these injuries from the police, some of the injuries, but there wasn't enough evidence to show that he got all of the injuries from the police. As to whether or not he was actually tortured, there is not enough evidence either . . . it just seemed to me they were just really mad at this guy for shooting one of their buddies, and you know a couple of these guys took the liberty of letting their emotional attitude toward this guy show. They were just acting out their anger toward this guy. That is something we agreed upon. . . . [But] it is kind of hard to find someone responsible for something so serious without an actual witness coming forward, a neutral witness coming forward and saying, "I seen him do it." . . . We did agree that he got those injuries from somewhere, but as far as being specific as to who actually did this

damage, there just wasn't enough evidence. . . . You know convicts, a lot of these guys are streetwise and they're pretty good at bullshitting.

Gall's response offers a glimpse into the jury's thinking, demonstrating how jurors overlooked the powerful evidence Wilson presented to them out of sympathy for the officers. The officers were simply "emotional" and "acting out their anger"—anodyne phrases that one might apply to a toddler having a temper tantrum. It is illegal for police officers to use excessive force against a criminal suspect, yet the jury both excused this behavior and refused to call it torture.

Members of the jury didn't only question Wilson's credibility. To Gall, a man like Porch could not be considered an "actual" or "neutral" witness, either, because he was a criminal—and criminals, according to Gall, are by definition untrustworthy, "good at bullshitting," which is another way of saying that Wilson and the others were lying about torture. Perhaps this is why Coleman's testimony did not carry much weight either. Even though he was a white man, Coleman was still a convict, and that fact might have made him unreliable. After all, despite Coleman's testimony, the jury still believed that there was a "de facto policy" that encouraged police abuse at Area 2. This suggests that Taylor's new theory about the systematic and routine nature of torture at Area 2 had, in fact, persuaded them to a degree.

To issue a verdict that Andrew Wilson was an exception to this policy meant that at least some of the jurors had to be innately suspicious of Wilson but at the same time identify with the motivations of a man like Burge. As a result, a torturer remained on the police force. Likewise, the police officers who joined Burge in committing acts of torture were also protected.

This is what I wanted you to see. Gall's statement is exactly the kind of thinking that was pervasive across all levels of the city's government. So, when the jury acknowledged this wrong but refused to compensate Wilson, they were merely parroting the point of many, many people, from citizens, to police officers, to the state's attorney, to judges, to politicians in your city. It is this pervasiveness that allowed the black box to swallow up so much clear evidence of torture and that allows the City of Chicago to put justice on pause until the People's Law Office appealed the verdict in Andrew Wilson's second civil trial to the US Court of Appeals for the Seventh Circuit.

• • •

As you might imagine, Wilson's legal team eagerly anticipated the outcome of its appeal. But just before hearing a decision, something important happened. The Chicago Police Board—a civilian body independent of the police department that hears disciplinary cases that involve Chicago police officers—held hearings for six weeks in February and March of 1992, to determine whether Jon Burge should remain on the force. Although the board refused to call him a torturer, members did conclude that Burge "did . . . physically abuse or mal-treat" Wilson, and that as commanding officer he did not stop others from engaging in the abuse, nor did he secure medical attention for Wilson. It was on these grounds that, on February 10, 1993, the board finally fired Jon Burge.

Eight months later, on October 4, 1993, a three-judge panel from the US Seventh Circuit Court of Appeals issued their decision on whether Andrew Wilson would be granted a new civil trial. In the decision, Chief Judge Richard Posner expressed awe and disbelief about what happened in Judge Duff's courtroom. In ruling that Burge's prior acts of police "abuse" were "immaterial" to Wilson's case, Duff had stretched the concept of relevance "beyond the breaking point," Posner said. He added that in a civil trial, it was Burge who had to defend himself, not Wilson. Kunkle should not have been able to in-troduce "inflammatory evidence" about Wilson's character that had little or no relevance as to whether he had been tortured. Wilson's lawyers should have been able to tell the jury that Coleman had a his-tory of lying on the stand. Kunkle had been allowed to "turn the trial of the defendants into a trial of the plaintiff," and Posner thought that Judge Duff was to blame. "Even a murderer has a right to be free from torture," Posner said, "and the correlative right to present his claim of torture to a jury that has not been whipped into a frenzy of hatred."

Because Posner agreed with Flint Taylor that Judge Duff's actions in the trial prohibited him from proving that Wilson's constitutional rights had been violated, he sent the case back to federal district court. US District Court Judge Robert Gettleman replaced Judge Duff as the case's arbiter. Wilson's attorneys asked Gettleman to adopt the findings of the police board rather than go through a third federal trial that would largely repeat the hearings held by the board. There was legal precedent that allowed Gettleman to act on the police board's findings regarding Burge's guilt and then hold a hearing to address the question of damages. That's just what Judge Gettleman decided to do.

In the summer of 1995, Judge Gettleman granted Wilson's motion of summary judgment, ordering the city to pay more than $1 million in damages. According to Gettleman's ruling, $900,016 was to be paid to Wilson's attorneys. Jeffrey Haas, John Stainthorp, and Flint Taylor had represented Andrew Wilson at every stage throughout his civil case. The tireless lawyers from the People's Law Office had recorded more than six thousand hours of work on the case, and until that point had not received any compensation. (By contrast, over the same period, the city had paid almost $850,000 to William Kunkle.) Gettleman also ruled that $100,000 was to be paid to Wilson, which would actually go to the families of the slain officers because of the judgment I mentioned earlier.

It is important to note that the knowledge that torture had occurred did not translate into any organized attempt to provide relief for the Area 2 victims. Nor did the verdict mean that the City of Chicago would begin indicting or investigating other police officers in Area 2 who had also been accused of torture. The only legislation that emerged after Wilson's second civil suit was a bill signed by Governor Jim Edgar in 1992. The bill was meant not to help torture survivors but to protect the torturers of the future. It established a five-year statute of limitations for police brutality. The rationale? The police board had disciplined Jon Burge nine years after he tortured Andrew

Wilson, and the supporters of the bill believed it was a tragedy they were able to do so.[11]

What I personally consider a tragedy, however, is this: after Burge was dismissed by the Chicago Police Board for "physical abuse," after the *Chicago Tribune* and *Sun-Times* called for a judicial inquiry into cases involving prisoners on death row who had confessed at Area 2, after Amnesty International investigated the allegations that Chicago police officers had tortured criminal suspects, after the Chicago Police Department Office of Professional Standards reported that police violence included "planned torture," and after the jury in Andrew Wilson's second civil trial noted a de facto policy of "police abuse"—after all of these things, Jon Burge would never face criminal charges for torture. Without such a public airing of the truth, the full knowledge of Burge's torture operation has disappeared, just like Burge's torture device, buried at the bottom of a body of water, never to be seen again.

PART II The B-Team

An Open Letter to Police Superintendent Eddie Johnson

Before I begin, I want to offer belated congratulations for your appointment to the position of superintendent of the Chicago Police Department on April 13, 2016. I have been following the appointment closely. I noticed that a month before that, when mayor Rahm Emanuel named you interim superintendent, it seemed the Chicago Police Board might try to block your appointment—especially since the mayor rejected the board's favored candidate and picked you instead.

While following the circumstances of your appointment, I grew more and more intrigued by your candidacy because of what you seemed to represent: hope for repairing the broken relationship between the police department and the Black community. In the local reporting much was made of the fact that you were born and raised in Chicago, and that you grew up in the notorious Cabrini-Green housing project. Reporters also made much of the fact that you had held just about every rank in the Chicago Police Department—from patrol officer to chief of patrol. You even served as a police commander, as Jon Burge once had.

But the mayor made it clear that you didn't get this position based on your qualifications alone. He saw you as a "bridge to the community." This is what I wanted to talk to you about: your role as a bridge.

The difficulty of building trust between the police department and the community cannot be underestimated. I know this isn't lost on you. Your predecessor, Garry McCarthy, was fired in 2015 amid outrage and protests following the video footage of a white officer shooting a Black teenager, Laquan McDonald, no less than sixteen times. You must be well aware that it wasn't just the mayor, but many Black and Latino aldermen who wanted a native Chicagoan of color to fill this post. From listening to your interviews after accepting this position, I know that you want to take responsibility for the police department's legacy of violence. I also know that you hope to end those violent practices.

What worries me is that the mayor, the aldermen, and the fifty city council members who voted unanimously in favor of your appointment are all behaving as though because you are African American and from Chicago, that will be enough to spark change. I agree with them that these are critical assets that many of your predecessors did not possess. But I disagree that these assets in and of themselves will ensure your success or allow you to create the changes needed within the police department to instill legitimacy. To effect change, you will have to reckon with the history of police violence, corruption, and scandal that you have inherited as superintendent, particularly as it relates to the legacy of torture.[1]

I'm fairly certain that by the time you were sworn in you had a lot of experts telling you about the incredible burden that torture has placed on the city. But the knowledge I can pass on is different from the issues of police morale or the economic costs of police violence, and it will also be different from any analysis that politicians and lawyers and lawmakers and bureaucrats have given you about the opportunity costs of addressing police torture.

They might have briefed you about Jon Burge and the Andrew Wilson case. But since Burge and the officers closest to him are now widely regarded as the ones responsible for the torture inflicted at Area 2, my guess is that you did not learn much about the other police officers working in Burge's vicinity when Wilson was brought in and tortured. I believe that it is these officers, especially the Black cops—often overlooked because they did not commit any crimes—who allow us to understand torture and its culture more deeply than your typical sources. It is only by making sense of what this marginalized group went through that you can appreciate the different ways that torture effects all Chicagoans across this great city, many of whom would like to be able to rely on the police—but feel like they cannot.

I'm aware of this distrust from studying the problem of police torture. I have found that the institutional culture of racism within Area 2 not only helped sow seeds of distrust between the police and the community but also helped torture to grow. Even though a host of white officers have been far more essential than Black officers in establishing and perpetuating this institutional racism, I want you to focus on how the Black officers had to navigate the discrimination they encountered. It is by paying attention to the most vulnerable within the police department that you can broaden your understanding not just of torture itself but also of the many related aspects of life in Chicago that police torture has affected. These Black officers were adjacent to the torture—both complicit in it and victimized by it—so by paying attention to their marginality, you can better see the entire government structure that allows torture to take place.

• • •

Before telling you about these Black officers in this letter, I must first tell you about the man they were up against, because by describing what Burge was like, and what inspired him, you can truly appreciate their struggles.

I have studied life in Area 2 for more than a decade; and I have stories to share that may be helpful to you as superintendent. During your decades on the police force, I'm sure that you've been pressured by individual cops to do something unethical or illegal. You may have dismissed these advances, or even reported them, and then occupied yourself with the details of everyday life at the precinct. Since being confronted with illegal behavior on the job oftentimes affects people on an individual level, it can be difficult to take a bird's-eye view of things to see the impact on the entire culture of a police district. That's why I want to tell you about Area 2.

What I'm going to tell you about Jon Burge and the police officers at Area 2 will, at times, seem stranger than fiction. Perhaps this is because, in some respects, Area 2 presaged a fiction—specifically, a television series that debuted ten years after Burge began his program of torture: *The A-Team*.

On more than one occasion—while interviewing former officers, or slogging through city archives or the court testimony in which torture survivors describe what Burge did to them—it has seemed to me as though Burge's exploits, so fantastical and dastardly and shocking, could have been cut straight from the TV show. This makes a certain kind of sense, I suppose, given that the show was inspired by the war in Vietnam, the same war in which Burge likely witnessed torture.[2]

Each episode of *The A-Team* begins with a voice-over, reminding us of the show's very specific origin:

> *Ten years ago a crack commando unit was sent to prison by a military court for a crime they didn't commit. These men promptly escaped from a maximum-security stockade to the Los Angeles underground. Today, still wanted by the government, they survive as soldiers of fortune. If you have a problem, if no one else can help, and if you can find them, maybe you can hire . . . the A-Team.*

In the show, during the Vietnam War, a Colonel Morrison orders his unit of Green Beret soldiers to rob the Bank of Hanoi. In Morrison's thinking, doing so would help end the war. The unit succeeded, but upon returning to base, they discovered that the Viet Cong had killed Morrison and burned his headquarters to the ground. Having lost their leader and headquarters, these men—the A-Team—had also lost all proof that they were acting under legitimate orders. Arrested and placed in a military prison, the crew escaped before standing trial. The veterans became mercenaries: working as freelance hired guns, killing, fighting, and kidnapping for anyone who could pay their fee—that is, anyone who was essentially a "good guy" who had in some way been wronged.

The leader of the A-Team was John "Hannibal" Smith, his nickname a nod to the Carthaginian commander. During the pilot episode, Sergeant Bosco "B.A." Baracus, the team's tough guy (played by Mr. T, the flamboyant Black actor, who I looked up to as a youth) explained that the Carthaginian "took his army over the Alps into Italy. He used elephants to carry his equipment. Nobody thought you could take an army over the Alps. But Hannibal did. Caught the Romans sleeping and beat 'em up."

Among Vietnam vets, "A-Team" was shorthand for the elite Special Forces known as "Alpha" units. Given that the US government gave Jon Burge medals for the feats he performed in Korea and Vietnam, it makes sense that he thought of himself as a hero, and he thought of the tough-guy methods he used in Vietnam as an essential part of his heroism. No wonder he brought that mentality back to Chicago. He even referred to the police officers in his inner circle as the A-Team.

I grew up loving *The A-Team*. The episodes were in syndication when I was in middle school, and I watched them, one after the other, after my parents went to bed. I cheered on their unforgiving brand of heroics. I knew they were campy and ridiculous, but I couldn't help myself. They still were exciting and addictive. Then, about a decade ago, long after I had forgotten about these childhood heroes, I sat down in an archive. The trial transcripts wrenched at my heart as soon as I started reading them. What bothered me most was how on the TV show, the Viet Cong soldiers they fought with constantly and engaged in shootouts with survived all sorts of mayhem with no ill effects. The message was that wartime violence was something that a person could easily recover from. Now I know better than to believe that lie.

The casual, even humorous way the producers of that show enacted cartoonish scenes of the A-Team throwing enemies off buildings, tipping over cars, and beating people up with metal pipes became horrifying when I realized that this happened in real life. I felt sick knowing that I rooted for the heroes of this show as a child, only to realize later that I identified more with the dispossessed people from faraway places that these "heroes" were killing. This funny misgiving overcame me: my childhood heroes acted like Jon Burge.

Some of the commonalities between Burge's cops and the characters on the show seemed trivial at first. For example, like Hannibal, Burge was known to wear loose-fitting safari shirts, carry a nickel-plated handgun, and repurpose old mechanical parts for weaponry. However, in considering these seemingly disparate details, I began to discern a common theme: Burge's elite squad members, like the fictional A-Team, defied the rule of law to pursue their own version of justice. Neither of these teams was accountable to anyone or anything. The show rationalized the use of extrajudicial means to accomplish whatever the team deemed necessary and made that flouting of the law seem heroic. Burge, it seemed, followed suit.

More than anything else, Burge and his men were proud of themselves, proud of their accomplishments in tracking down so many men they considered menaces to their city, and they protected one another in their quest to fight against "evil." Speaking as a character witness on behalf of the former police commander, one of Burge's colleagues even said: "If I was on my way to heaven, and Satan himself was trying a final time to take my soul, I would want Jon Burge watching my back."[3]

For Burge, the number of criminals he punished and the confessions he forced from them garnered the admiration of his colleagues and led to many commendations and promotions over the years. Burge advanced from patrolman to detective to sergeant to lieutenant to commander, with a Purple Heart and the Vietnam Cross of Gallantry along the way. And lest you forget, all of this happened with the blessing of the superintendents he served.

Many reporters and activists have considered how your predecessors were complicit in legitimizing and sustaining this culture that permitted torture. One of them, Richard Brzeczek, recently argued that a code of silence in the police department has not just led to but also encouraged police corruption over the years.[4] But hardly anyone has investigated the institutional culture of Burge's Area 2 or how the social exclusion of Black officers enabled him to torture. I know from experience that there is much to learn from such an investigation. And this is why I am writing to you now.

An Open Letter to the Late William Parker

You died in 2008, and I know that while you were living, you sometimes felt like an outcast. You felt as if the entire Chicago Police Department had conspired against you. You felt as though your efforts to call out police misconduct and torture were in vain. But I'm here to tell you they were not. Your life and career have been enormously helpful in identifying enduring problems within the Chicago Police Department. If I have any say, your legacy will be one of an untiring whistleblower. Although you might not have seen the kind of change you wanted to see in your lifetime, you have taught me key lessons about the conditions that permitted Jon Burge to terrorize the Black people of Chicago. I would like to pass those lessons along.

My open letter to the current superintendent of the Chicago Police Department, Eddie Johnson, was informed by what I learned from you, about your time working under Burge's command. Superintendent Johnson faces enormous pressure to act, to fix social problems, and to make clear his intentions for improving the city. After reflecting on your life, I felt an urgent need to address him, so that he can figure out the steps he would take to deal with police corruption. I believe that sitting with the reality of torture and discrimination, reflecting on it, is more important than acting hastily to fix the problems that the phenomenon of police torture has created. This is because the wrong solution can actually make things worse. I have to credit you with that insight more than anyone else. You helped me realize that to answer the question of how torture becomes accepted among police officers, you must first understand what goes on in a precinct, where a code of silence among police officers breeds divisiveness and exclusion.

In terms of the institutional culture at Area 2, I also learned from you that the problem of police torture does not begin and end with a dangerous man named Jon Burge, as many have assumed. A major catalyst for torture was not even a person at all. It was a desire common and seemingly fundamental to our capitalist worldview: career ambition. Yes—career ambition allowed police officers to benefit from keeping quiet about torture, and it punished them for speaking out. It is tempting to see ambition as a neutral desire, a desire that has nothing to do with race. But when your minority status marginalizes you and makes you different, the ambitions of others can put you in a horrible bind. Your life and career make a prime example of this point.

• • •

After learning that the officers closest to Burge were considered his "A-Team," I needed another letter to denote those farthest from his inner circle. What if Area 2 also had a B-Team? If everyone on the A-Team was white, then the police department's B-Team was all Black. If the A-Team comprised soldiers of fortune, then the B-Team comprised soldiers of misfortune—cops plagued by adversity and setback. If the former squad operated outside the law, acting under its own authority, which was the only authority its members recognized, then the latter could be characterized by fidelity to the law, a fidelity that hindered its members' ability to gain power. If the captain of the A-Team was Jon Burge, a man who might have viewed himself as a Hannibal-like figure, the storied commander who crushed his opponents at any cost, then the captain of the B-Team would have to be you, William, whose career is surely a cautionary tale for Black officers in the Chicago Police Department. Even for those Black officers who would have never heard of you, or would never get to meet you, the fact that they were deprived of your dignified example, I think, is a shame.

In the fall of 2009, I came across your sworn statement in the torture case of Aaron Patterson. Patterson was one of the four men who, in 2003, would be granted an innocence pardon by Illinois governor George Ryan on the basis of having been tortured into giving a false confession. But soon after I found your testimony, I discovered your obituary. I have since searched for your name in various newspaper articles and archives, and I have come to know your story well. The more I learned, the more your career disturbed me. What still bothers me more than anything is not the trouble you seemed always to find yourself in—the controversies that gravitated toward you as though magnetically attracted to you—but rather your excellence. You were an outstanding officer. And you suffered numerous indignities and demotion. Indeed, you embodied the irony of "Black excellence," the notion that a Black person has to work twice as hard to achieve half as much as his or her white peers.

While researching your life to find out what led you and Burge to cross paths, I learned that you were hired out of the National Guard and joined the Chicago Police Department in 1957. At the time, you were one of fewer than one hundred Black officers on the force (out of approximately ten thousand CPD employees). Chicago in the late 1950s was a deeply segregated city with profound racial divides—and this was certainly true of the police department, which was an accurate reflection of the society it served. To thrive in such an environment was no small feat. No doubt you had learned from your time in the Guard the discipline you would need as a patrolman. I was impressed to find that you were promoted to detective within six months.

Still, looking into your life made it plain to see how exceedingly difficult it was for a Black officer to rise through the ranks in this overwhelmingly white profession without suffering major setbacks. The color of your skin would, again and again, prove a liability. But

I noticed another problem, perhaps even more damaging than your skin color: your fidelity to the law. Your colleagues described you as having such a strong sense of appropriate conduct that you never even permitted yourself the guilty pleasure of using foul language.

This propriety comes across in a December 13, 1991, letter you wrote to Flint Taylor, the civil rights lawyer who has been creating headaches for Chicago's mayors since the late 1960s. What has been extremely helpful in my efforts to document police torture is how you began the six-page letter: by explaining your three reasons for writing it. First, you wanted to break "the code of silence within the Chicago Police Department"; second, you wanted to make Taylor aware that you had worked in Area 2 with Burge for a little over a year, from September 14, 1972, to November 8, 1973, during which time you "had an occasion to witness Burge commit an act of brutality"; finally, you submitted a detailed chronology, documenting your time on the force, which contained "the facts and circumstances" surrounding the ongoing violation of your "rights and privacy" over twenty-eight years.

In the letter, you expressed hope that Taylor might review the document and perhaps represent you, because you were contemplating suing the Chicago Police Department. (As far as I can tell, the suit never went forward.)[5]

What impressed me most about this letter was that, throughout your career, you were willing to stand up and express indignation when witnessing any form of injustice. That admirable quality seems to have been part of your personality, which was perhaps why you were drawn to the police force in the first place. However, I couldn't help but notice that this did not endear you to your fellow officers, who viewed you as a petulant child standing on a soapbox, protesting everything they were doing wrong.

Indeed, the more your peers got to know you, it seemed, the more they shunned you. Even early in your career, you seemed to inspire a crowd of detractors. Before you knew it, a vast sea of dissent had swelled beneath you—fellow cops intent on destroying your career. Throughout your time in the department you would ride waves that would sometimes recede but would nevertheless eventually sweep you away. How did you survive in such a toxic environment?

Your colleagues seem to have hated you in a deeply personal way. Nevertheless, you did not seem to know how to behave any differently—a principled policeman in spite of yourself, you couldn't help but antagonize them because your exemplary behavior threw their own faults into sharp relief.

I have to admit that, even to me at first, you did seem something of a prude. As you said in your letter: "I became labeled a (big anal opening). The reason being, I refused to accept free coffee and rolls. More exactly, one of the officers in the district noticed that I always insisted on paying. Consequently, he brought it to the attention of the other district personnel. Finally, one day the officer came to me and stated: 'If you don't want to accept the coffee and roll for free that's your business. But don't mess up a good thing for everyone else.'"

I could just imagine the running joke around Area 2:

Parker is so uptight.
How uptight is he?

He's the only cop on the force that won't accept a free doughnut . . .

All of which is to say nothing of the fact that in your letter to Taylor, you would not even reproduce the epithet they had called you.

When I first read about the doughnut controversy, I assumed that such banter was largely hyperbolic, that you were overreacting. But as I read farther, and as you recounted other major hurdles in your career, I realized that you'd had the right perspective all along. The events you described should not be taken lightly, for such small abuses of power suggested the much greater abuses that were already going on. Something as innocuous as a free doughnut does suggest the pattern of larger abuses of power that were happening throughout the Chicago Police Department.

I noticed how you became increasingly less inhibited as your letter to Taylor went on, describing problems on the force and how your colleagues reacted to you. Clearly, your colleagues wanted you to leave them alone, with respect not just to free doughnuts but also to other, more serious situations. I learned from your story how small infractions could pave the way for larger abuses. One cop transgresses the law. Another cop protects. Those same mechanisms later shielded Burge's torture operation.

In reflecting on the code of silence within the Chicago Police Department, I often find myself returning to this quote (also from your 1991 letter): "Then there was the incident in 1964 or 65 where I was present when an alleged rapist was being brutalized by two officers. I became so upset, I just went in and took the offender back to the lock up, and told the officers I did not like the way they were trying to make him admit to something that he may not have been guilty of. The following morning, I was called in by the unit commander (Lt. James Riordan). He told me he had heard about what I had done. The fact that it had happened could not be changed. However he strongly suggested that in the future I should not be involved with other officers and their prisoners, for the same reason that it was none of my business. Instead, he suggested that I leave the presence of any future situation where I might be prompted to butt in."[6]

I learned from your own words that much of your time on the force was marked by feelings of exclusion and isolation. Nevertheless, above all else, one unforgettable encounter with Jon Burge seems to have determined your trajectory, causing your superiors in Area 2 to torpedo your career in such a way that you never entirely recovered.[7]

• • •

When thinking about what it must have been like to be an honest cop under a corrupt boss, I often return to a chilling incident you described in your correspondences with Taylor. You said that, in 1973, nine years before the most infamous case of torture in your city's history, you were typing a report in the hallway on the second floor of Area 2 police headquarters. All of a sudden, you heard a loud scream coming from inside one of the rooms. You ran into that room, where

you observed a criminal suspect who was handcuffed to a radiator—
"Old Smokey," as it was called back then by cops in Area 2.

The man chained to the smoking-hot radiator sat in the corner,
whimpering and pleading for mercy. "What's going on?" you asked
Burge and a few other members of the A-Team who surrounded
the man.

"None of your business," Burge replied. Pointing to the door, he ordered you to leave. Back outside in the hallway, other detectives were
busily typing their reports. The way those naturally curious and typically suspicious detectives ignored the screams of the chained man
led you to believe that they had grown accustomed to such outcries.

That scene still haunts me.

Even before you burst into that room, you were never allowed
weekends off, and you were given a broken radio so you could not
call for backup. After you stormed into Burge's interrogation room,
however, things got much worse: roughly a year after witnessing "Old
Smokey" in action, you were transferred to another precinct and de-
moted from detective back to your original civil service rank of patrolman. I can only imagine how hard that was for you to cope with.

Considering the adversity you faced, it is admirable that you remained determined to do the right thing, no matter the consequences.
Had I encountered the same dilemma and suffered the same fate, I'm
not sure what I would have done. Had I been compromised by an
inferior rank and been made both complicit in torture and powerless
at once, I'm fairly certain that I would have been reduced to a shadow
of my former self. After suffering the decades of discrimination you
faced, after seeing the years of torture that you saw, my faith in the judicial system that I was upholding by virtue of my occupation would
have been shaken. I do not know what I would have done, especially
had I believed in the law as deeply and thoroughly as you.

The fact that you witnessed torture, and documented it, was more
important than you could have known when you wrote Taylor that
letter in 1991. It provided him with insight and evidence that Burge
had tortured before. That statement, Flint Taylor told me, was "one of
many pieces of important evidence" that resulted in a settlement for

one of Burge's torture victims in 2008. But even more than your statement, your career on the police force foreshadowed what it would be like for Black officers to work in Jon Burge's precinct.

If the reality of torture at Area 2 was an immovable rock, and the ambition to succeed within this precinct was the proverbial hard place, you told the world what it was like to be stuck in between. And I, for one, am grateful for that.

An Open Letter to Doris Byrd

I had not planned on writing you until recently. I was hesitant to write a retired cop because I thought you might want to put your days of thinking about police torture behind you, especially since I tried to contact you and never received a reply. My idea was actually to compose another letter to the superintendent of the Chicago Police Department, Eddie Johnson, telling him about the Black officers who worked at Area 2 under Jon Burge's command. I had already written an open letter to him.[8] In that letter, I told him that the most marginalized cops in a police precinct can be valuable assets because they often have the most to teach the high-ranking officers (assuming those officers are willing to listen and learn). I had hoped your 2004 statement in the Aaron Patterson case would help him see Area 2 precinct through your eyes—the eyes of a Black woman—as it was then. I thought that seeing a precinct in which power was abused so thoroughly and so blatantly would help him avoid repeating the mistakes of the past. I wrote a draft of this letter, and then I shared it with a small group of Chicago residents, so that I could get their perspective on what I should say. You may be wondering why.

Before publishing any open letter that I write to a public official it is my scholarly practice to share these letters with Chicago residents to see if there is anything they feel I need to add or emphasize, to expand or erase. The reason for this is that my insights are relevant only insofar as they matter to those residents and can, in some large or small way, have an impact on their lives. My scholarship, in other words, is meant to amplify their concerns. I'm writing you now, Doris, because after Chicago residents read a previous draft of this letter, your career became a touchstone among this group of people: your career, they said, epitomized the evils of complicity and how evil deeds can become an everyday aspect of someone's life.

I imagine that when you decided to make a statement on Aaron Patterson's behalf in 2004, you did not think that strangers would read about it years later and look at you with contempt for being complicit with Jon Burge's crimes. I imagine that your knowledge of police torture haunted you and tainted your entire time on the police force. That's at least part of what made you speak up all those years later, after you retired, right? Your willingness to make a statement suggests that you were at least trying to make amends for the role you played in perpetuating police torture.

Given that you seem to be trying to rectify the wrongs of the past, I thought you might want to know what residents thought about your actions then and how those actions influence their feelings about the police today. I'm writing this letter in the hope that your work in making amends is not done. Perhaps you don't want to stop at helping to exonerate Patterson. Perhaps you want to focus your efforts on the police officers who think torture is still a necessary evil. Perhaps by hearing from these residents you can work to change the institutional culture of the Chicago Police Department from within. If there is any part of you that still wishes to atone, this letter is for you.

I understand the difficulties that Black officers like you faced. I also understand that, in the grand scheme of things, no one person can change the institutional culture of the Chicago Police Department without help. By focusing on your hardships in this letter, I do not want to give the impression that Black officers are chiefly responsible for torture at Area 2. But I do believe that you all are more essential for changing the institutional culture. Precisely because you were seen as outcasts, because you were treated unfairly, because you were taken for granted and often ignored, you have intimate knowledge about the hierarchical structure that protects the powerful.

From learning about your career, I noticed that there were whistle-blowers working at Area 2 who you watched and observed closely—a man named Frank Laverty was one. But you and several other Black officers who worked at Area 2 in the mid-1970s and 1980s—namely, Sammy Lacey, Jack Hines, Lucius Moore, and Walter Young—decided not to follow in the footsteps of those whistle-blowers. Instead, you viewed the actions of those cops as examples of what not to do. You all were caught in an awful situation: working as part of the Chicago Police Department as the first accusations of police torture became public, starting in the early 1980s. And I sympathize—I really do.

As far as I can tell, you were screwed no matter what you did. I have often wondered what your daily life at Area 2 looked like. Did you leave the break room whenever Burge came in? Did you make small talk with him? Did you wait to see which cases he was assigned to, then ask for different assignments? It seems that the anxieties of working in this environment—not to mention the corrosiveness of torture itself—prevented many of you from becoming the kind of cops you wanted to be. Not because you participated in this brutality, but because the other options available to you were also fraught with peril.

Despite my own sympathy for the danger you faced, when I described this danger to Chicago residents, they were not at all convinced that they should feel sorry for you. They lamented the fact that to remain on the police force, officers like you decided to make a devil's bargain. You did not say anything. You became complicit in torture through your silence. You accepted the bargain as a condition of your job, which is to say, of your livelihood. They weren't concerned that your choices did not spare you negative consequences and routinized reprisals from white superiors or that you suffered from an unwritten policy of consistent exclusion. They felt that the issue was cut and dry: You had a duty to stand up to anyone you suspected of being a torturer. And you did not. As a result, you were part of the problem.

At first, I naïvely thought that I could complicate this moral stance by giving these residents a sense of the scope of Burge's torture operation. To do this, I began my discussion with a letter dated March 6, 1989. It was delivered to the doorstep of the People's Law Office by a police insider, an anonymous source named "Deep Badge." Deep Badge had written a list of Burge's friends as well as his enemies, which he (or she) sent to the lawyers who were defending Andrew Wilson so that they would "treat those subjects who were not involved [in torture] with leniency."

For your convenience, the list is here. Many of the names are likely familiar to you:

BURGE'S ASSKICKERS

Sgt Jack Byrne (his main man—check his IAD record)

Det George Basile (his close friend)

Det Pete Dignan

Det Frank Glynn

Det Fred Hill (his involvement got him a choice job at 26th St)

Det John Paladino

Det John Yucaitis

WEAK LINKS

Sgt Frank Lee (went to Area 3 to get away from Burge)

Sgt Joe Nolan (Burge dumped him)

Sgt Mike Hoke (He and Burge constantly were arguing and backstabbing each other)

Sgt Tom Ferry (Burge dumped him)

Sgt Tom Bennett (an attorney and he and Burge broke up with some anger)

Det Ray Binkowski (talks a lot)

Det Doris Byrd

Det Robert Dudak

Det Pat Hickey (Burge hated her because she was a woman)

Det Bill Kushner (escaped because of Burge and Byrne)

Det Frank Laverty

Det Walter Young

Det John McCabe

As you can see, your name appears, seventh in the "Weak Links" column. We now know that the A-Team had to be slightly larger than the seven people Deep Badge mentions here. We've learned from the proceedings in civil suits that approximately twenty-five officers have been accused of joining Burge in torture. Indeed, people spend so much time on Burge that they often forget about his accomplices—the people in the room with him when he was torturing Black criminal suspects.

You might know that John Byrne is said to be one of those accomplices. In a sworn deposition taken in a state court postconviction case on March 1, 2001, Byrne denied torturing, abusing, or witnessing torture.[9] Nevertheless, the claims of many of the torture survivors, including those of Gregory Banks, David Bates, Darrell Cannon, Stanley Howard, Lee Holmes, Philip Adkins, Marcus Wiggins, Aaron Patterson, and Thomas Craft, specifically mentioned Byrne and have been validated by judgments won in court and, in some cases, settlements.

Like Burge, John Byrne was never tried for torture. But even though the US Attorney eventually prosecuted Burge for perjury and obstruction, the Department of Justice has failed to pursue such charges against any of the other police officers who have taken the stand and claimed ignorance of Burge's torture operation. Time and again, these officers have testified in court that they did not witness or participate in, or were otherwise aware of, torture at Area 2.

In 1990 the Chicago Police Department Office of Professional Standards' Goldston Report—named for the Office of Professional Standards' investigator Michael Goldston—cataloged more than fifty instances of "methodical" and "systematic" torture involving Burge and police officers under his command. But were you aware that in subsequent reports specific officers were named in as many as thirty-five cases? Peter Dignan was named in seventeen cases, John Paladino in thirteen, John Yucaitis in twelve, Daniel McWeeny in eleven, Anthony Maslanka in ten, and Robert Dwyer in nine.

While Jon Burge was named as someone directly involved in torture in thirty-five torture cases, twenty-one Area 2 detectives and supervisors were identified in connection to at least five separate cases. All together, whether through testimony or reports in one or more of the torture cases, a total of sixty-seven officers were identified by survivors as having direct knowledge of torture. This figure suggests that even though the A-Team is said to have been relatively small, a little less than ten cops, its influence throughout the Chicago Police Department was much more pervasive.

. . .

From your statement, it seems that the group of Black officers you confided in numbered slightly fewer than the A-Team—that is, around five or six people. Even so, in this letter, I refer to the Black police officers you worked with at Area 2 as "The B-Team" to distinguish them from the rest of the "weak links" who were more privileged than your group.

What separated the Black cops from Deep Badge's general list of weak links was that you all didn't have the resources or connections to avoid Burge or to leave Area 2—you could not transfer, like Frank Lee did, to "get away" from Burge, and you could not "escape" like Bill Kushner did. Nor could you afford to constantly argue with Burge or "backstab" him like Mike Hoke. Unlike the white men whom Burge disliked, your B-Team wasn't on his bad side because of your personal beef. You all had more in common with Pat Hickey, whom Burge "hated" because she was a woman. Your very existence was the issue. In Burge's macho, war-laden vision of the world, any officer who seemed frail or was without military experience, or was gay, or Latino, or Asian would also be excluded.

It seems that the chief difference between your B-Team and all the other people Burge shunned was that you banded together because you were socially excluded in the same way, which is to say, because your race in particular made you pariahs at Area 2.

From my studies I have found that there were several other factors that qualified an officer for membership in the B-Team, as opposed to Burge's A-Team of officially sanctioned torturers. Among the most prominent were race, willful ignorance of what went on in certain Area 2 rooms, the ways you were marginalized on the Chicago police force, and the kind of information you would not be privy to—both because the information was willfully kept from you and because you willfully chose to stay away.

Speaking of this last factor—that, as a Black cop at Area 2, you were not privy to the same amount of inside information as everyone else—I've always been fascinated by the mention of "street files" in your statement. Street files, according to reporter John Conroy, were documents that were not turned over to defense lawyers because they contained "inconvenient truths that could hamper the prosecution" of a criminal suspect. These files included memos about other possible suspects, crime lab reports that could help exonerate a given suspect, and other documents that might damage the case against the people the police were convinced had committed a crime. In my discussions with Chicago residents, we spent a lot of time talking about these files, because they seemed to exemplify the fact that police officers at Area 2 were not interested in discovering the truth. They were more interested in arresting and then punishing people who they had already decided were guilty.

· · ·

I must admit, Doris, that while reading your statement about how certain information about police torture was concealed at Area 2, the residents I spoke with were struck by your description of Frank Laverty's demise. We didn't skip anything during our discussion of your statement. I presented residents with the full story because I wanted them to understand the dilemma Black officers working under Burge in Area 2 faced: you had to risk your careers by going out of your way to avoid being confronted by unconstitutional and inhumane torture. The result was an awful contradiction. You were forced into complicity with Burge's crimes, and at the same time you were powerless to stop those crimes—or at least that's what it seemed like from your statement about Frank Laverty.

The Chicagoans I talked to thought that you must have cared deeply for Frank, because they could sense your angst as you described how the tide turned against Laverty in 1981, when he helped investigate a case the A-Team had already been working on. George Jones, the son of a Black Chicago police officer, had been charged with the murder, battery, and rape of an eleven-year-old girl. All the evidence against Jones was circumstantial. What's more, Laverty presented evidence to the assistant state's attorney, Larry Hyman, and wrote a memo to his supervising commander, Milton Deas, telling them that he suspected someone else. The real perpetrator, Laverty said, was a different man (also named "George") who had committed another rape and murder. Although this evidence pointed away from Jones, Deas buried this information in the street file he maintained on the Jones case. This was a clear violation of the state's constitutionally required duty to turn over potentially exculpatory evidence to the defense.

Laverty brought the evidence that exonerated George Jones to Jeffery Haas, who was defending Jones. Soon after, Laverty came to court and testified on Jones's behalf about another possible suspect. In doing so, Laverty exposed a practice of hiding evidence in street files that had been going on for decades in police districts across the city.

After this, Laverty was met with cold stares and veiled threats from his fellow officers. Burge's hostility toward Laverty escalated. As you told it, one day, Laverty left his desk and headed for another room, apparently searching for something—typewriter paper or a work memo. Burge, in full view of many of the police officers from Area 2, followed Laverty. Just as he was about to exit the room, Burge drew his nickel-plated handgun and pointed it at the back of Laverty's head. "Bang," Burge said.

In this word—*bang*—you saw the end of Frank Laverty's career, if not his life. You saw George Jones sitting in a prison cell for a crime that he didn't commit, a crime that other officers knew he was innocent of. You saw your own son being grabbed by the A-Team, and you knew full well that you couldn't protect him, your own flesh and blood, even though you, too, were a cop.

Shortly thereafter, Laverty was removed from active duty. He was reassigned out of Area 2 and sent to the Recruit Processing Department, downtown, where he spent his days watching police recruits piss in plastic cups.

There was one bit of good news—George Jones was eventually exonerated of his accused crimes. Yet from your perspective, the message was clear: Laverty was punished for standing up to Burge, banished forever to the belly of low-level police bureaucracy—and it was likely that only the color of his skin shielded him from worse consequences. Laverty's decision to testify on behalf of George Jones no longer seemed inspiring. Instead, it seemed a cautionary tale about the consequences of crossing Burge.

Reflecting on these events twenty years later, you said, "I took it as a message about what would occur if I ever did come forward and break the code of silence." I pointed Chicago residents to this quote for a particular reason. I hoped it would help explain how Burge and the A-Team perpetuated an institutional culture of silence at Area 2 through intimidation and threats. Until Laverty's demotion, you had made it your mission to avoid Jon Burge. But now you were beginning to think that avoidance was not enough. For instance, avoidance could not keep you safe if you walked into an interrogation room and stumbled upon a criminal suspect with clamps attached to him, pleading for help.

So with no sergeant, no state's attorney, no superintendent or mayor on your side, this is what you decided to do: you developed ways of remaining willfully unaware of anything that might compromise your ability to rise in the ranks of the police force or put you at personal risk. When it wasn't your shift, you stayed out of Area 2 precinct as much as possible. Whenever you got wind that the A-Team was on the verge of giving a criminal suspect the "Vietnamese treatment," you hit the street to pursue leads, or you took your paperwork home so as not to be within earshot of a suspect's pleas. You and all the other B-Team members who followed in William Parker's wake even came up with a name for this willful circumvention: "the ostrich approach." You all came to a consensus on what you would need to do to survive. Unlike Parker, you all became experts at burying your heads in the sand, seeing and not seeing, learning to know what not to know.

This business of not knowing was made easier by the way Burge systematically excluded you all from the precinct's most important cases. This was illustrated on February 9, 1982, the day Officers Fahey and O'Brien were shot. As the manhunt began, Sammy Lacey, a B-Team member, learned that officers were taking suspects to police headquarters downtown. Although he was off duty, Lacey went to see if he could help with the investigation. When he arrived, he asked Burge whether there was anything he could do to assist. Burge told him there was not and assigned him to guard a witness at a Holiday Inn, miles away, on an unrelated case.

Later that evening, Lacey came across information he thought might help solve the crime. His former partner Daniel Dixon had called him shortly after Fahey and O'Brien were shot. Dixon knew that the slain officers had pulled over suspects who had recently committed a robbery. That particular robbery fit the modus operandi of a case Dixon had previously investigated, in which two brothers had robbed a camera store at 115th and Michigan. Dixon told Lacey that the suspects' car was brown and that he would call back later when he remembered their names. (At that point the A-Team had an all-points bulletin, or APB, out for a burnt-orange-colored car.)

Lacey approached Burge and explained the particular detail of what he thought was a reliable lead. Burge seemed annoyed: "We know what we're doing," he said dismissively. Days later, Dixon would confirm that the two suspects he had been referring to were, in fact, Andrew and Jackie Wilson.

After Burge ignored his lead, Lacey began to wonder why. He concluded that the reason the B-Team wasn't being allowed to help was because of essentially an open secret. The mayor at the time, Jane Byrne, was furious when she learned that two police officers had been shot. As a consequence of her rage, she granted Jon Burge a "mandate to do what he had to do" to clear this case, and police superintendent, Richard Brzeczek, appointed Burge to lead the manhunt. You, and I'm guessing every other Black officer who knew Burge, believed that he had official sanction to use methods that might best be kept quiet, and because you were not members of Burge's team and had not established yourself as an officer who was willing to torture suspects— and, of course, because you were Black—you were excluded.

On February 14, 1982, five days after Fahey and O'Brien were shot, Lacey arrived at Area 2 and found news anchors from the local television stations surrounding the building. Several black cars, the kind the top brass traveled in, were parked nearby. Lieutenants, commanders, and superintendents were inside. Clearly, important news was breaking. *This must mean they finally captured Fahey and O'Brien's killer*, he thought.

As Lacey busied himself with work, he began to hear noises coming from one of the interview rooms. "It was sort of like chairs and furniture were being moved around," he said. Next, he heard what he thought was a scream. Hearing those noises and knowing that they probably came from the suspect, he decided to employ the ostrich approach. He stopped what he was doing, promptly filled out a request for time off, and walked upstairs to turn the form in to the precinct secretary.

This image—of Lacey trying to physically remove himself from the scene of the next crime, to avoid being implicated in police torture— makes me think of William Parker. Lacey and Parker dealt with their marginalization in opposite ways: Lacey tried to ignore the illegal actions of the cops in his midst while Parker tried to call them out on their hypocrisy. Both of these contradictory approaches, of course, were by-products of their social exclusion. The major difference was that Lacey felt incapable of changing the system and thus became complicit in it; Parker held out hope and tried to intervene.

Just like Parker, Lacey heard screams outside of the interview room. But rather than having to face the disquieting eyes of a criminal suspect chained to a radiator, he did not go in. Lacey filled out a form for time off and walked away. When he left Area 2 that day, instead of continuing his police work, he drove straight to church. And there, I assume, he prayed.

Likewise, Doris, you told Aaron Patterson's lawyers that you knew that, as part of the citywide dragnet, Burge and his A-Team were kicking down doors in African American communities, stopping people on the street at random, arresting people, and bringing them in to be interrogated, sometimes brutally. During the Wilson manhunt you observed a Black man attached to a radiator in an interview room at Area 2. Even before this dragnet, residents who had been interrogated at Area 2 would stop you on the street and tell you about the telephone books they were beaten with, the plastic bags they were suffocated with, and the black box they were shocked with. You also knew that the less you said about the many abuses that occurred along the way, the better for your career.

Why were you willing to speak out now, in 2004, Flint Taylor wanted to know, whereas before you were not: "And so the reason you're talking to me on the record now is that you're free of being a police officer and you've retired?"

"I retired," you said. "Yes."

"And you have your pension?"

"Yes, I have my pension. And if they haven't taken Burge's, they sure as hell won't take mine."

• • •

Maybe it was my own fault for organizing a group discussion around this particular passage in your statement. I just wanted residents to know that your pension was a major consideration because that fact seemed to be evidence that you were torn about what you heard outside of interrogation rooms—proof that what you heard really bothered you. But for these residents, the fact that you thought ahead to your eventual retirement before acting on injustice meant that you had the capacity to act morally, and they were infuriated that you did not.

The most heated conversation about you and the B-Team came

toward the end of our discussion of your statement, in fact, when we reflected on the question that Taylor asked you about your pension. Your answer, as you might imagine, was extremely controversial. These residents were troubled by the fact that you seemed to benefit financially from keeping quiet, all while allowing so many others to suffer.

Evelyn said, "I'm sorry, but that's just selfish. She's only worried about her pension."

"I agree," David said, "but it's not a simple issue. Because even in the workplace now, wherever you work, it's always hard to be the whistle-blower. Everybody's looking at you, and you become sort of the bad guy, even though you're trying to do the right thing. It can jeopardize your job if you have kids. It's just — I mean, somebody definitely should have said something . . . but it's just hard."

Other residents were likewise put off by the fact that Lacey went to church rather than intervening on behalf of vulnerable residents.

"What bothered me was this part," Evelyn said, "when Lacey heard the screaming and didn't do anything. It disturbed me that he left, and went to *church*?"

Evelyn said this as if she were asking a question, as if she could not quite comprehend why he did not take action against Burge back then.

"But who should they have called?" Sharon asked the group. She seemed to sympathize with you and the B-Team. "They *are* the police."

"They could have contacted the Department of Justice — the federal government," Carl said.

"Somebody, yeah," Katie agreed. "That's why I think they bear some responsibility, because they are there to serve and protect."

After your discussion of Laverty, and your explanation that you had to remain silent if you wanted to keep your job, the residents I spoke with perceived you as having evaded your duty to serve and protect the people who were tortured at Area 2. They felt that you had shirked your responsibility to ordinary citizens like them as well. They believed that any cop who had knowledge of Burge's operation had betrayed a sacred oath as a public servant.

"Yeah, it's hard," Cliff said. "But you could change your line of work if you have integrity."

"I've sacrificed a lot in my life to be a person of honesty," Nick interjected. "I could have had a well-paying career in corporate America. But I chose not to lie and cheat people. I'm not saying that to toot my own horn. All I'm saying is, sometimes somebody needs to sacrifice. You might not care until it's your kid that dies or gets tortured. Then you'll be running around saying, 'No one's helping me out.'"

When Nick finished speaking I better understood the nature of the criticisms these residents were leveling at you and the B-Team. Many of them felt that they themselves had sacrificed material things to live a life of integrity. They also thought that their fate was tied to the vulnerable Black people who had been tortured. In pointing this out, they reiterated the idea that purposefully allowing these people to suffer was betraying the race.

Mikki and Nick both made these points clear. "I agree with Nick," Mikki said. "A lot of my friends are police officers," she continued. "They make like $80,000—which is good money compared to me. I'm a part-time CPS [public] schoolteacher. I make $29,000. But they're jerks. They talk about all the tickets they write. They write poor, Black people tickets all day. They're not really fighting crime. They're just tormenting good people."

"The sad thing for me," Nick said, "when I think about the B-Team, is that you had people of color being oppressed, and then you had people with power of the same race that could've done something to stop it, but they didn't. That, to me, is a shame. Like if somebody is taking advantage of somebody from my race, I'm not just going to sit there and do nothing. And the fact that the B-Team didn't do anything, to me means that they're cowards."

Perhaps you are thinking, Doris, that calling you a coward is a strong insult. Maybe you feel like you don't deserve the label. But there is no need to sanitize these residents' expressions; it helps no one. Instead, I want to convey their anger and disappointment in all its bitterness. If you truly want to make amends for your complicity in police torture, then you must reckon with their feelings.

These residents expected Black police officers to hold themselves to a higher standard. After all, you were the same race as many of the focus-group participants, and they considered themselves to be part of the population that was most likely to be tortured next. Statistically speaking, they were right. They felt that, if not your sworn oath to protect the public at large, then at least a sense of racial solidarity should have compelled you to step forward. Since you did not, a special kind of disappointment—a disappointment of the "I expected more from you" variety—was directed toward all the Black cops in your precinct. But resentment was aimed in your direction, in particular, after they heard your explanation for keeping quiet.

That's another reason I'm writing you now. I know it felt like you were powerless at the time, working within arm's reach of a sadistic man like Burge. But that powerlessness, which is to say, your marginality, was also your greatest strength. Your powerlessness kept you at a distance: close enough to observe but not involve yourself directly in torture. Your powerlessness kept you in a position to expose this practice. You did not draw on the strength of your powerlessness until decades after some of the most extreme forms of torture on record occurred. But it's not too late to intervene in the future. You can tell marginalized cops working in Chicago's precincts now about all of your regrets. You can tell them about what you did know and what you did learn, even while working at a place where secrets were the supreme form of currency. You can teach other marginalized officers how to investigate their own workplace and to search for corruption. I bet they'll listen and respect you more than they do someone like me who has never worn the badge.

I know this extra burden is in no way fair. I know it places added pressure on people who already have less status and prestige than their privileged counterparts. But I also know this: the only way to change the institutional culture that turns silence into the handmaiden of torture is to develop a dissenting voice.

We must all learn to use our voices when the occasion demands. I am still learning how to use mine. And I hope you will consider using yours to expose the problem of police violence in your city.

An Open Letter to Police Superintendent Eddie Johnson

You and I both know that it's your job to make sure that the public is able to make complaints against the police and, when they do, that there is a fair and honest investigative process in place. Because you oversee and implement this system of police oversight, you are the public liaison between the police department and the residents of your city. You are also a career cop who grew up in a part of the city in which residents have long had tensions with the police. Therefore, I'm sure you know just how important it is to foster a healthy institutional culture within your department.

To accomplish what is necessary for Chicagoans to feel that the police are on their side, you need to rethink the role of the police in your city. For that you must look inward and conduct a moral audit of the police department itself. In this letter I would like to point out what you might look for while conducting this audit.

Remember when I wrote you last I said it was important that you learn about the Black officers who were complicit in torture, because their marginality allows us to see how the chain of command was corrupted at Area 2? Well, Area 2 will be a test case for the audit I'm asking you to conduct. This police district will serve as an example of what can go wrong when trust and legitimacy within a precinct has eroded.

• • •

I'm sure you know that Area 2 consisted of an A-Team that did horrible things and then a slightly larger group of people who opposed Burge. Included on the opposition's side was a group of Black police officers whom I've taken to calling "The B-Team." In my thinking, the A-Team epitomized everything wrong with the Chicago Police Department: it is racist, it is secretive, and its officers and leaders believe that the police department has the right to operate above the law. By contrast, the B-Team epitomized the best hope for the future: they were marginalized, and much can be learned from the most marginal within the department. The problem is, though, they never realized their potential to teach us because they were afraid to speak up. This was a group of Black police officers who wanted to do the right thing but being excluded in their jobs made them feel powerless.

As you are a Black officer who has risen through the ranks, I'm sure you've had your fair share of setbacks. You probably have a lot of insight into what can make a police officer feel powerless. I'm also confident that you know much more about the police chain of command than I do. But from studying the inner workings of Area 2, I have learned that when high-level officers abuse their power, lower-level officers learn to ignore those abuses. This kind of corruption is important to understand because, if left unchecked, it can ultimately facilitate torture and protect torturers.

The reason I know so much about Area 2 is because the Black officers who used to work there told their story to Flint Taylor, a lawyer from the People's Law Office, who was representing a torture survivor named Aaron Patterson. Had you been a little older, or joined the police department five or six years earlier, you might have even worked with them as a member of the B-Team. I'm sure you may know some of them. Does the name Walter Young ring a bell?

In 2004, after Young had retired from the force, he gave a statement on behalf of a torture survivor named Aaron Patterson. Patterson had filed a civil suit against Burge and the City of Chicago. Most chilling about Young's statement was his description of how torture could occur even in the absence of any direct order. Young said that there was "an implication that if you were a detective, you were supposed to know how to get information. I have never been directly ordered to mistreat a prisoner." Young was supposed to use his wherewithal to obtain the necessary information. This is a critical point about what happens within the precinct.

When Young gave his statement in 2004, the American public was not yet flooded with viral video footage of Chicago police officers gunning Black Chicagoans down in the street, such as the videos of Harith Augustus in 2018, or Paul O'Neal in 2016, or Laquan McDonald in 2014. These spectacular episodes of police violence, which today seem to pop up in our news feeds constantly, seem to provide proof that the police department's crisis of legitimacy consists of a problem between cops and the communities they patrol. But if we look at Young's statement, we see that this crisis actually begins within the precinct walls. Area 2 was a prime example of how an inequitable work environment can consolidate power in the hands of the corrupt. So, Superintendent Johnson, if you do not wish to repeat the problems of the past, take note of two kinds of corruption that made it easier for torture to take place at Area 2: how cases were investigated and how internal grievances were handled. Ensuring that these issues are adequately dealt with will at least be a start in addressing the lack of trust people have in the Chicago Police Department.

• • •

In his statement, Young described how specific duties were allocated within the precinct. "There was a case management sergeant," he said. "When tips came in, you had what was called 'hot cases,' that is, cases where the offender was known. Those would be assigned to certain detectives." Most often they were assigned to A-Team members.

To illustrate his point, Young offered a hypothetical example in the form of Joe Willie Stupid. "Say Joe Willie Stupid went out and robbed somebody, and then a day later he came home and knocked his girlfriend in the eye. Well, his girlfriend might get pissed off. And if she gets pissed off enough, she might get on the horn and call the station. 'Remember the guy who committed the robbery?' She might say. 'That was Joe Willie Stupid. And he is here.'"

Homicides were at the top of the list of hot cases. They conferred the most prestige on the police officers who solved them. If the case management sergeant received a tip that might quickly lead to the arrest of a murderer, he would contact members of the A-Team. Of course, arresting suspects in this kind of high-profile case was the ultimate prize, much better than simply arresting a robbery suspect like Joe Willie Stupid.

The case management sergeant classified other tips differently.

Some tips, for example, were associated with "cold cases," which were more difficult to solve. Cold cases were assigned to the B-Team. Because of this practice of funneling cold cases to the B-Team, it was difficult for them to develop an arrest record comparable to that of their peers. This, then, was how Burge concentrated power and prestige in his favored A-Team—the only officers he truly trusted.

During their time working at Area 2, Young and the other B-Team members believed that they were excluded from the highest-profile cases because Burge was a racist who did not want to work with Blacks. They had no idea that their exclusion served a purpose. It kept them from directly witnessing torture and being able to prove that Burge was breaking the law. This, Superintendent, is how the seemingly mundane issue of case management within a police precinct is related to the larger crisis of legitimacy. This is why police officers must also have a way to voice complaints that is not corrupted by the code of silence. If they had this in the past, more police officers at Area 2 might have worked on the same cases at the same time as Burge, which would have probably put them in position to witness torture. Such direct knowledge would have increased the likelihood of someone stepping forward. Instead, when the B-Team tried to complain about their caseload, they were further marginalized.

· · ·

In the fall of 1982, members of the B-Team decided that something needed to be done. At the time, Officer Sammy Lacey in particular felt he had nothing to lose, mostly because of racial tensions that were calcifying at Area 2.[10] It wasn't just accusations of torture that bothered the Black officers. They hated Burge because he was preventing their career advancement. The fact that they were Black didn't automatically mean that they were going to fight valiantly on behalf of their community. First and foremost, they were motivated by their own self-interest.

This is an important point to make to someone like you, Superintendent Johnson, who is often portrayed as an advocate for his community. You cannot expect police officers to expose corruption because that's what you would do, or because it's the right thing. As superintendent, you must find a way to incentivize good behavior. If you do not, then your officers won't deem it worth their time to disrupt the status quo when presented with an ethical dilemma. At least that's what happened at Area 2.

When the B-Team took their complaint on the lack of opportunity to solve homicide cases to someone who outranked Burge, the person they confided in refused to rock the boat. After carefully considering which higher-up would most likely be supportive of their cause, they decided on Leroy Martin. Martin was among the few Black commanders on the police force in the 1980s. Sure, others, like Commander Milton Deas, also outranked Burge. According to the B-Team, however, despite their relative rankings, "Deas answered to Burge, Burge didn't answer to Deas." Martin therefore seemed a better choice. Lacey and Byrd figured that, since Martin had once been in their position and had managed to ascend the ladder, he must have had similar experiences. Even more important, Martin seemed to be an independent person, someone, they thought, who might be able to reason with Burge.

Determined to change their situation, Lacey, Byrd, and another Black officer, Jack Hines, went to Leroy Martin's office. Surrounded by his accolades and awards, which were positioned neatly on the shelves, Martin looked keen and steady in his environment. They were not asking for a handout, the Black officers said to him. They just wanted a shot, a chance to pursue the highest level of police work. Martin seemed to sympathize with their plight. "Don't worry," he promised. "I will investigate the situation."

The next day, Burge called several members of the B-Team into his office. Hopeful that Burge was about to assign them a new caseload, they grew excited. Instead, Burge yelled at them for going outside the chain of command. Wildly agitated, Burge beat the desk with his hand and spewed a vileness that reminded Byrd of fights at the South Side taverns she often had to break up. Burge was furious at what he regarded as their betrayal. If they had a problem, they had better talk to him first. "Don't you ever go above my head again," Burge said—a stern warning.

Members of the B-Team came to believe that Martin had sold them out. They think he called up Burge and told him that he should control the officers under his command. Their feelings of betrayal should help you see this: not every Black officer in the Chicago Police Department was a member of the B-Team. Some Black cops believed that Burge had the right to assign homicides to whomever he wanted. Worse yet, some also believed that criminal suspects needed to be roughed up sometimes, too. Given his reaction to the B-Team's complaint, maybe Martin held at least one of those beliefs. Like you, Superintendent Johnson, Martin served as superintendent. His term was from 1987 until 1992. But that doesn't mean he was a trusted ally for police officers who wanted to point out unfair treatment.

Upon learning about the story of Martin and the B-Team, Barry, an army veteran whom I interviewed for this project, pointed out that this was a perfect example of how the chain of command contributes to the crisis of legitimacy. "There's a culture of silence connected to the chain of command," Barry said. "You see that when the B-Team went to Leroy Martin. You can't go through the chain of command. You can't go around the chain of command. That's why the officers that are breaking the law have impunity."

Barry continued: "Eventually you realize that there's no place to get justice. You realize that you can't go through the system itself, that no one is policing the police. You see that there's no escape."

Maybe Doris Byrd would agree with Barry: in her 2004 statement in the Aaron Patterson lawsuit, she said the incident with Leroy Martin twenty-two years earlier was the moment at which she finally understood that Burge was not subject to any oversight. If the system was corrupt, and if there was no place to get justice, then Byrd would keep her head down and quietly take advantage of that system.

I wrote an open letter to Doris Byrd in which I expressed regret that her complicity helped to perpetuate a law enforcement structure that permitted torture. Now I might add that the silence of everyone on the B-Team also protected Burge's interests, legitimizing his monstrous acts. Even though they had some sense of what was inside the black box of police torture, these officers either did not, or felt they could not reveal its contents.

As superintendent, your task is to see how a culture of silence can obscure our direct knowledge of police torture. You must be determined to understand how the history of police corruption impacts the people you serve. So before you take to the streets and attempt to build bridges of trust with residents, I believe you must begin with the culture within your own precincts. A bridge cannot stand if its foundation is cracked.

An Open Letter to Police Superintendent Eddie Johnson

In my previous letter I urged you to conduct a moral audit of the police department—to take a long, hard look at the internal dynamics of your police precincts—and to fix those problems before offering an olive branch to the public. I believe you will never be able to form a true partnership with the public if your precincts are corrupt. In this letter, I want to make a related claim, and that is this: if you truly want to instill legitimacy in the police you must seek to change the present reality that the police can injure, maim, murder, and torture people and only experience the most minimal forms of sanction.

Because you are superintendent, I'm asking you to advocate for prosecuting police officers as you would anyone else who breaks the law. I think this would mean a lot coming from you. Sure, the mayor or another elected official could do it. But it would likely be seen as a disingenuous attempt to shore up votes. Coming from you (the person who was the choice of city council members and the mayor) such an ethical stance could actually make a difference. You could effectively make the case that to be the bridge between the police and the community that everyone wants you to be, the public has to see that no one is above the law, including the police. That would be something concrete that could actually spark change. In fact, adopting such a stance is necessary for repairing the police's relationship with the public. But even more than that, holding your fellow officers accountable for their crimes is simply the right thing to do.

• • •

I know what you must be thinking—that several Chicago police officers have been held accountable for torture. I realize that twenty years after Andrew Wilson was tortured, the Cook County judiciary did eventually launch an investigation. On April 24, 2002, Paul Biebel, presiding judge of the Cook County Circuit Court, appointed two lawyers—Robert D. Boyle and Edward J. Egan—as special prosecutors and tasked them with looking into torture. But there were several flaws with this investigation that prevent me from considering it a successful attempt to hold the police accountable for their crimes.

After four years of investigation, the special prosecutors found beyond a reasonable doubt that Jon Burge and John Yucaitis "committed armed violence, intimidation, official misconduct and aggravated battery," and they found that, on February 14, 1982, Wilson had in fact been subjected to abuse and mistreatment in Area 2's interrogation room. The special prosecutors also found that Burge and Yucaitis had committed perjury at Wilson's first civil trial and that a number of other Area 2 cops had "abused" criminal suspects. According to the special prosecutors, Burge's superiors knew about his abusive behavior. In fact, your predecessor, former police superintendent Richard Brzeczek, was found guilty of "dereliction of duty" because he did nothing to stop it.

But I do not think of these findings as a genuine attempt to hold the police accountable because Boyle and Egan failed to label Burge and Yucaitis's actions as "torture." The prosecutors interviewed doctors who had treated hundreds of torture survivors, and those doctors found psychological markers consistent with torture. Yet the special prosecutors opted for more sanitized terms like *misconduct* and *abuse*.

How is that possible? How could Boyle and Egan consider the many people who claimed that they had been suffocated, beaten, electrocuted, and prodded in their genitals the victims of mere misconduct? How could they call electrocution something as tepid as abuse?

You only have to look at the incentives they had for downplaying torture to see why this happened. Both Boyle and Egan were former Cook County assistant prosecutors. After Boyle left the Cook County State's Attorney's Office, he became a partner in a firm headed by Morgan Murphy Jr., former congressman and member of Richard J. Daley's inner circle (not to be confused with his son, Richard M. Daley, or "Richie," who was state's attorney when the torture scandal began). As a longtime operative of the Democratic political machine in Chicago, Boyle had every reason to downplay the widespread ramifications of police torture. Indeed, while Boyle would condemn Chicago's former police superintendent, Richard Brzeczek, saying he "did not just do his job poorly, he just didn't do his job," he would reserve only mild criticism for Richie Daley, "We accept his explanation, but would not do it the same way he did."[11]

The other special prosecutor, Edward Egan, came from a family of police officers: his grandfather, father, three uncles, two brothers, and two of his nephews all had served, holding ranks from sergeant to captain to detective. One of those nephews, William Egan, worked under Jon Burge at Area 2. Judge Biebel might not have known about this connection before he assigned Egan to the torture cases, but he should have—and if he didn't, Egan should have made Biebel aware of it. But that did not happen.[12]

As you can see, many well-placed people, in various capacities, had good reason for keeping Jon Burge safe from prosecution. Whether it was intentional or not, the investigation was flawed from the start. Perhaps this is why even after determining that Wilson and fifty other men were "abused," the special prosecutors failed to bring criminal charges against any members of the Chicago Police Department on the grounds that the statute of limitations had passed. I'm aware that they found your predecessor Brzeczek guilty of *something*. But "dereliction of duty" is most often associated with falling asleep during the night shift or getting drunk on the job. It's a slap on the wrist, as I'm sure you know. It is hardly a crime.

With this judgment the prosecutors dismissed claims of torture in two ways: by labeling the violence Wilson suffered as "abuse," as opposed to the torture it certainly was, and by arguing that, even if torture had occurred, it was too late to hold anyone accountable for it.

Egan and Boyle also dismissed—again because of the statute of limitations—a wealth of evidence establishing a widespread cover-up of the torture scandal, if it could even be called a cover-up, given that the torture took place in plain sight.

. . .

In recent years you have tried to change the public face of the police department. You want to prove to the public that police officers are friendlier than in the past, that they are willing to listen and learn. You've initiated programs like "Coffee with a Cop" where residents can meet with the officers who patrol their neighborhood and discuss anything that may be bothering them. The problem with programs like this is that trust is delicate. It is not something that is easily developed or maintained over a shot of espresso. Trust is something that's earned when residents witness a tangible change in the way they are treated by the police over a sustained period of time. It's also earned when the police themselves face repercussions for breaking the law.

The Chicago residents I have spoken with just want the police to be treated like everyone else when they violate their own codes and break the law. In this regard, the issue of police torture is important because it exposes the unfairness of our current systems of accountability. You see, police torture exists on a spectrum—what you might have referred to in the police academy as "the use-of-force continuum," which begins with mistreatment, like verbal assault, and ends with horrific forms of violence like what happened behind closed doors at Area 2. I do not think it is possible to understand the issues of trust and legitimacy outside of this continuum.

I'm sure that if a Chicago resident told you that she experienced even a minor form of police abuse you would advise her to report the incident to the Chicago Police Department. But the reason many residents do not is because of this use-of-force continuum, and how normal it is for many Black people to be mistreated by cops. They believe that if cops like Burge have never been held accountable for even extreme acts of torture, then nothing will happen to the police officer who harasses them or roughs them up. They believe that high-ranking officials will ultimately do nothing to protect them and will likely defend the officer who mistreated them. The assumption that cops will not be held accountable for their transgressions is rooted in your own inability to address forms of extreme police violence like torture. This is why a rift exists between the police and the community.

I know that you are aware of the lengths activists in your city have gone to hold the police accountable for the violence they have inflicted on residents. I also know that your record of working with residents to solve their problems is part of the reason the mayor appointed you to be superintendent. I guess that's why I was disturbed by the comments you made in your acceptance speech. "The countless incidents of courage and professionalism," you said, "far outweigh the few examples of excessive force." That quote really troubled me. It bothered me because these incidents of police violence are not few and far between. Nor are they "isolated," as you also have implied. Given your upbringing, you must be aware that there are neighborhoods in Chicago where getting stopped by the police can be a daily—sometimes hourly—occurrence. There are neighborhoods where it surprises no one when the police gun down an unarmed teenager. These are the neighborhoods where Jon Burge hunted Black people.

But even if we agree to disagree on how often police violence occurs, you have to admit that what is not isolated in Chicago's low-income Black neighborhoods, what is reliably consistent, is the fact that police officers hardly ever face any form of legal sanction when they kill, torture, or otherwise injure city residents. That is what I want to talk to you about.

I imagine that during your twenty-nine years as a Chicago police officer you must have attended countless community forums addressing police violence. And yet your comments lead me to believe that you are misunderstanding the full extent of what takes place during such gatherings. Residents are not merely complaining about what police officers have done wrong, they are searching for the accountability that police officers have escaped for as long as the police have existed in this country. It is my experience that in these settings police torture often becomes a prominent issue. But I no longer think this is merely because talk of torture can trigger a sense of injustice. After reflecting long and hard about these forums, I now think of police torture as a touchstone for all the other incidents of extrajudicial force that police officers get away with every day.

Even after the city of Chicago's municipal government offered a public apology to torture survivors and paid fifty-seven of them a monetary settlement, after torture survivors have been released from prison, after the city paid for their college tuition, after the city promised them job training and counseling, after the city helped fund a Chicago Torture Justice Center—after all this, there is still a sizable string attached to these concessions. Reparations in Chicago have been delivered in the name of police torture, now seen as a historic injustice, and yet, no police officer has ever been indicted for torture, let alone tried or convicted of the crime. Your city government, in other words, has created a world in which the tortured exists but torturers do not. This contradiction is a stain on your police department. It is part of what makes your talk of trust and legitimacy ring false.

· · ·

Going forward, any idea of legitimacy must include the principle of accountability. Cops who commit heinous crimes can no longer be shielded from severe repercussions. As you know, Burge was eventually indicted, but the crime was perjury and obstruction of justice. By the time charges were brought against him, the statute of limitations on torture had run its course. When his case finally went to trial, I followed it closely. As the case progressed it only solidified the idea that the system is rigged against residents who experience police torture, and that current ways of holding the police accountable are wholly inadequate. A funny thing is that I came to these conclusions despite street and brutally tortured until he confessed to a murder. He said, 'I had the body of a man; but I was a child inside.' He remains in prison for a crime he insists he did not commit, being abandoned by family and friends who trusted that the police would not have charged him had he not done the crime. The grandmother who stood by him, died while he is in prison, a graying, middle-aged adult. Imagine the loss."[13]

After summarizing this letter, Lefkow expressed her outrage at the position taken by Burge's lawyers. They essentially argued that if someone did the crime, they deserved to be tortured. "I am frankly shocked," she said. "Even if counsel only means to say that none of these people can be believed because they are criminals, the mountain of evidence to the contrary completely belies that position." She also cited friends and family members of Burge's who were grateful to him for his work on the police force, and fellow officers who praised his mettle in dangerous, life-or-death situations.

Then came the moment of truth. Addressing Burge, she said to him: "You denied any knowledge of torture of the plaintiff or of any other torture or abuse having occurred under your direction or command. . . . Unfortunately for you, the jury did not believe you, and I must agree that I did not either." "The torture must stop right here and right now, in this courtroom," she concluded.

In the end, you may recall that she went well beyond the sentencing guidelines of twenty-one to twenty-seven months; she sent Burge to prison for fifty-four months.

• • •

Is a long enough sentence? Many Black Chicagoans think not. The horrors that Burge inflicted, they say, cannot be measured in time served. I agree with them. I wonder if you do, too. If so, I'm asking you to advocate for Chicago residents and address their desire for accountability.

Should police officers under your command believe that even if they were to torture more than one hundred men, then the worse that can happen to them is a light prison sentence that they will serve

the fact that what happened at Burge's perjury and obstructi
went as well as it could have gone. Burge's peers found him g
all counts.

I must admit that before Burge's verdict was read, and tl
of his sentencing was left to Judge Joan Lefkow, I was ra
anxiety about how she might rule. In anticipation of the
I researched her background. An alumnus of Wheaton (
later Northwestern Law School, like you, she had lived in
a long time. I got the sense that she knew how much thi
to the City of Chicago and the State of Illinois. But in her
tory, I also stumbled across headlines that were imposs

Did you know that she had experienced a life-shatt
her own, just five years before Burge's trial began? As
a father, I cannot fathom what it would be like to se
on February 28, 2005, when she came home to find t
and her mother had been gunned down in her basem
been nearly impossible for her not to feel implicat
Bart Ross, a former plaintiff whom she had ruled a
malpractice suit, had shot them to death. Member
caught the killer. As Lefkow said during the sent
hardly a sufficient word for how I feel about the t
of the people who helped me and my family in

Nevertheless, despite the debt she felt to the
the evidence against Burge soberly and on i
heard testimony from a number of witnesse
During several days of sentencing hearings, s
porters and opponents of Jon Burge. In he
tioned the people who had come to court
riences of torture. Some of the content,
appalling. A number of torture survivors f
city, they had told her, because they we
burned, suffocated, or electrocuted agair

"One statement from a prisoner," she s
the longest. This man reports that he ha
He stated he was 17 when he was arre

only a fraction of—if Burge should be their cautionary tale of what happens to corrupt cops, and until his death in September 2018, he lived in Florida where he was content to collect his $4,000-a-month police pension—should your officers take this reality for granted, Superintendent Johnson, then why wouldn't every single one of them believe that he or she is above the law?

This is not a rhetorical question. It is one that you must answer because if you cannot, then your efforts to improve the relationship between residents and the police will all be in vain.

PART III Charging Genocide

An Open Letter to Josephine Grayson

Please forgive this unsolicited letter. You don't know me, or I, you. And yet I feel compelled to write you—to let you know, if you don't already, about the political activism that has continued in your name.

In the past several years, I've learned a lot about the organization that you belonged to, the Civil Rights Congress, and its twinned strategies of litigation and demonstrations, aimed at calling attention to racial injustice in the United States. I want to tell you about the eight young people in Chicago who made me aware of this important political legacy. Inspired by what you and your companions in the Civil Rights Congress did in 1951, they compiled a report on police violence in Chicago. In 2014, a few years before I started to type this letter, these eight young activists— Breanna Champion, Todd St. Hill, Malcolm London, Page May, Asha Rosa, Monica Trinidad, Ric

Wilson, and Ethan Viets-Van Lear—took your legacy all the way to the United Nations.

What ties these young people to your legacy?

Sixty-five years after you lost your husband to the electric chair, a Taser in the hands of a policeman killed a close friend of those eight activists. Sixty-five years after your husband was tried, convicted, and given a death sentence in Virginia, African Americans are still much more likely than whites to die under the aegis of the state, whether by such legalized means of state-sanctioned murder as lethal injection or the electric chair or by the hands of a policeman on the street. Many decades ago, these realities prompted you to ask, "How many more African Americans must die this way?" These young activists from Chicago have the same question.

Following the death of their friend Dominique Franklin, these eight young men and women began coordinating meetings in community centers and schools across Chicago to discuss their plans for exposing and protesting police violence. When asked to explain the controversial name of their organization, We Charge Genocide, one group member, Page May, pointed to the rich history of activism her group was trying to invoke.

On October 22, 2014, I listened from the crowd as Page addressed an audience at the Hull-House museum located on the Near West Side of Chicago. Page said: "In 1951, an American group called the Civil Rights Congress presented a petition to the United Nations entitled *We Charge Genocide: The Crime of Government against the Negro People.* The petition accused the United States government of subjecting African Americans to premature death in a calculated manner. It got international attention because it documented over one hundred and fifty racial killings of Black people, mostly by law enforcement officers."[1]

Unable to mask the pride that this instance of activism evoked in her, May told the crowd how a number of people like you, Mrs. Grayson—people whose lives were devastated by a racially biased criminal justice system—had signed this petition. Not long after you signed, the petition was presented to UN officials in two different venues: first in Paris, where the General Assembly held its meetings at the time, and then in New York.

This petition, which I found in an archive at the Stony Island Arts Bank on Chicago's South Side, shows your name in the second column, fourth from the top—one signature among nearly one hundred. Now, when I get word that the police have tortured or killed someone—usually someone young and Black—I often find myself reading the petition again and again, start to finish. Poring over the stories it tells in its 237 pages, I am astonished at how current the document still feels. The horrors it chronicles are still very much part of life in the United States.

At the Hull-House, Page May did not mention you or your husband, Francis, by name. Instead, she referenced signees whose names the crowd might know, such as the world-famous actor and opera singer Paul Robeson, who was charged with delivering the petition to the UN Secretariat in New York; and the eminent sociologist and historian W. E. B. Du Bois, who had intended to go to Paris with the petition but was prevented by the US government from traveling abroad. Du Bois had been classified by the State Department as an "unregistered foreign agent." The United States had revoked Robeson's passport in 1950, or he might have gone to Paris, too.

And yet for all the civil rights icons like Robeson and Du Bois, there were and still are many more everyday folks like you, Mrs. Grayson, who found, and who still find, their lives upended by racism and violence. Often the people who stand on the front lines of these struggles are the people who remain all but invisible to history—not "great men and women," but everyday people who stand up for what they think is right. "It is because of this legacy," May told the crowd, "that we named our organization We Charge Genocide."

A desire to put an end to this history of violence against Black people inspired Page May and her group to follow in your organization's footsteps and present their case on an international stage. Their goal was a lofty one: testify in Geneva at the UN Committee against Torture. They had no credentials or official expertise, and certainly no experience addressing a global conference. But they did share a mission with your organization, and they hoped to follow in your footsteps.

• • •

The group's rallying cry was "We charge torture. We charge genocide." They used these sentences in their press releases and speeches and on the website, and they chanted them during protest marches and rallies. When I first heard the group connect torture and genocide together in this way, I have to admit that I did not understand the link. Genocide extinguishes an entire group of people; torture is carried out against individuals, not groups, but it doesn't aim to kill. Torture terrorizes. It keeps people subservient. It debilitates and maims.

Yet the more I learned about the activism of We Charge Genocide, the more I realized that torture and genocide have a lot in common. Eventually, I came to understand how the group members thought about this relationship: police officers deliberately torture the most marginal groups in the United States; since African Americans are among the most marginal, they are disproportionately exposed to torture; and the deliberate exposure of African Americans to torture by our government is a form of genocide.

From We Charge Genocide's point of view, to live a life of perpetual debilitation, to be subjected to "slow violence" with no end in sight, is hardly to live at all.[2] Having one's humanity steadily annihilated, well, that *is* torture.

An Open Letter to the Late Francis Grayson

I was putting together a syllabus for an Intro to African American Studies class when I got distracted. I couldn't stop thinking about your death by electric chair in Virginia in 1951. So, I decided to write to you.

I am a professor who teaches college students about race relations, crime, and the law. Sometimes I discuss your case. I tell my students that you were one of seven Black men in Martinsville, Virginia, who came to be known as the "Martinsville Seven." In 1949, the seven of you were arrested for the gang rape of a white woman. Two years later, you were tried by all-male, all-white juries in six separate trials (two of you agreed to be tried together). Each trial took two weeks. All seven of you were found guilty and electrocuted several months later, in February 1951.

I tell my students that your case was not merely about rape. In the Jim Crow era, it was about whether Blacks were fit to live among whites or were sexually rapacious savages who could not be trusted in the presence of white women. Beyond that, it was about whether African Americans alone should face the electric chair for the crime of rape. In fact, from the time Virginia began using the electric chair in 1908 to the day you were arrested, the only men who had ever been executed for the crime of rape in the state of Virginia were Black. Sadly, this did not change for as long as the state continued to execute people for rape, which it did until 1961.

In my seminars, I sit with students at a large, round table and urge them to participate in discussions. I get them to process their conflicting feelings while I attempt to maintain a neutral facade, as professors are trained to do. I have always found it difficult to maintain that facade, though, particularly when teaching about historical injustice and social inequality. The mentors I have turned to time and again as a professor constantly question the notion of objectivity, even though the dominant perspective among social scientists is to defend objectivity at all costs. I have learned from my mentors that the proper attitude for a professor to take is not always one of neutrality, because not all of the issues we study are neutral. Some issues demand something different, something more. They require us to take a stance.

I tell my students about how you were arrested after you left work, while you were drinking alcohol near the train tracks with six friends, of how you and the other six defendants were interrogated while inebriated and without lawyers present. I tell them of the efforts of your wife, Josephine, in the years that followed, working sixteen-hour days to organize protests that you both prayed might secure your release.

Despite a lack of evidence in many cases, Black men in the rural South were often convicted of raping white women and summarily sentenced to death—and your case was no exception to that rule.

Writing you now has made me realize what I should do. This year, I think I will begin my seminar with William Patterson's "Summary and Prayer" from the 1951 We Charge Genocide petition:

> There may be a debate as to the expediency of condemning the Government of the United States for the genocide it practices and permits against the 15,000,000 of its citizens who are Negroes. There can be none about the existence of the crime. It is an undeniable fact. The United States Government itself, through the Report of the President's Committee on Civil Rights, admits the institutionalized Negro oppression, written into the law, and carried out by police and courts. It describes it, examines it, surveys it, writes about it, talks about it, and does everything but change it. It both admits it and protects it.
>
> Thus it was easy for your petitioners to offer abundant proof of the crime. It is everywhere in American life. And yet words and statistics are but poor things to convey the long agony of the Negro people. We have proved "killing members of the group"—but the case after case after case cited does nothing to assuage the helplessness of the innocent Negro trapped at this instant by police in a cell, which will be the scene of his death.
>
> We have shown "mental and bodily harm," but this proof can barely indicate the life-long terror of thousands on thousands of Negroes forced to live under the menace of official violence, mob law and the Ku Klux Klan. We have tried to reveal something of the deliberate infliction "on the group of conditions which bring about its physical destruction in whole or in part"—but this cannot convey the hopeless despair of those forced by law to live in conditions of disease and poverty because of race, of birth, of color. We have shown incitements to commit genocide, shown that a conspiracy exists to commit it, and now we can only add that an entire people, not only unprotected by their government but the object of government-inspired violence, reach forth their hands to the General Assembly in appeal.

Three hundred years is a long time to wait. And now we ask that world opinion, that the conscience of mankind as symbolized by the General Assembly of the United Nations turn not a deaf ear to our entreaty.

This statement is still terribly relevant more than a half century after it was written. Patterson was saying that in the United States, deliberate, coordinated, predictable, and systematic forms of debilitation encircle Black people like a cowboy's lasso, growing tighter when they try to escape. What your wife, Josephine, was fighting for on your behalf in the 1950s is still relevant today precisely because of how policing continues to pervade the lives of Black people in the United States, whether they are stopped at a traffic light, or given a harsh prison sentence, or tortured in police custody, or shot in the back while running from a cop. In this age of mistreatment, mass incarceration, police torture, and death, racially determined punishment continues to infect our modern legal system like a disease.

But, Francis, I am also writing to let you know how proud you should be of your wife. The last I've seen or heard of her in the media was in 2011, when I came across an article in which your granddaughter was interviewed.[3] In it, she said that Josephine no longer wishes to speak about the circumstances that led to your execution. Surely this is not because she wants to forget you or the legacy of your case. Perhaps the most straightforward explanation is that she has spent her whole life talking about you and after a while she grew tired, that her activism wore her out. Yet maybe, in refusing to carry on, she was unwilling to position herself as the spokesperson for a movement against injustice. Josephine always wanted the focus to be on the Martinsville Seven and the We Charge Genocide position, and that's why she probably doesn't feel the need to remind people about her place in history. Josephine loved you, and she fought to keep you alive. And today, in young people in Chicago, the kind of activism she embodied lives on.

· · ·

Josephine, and her activism, endures in people like Mariame Kaba. She is the Black woman who dreamed up the 2014 version of We Charge Genocide after a young man named Dominique — "Damo," to his friends — was killed by the police.

Mariame did not know Damo personally. All she knew was that his death had affected the lives of several young activists in Chicago whom she cared deeply about. They were devastated. Seeing them in pain brought her anger and sadness, so she began thinking of ways that his death could spark positive action. That's how she came up with the idea to create a modern version of the 1951 We Charge Genocide petition. Shortly after Damo died, she expressed this sentiment in a blog post: "Perhaps such an effort could serve as a container for our collective pain. Maybe we could transform our devastation into righteous and purposeful collective action."[4]

After gathering nearly fifty like-minded Chicagoans to meet and discuss her idea, she decided along with them that young people would drive We Charge Genocide. This, more than anything else, is why Mariame brings Josephine to mind for me. In the midst of leading the charge to transform her devastation into something productive, she insisted on sharing the spotlight, or that the spotlight not point at any single person. As she put it, "We Charge Genocide is not contingent on one person but is truly a collective and collaborative effort."[5]

Nevertheless, as an imaginative community organizer and long-time activist, she had an important role to play.

"No one is more important than her," Page May, a member of We Charge Genocide, says of Mariame. "You can't expect a seventeen- or twenty-year-old to know how to do this — to submit a petition to the UN. She let us know that it's okay to expect adults with more experience to help and support us."

If I could meet your wife, Josephine, or say anything to her today, I would not discuss your case, or ask her to sit down for an interview to further my own research. If I mentioned your case at all, I would tell her that I respect her refusal to speak about it.[6] The anthropologist Sherry Ortner first made me aware of the importance of this kind of refusal. She coined the term *ethnographic refusal* to refer to the practice by which researchers and their collaborators decide not to make available certain information for academic audiences. The purpose of withholding in this way is to ensure that communities can discuss the issues that have an impact on their lives in their own time and on their own terms. That is why I would not try to persuade Josephine to speak about you given that she has already refused.

Instead, I would hand her a letter that I wrote about a group of young activists who were inspired by the Civil Rights Congress, the organization that your wife leaned on to fight for your life, Francis. I would show her this letter just to make her aware of how much the 1951 petition matters to a group of young people who are grieving for their friend.

An Open Letter to the Late William Patterson

It was your idea, William, as president of the Civil Rights Congress, to create the original We Charge Genocide petition in 1951. When your petition was presented to the United Nations, the UN was a fledgling organization that had proclaimed itself "the conscience of mankind." In its six short years of existence, it had received requests for assistance from marginalized groups the world over. Indigenous peoples from European colonies in Africa and Asia had asked for help. So, too, had Blacks living in the United States. In fact, the We Charge Genocide document would be the third such petition the UN had received from African Americans, following one from the National Negro Congress in 1946 and a second from the National Association for the Advancement of Colored People in 1947. But the 1951 petition was the one that attracted the most attention, that stirred the most controversy, and therefore led to the most pushback from the US government. Even Eleanor Roosevelt, who years earlier had advocated—unsuccessfully, it must be said—for the passage of antilynching legislation, spoke out against it, calling it "ridiculous." She did not see how lynching, that is, the systematic and deliberate torture of Black people, could reflect a genocidal impulse at the heart of this country.

One of my favorite stories about the We Charge Genocide petition is how that document actually reached the United Nations. I find the story so unbelievable that I have always wanted to ask you whether it's true.

In 1951, the General Assembly had not yet moved to its new UN headquarters in New York, so to present the petition, you traveled to Paris. According to what I have read, upon arrival, you discovered that US government officials had gone through your luggage and confiscated all copies of the petition. Your name had also been removed from the UN agenda, erasing any official record that you had been scheduled to speak.

Such sabotage by the US government was not surprising. But your prescience in anticipating it, and your resourcefulness in defeating it, is quite remarkable.

Because of the possibility of foul play, which must have seemed likely since the Civil Rights Congress was a communist-leaning organization, and this was the height of the Red Scare, you mailed sections of the petition to several friends and allies in Paris and Bulgaria before your flight. After arriving in Paris, you visited each friend's home and collected the pages you had sent piecemeal and were then able to reassemble the document.

I have always found this workaround more fascinating than the government's theft. Sometimes I imagine being one of your allies in Paris. I receive your mailed document, knowing that the world's understanding of what was happening to African Americans might depend on my keeping safe a few carefully typed sheets of paper. It is a frightening and sobering prospect.

Reading the summary of the Civil Rights Congress's appeal to the UN, I can imagine how inflammatory this document must have seemed to many in power in the United States. I wish you were alive to tell me about your presentation of the petition. Your presence was erased from the official record, so there is no transcript of your speech. I can only assume that the US government was threatened by your words, because after your visit, you were so reviled in this country that your passport—like Robeson's and Du Bois's—was revoked.[7] And even beyond what must have been a fiery speech, I can understand the courage it must have taken for you to convince other activists, in the midst of their own individual struggles, to add their names to the petition. I am grateful you managed to convince them to associate with a leftist organization like the Civil Rights Congress at a time when the House Un-American Activities Committee was targeting it, and many of its leaders had been jailed—when the US government was trying to drive a wedge between it and other civil rights organizations like the National Association for the Advancement of Colored People.[8]

And yet I wonder how much it would trouble you to know, if you were still alive—or perhaps you do know, in whatever kind of afterlife there is—that many of the same issues you and the other writers of that petition raised in 1951 about the Black experience in the United States still exist today. One of these issues is how Black people are unfairly subjected to the use-of-force continuum. A modern-day group that calls itself We Charge Genocide has focused on this continuum, in which banal forms of aggression bleed into torture and death, shaping the experience of life. I wonder what you would think of your words being repeated in We Charge Genocide's own report: "Once the classic method of lynching was the rope, now it is the policeman's bullet." Police violence is an issue about which you were terribly prescient, indeed.

Thanks in part to tutelage from their community elders, the young people of We Charge Genocide realize that African Americans have been waging a battle against this dehumanizing continuum for a very long time. They understand the sacrifices you made, and they recognize that they can learn from your struggle, which helps them to contextualize their own. In fact, they feel they *must* learn from you. Their own desire to give testimony to the UN was part of their ambition to follow your path, and it was motivated by the same concerns you had.

But they did not request an audience before the General Assembly. There is now a different UN forum for such testimony, so they sought to appear at one of the hearings that the Committee against Torture now holds regularly in Geneva, Switzerland. These hearings are part of the committee's implementation of a treaty known as the Convention against Torture and Other Cruel, Inhuman or Degrading Treatment or Punishment, which was adopted in 1984 (although the United States did not sign on until ten years later).[9] Nations that are signatory to it must agree to take certain measures to prevent torture from taking place inside their borders, and they must appear once every four years before the committee's hearings to answer questions and testify about their adherence to treaty policies.

At these hearings, each country offers a report about its implementation of the convention's antitorture provisions. But in the weeks before that hearing, members of "civil society" — nongovernmental and grassroots organizations, political action groups, and others — are invited to submit "shadow" reports. These reports, which might offer information that is either not included in or is contradictory to the government's own report, are meant to inform committee members more fully about torture-related issues in that country and to serve as a check on accuracy.

In 2014, We Charge Genocide decided to submit a shadow report. This was remarkable — it is not common for youth-based organizations to participate in UN proceedings. In fact, no other youth-based organization did so that year. The document its members assembled was the result of a long, arduous process that began with a website. On the site, the group asked Chicago residents to upload stories about close friends and family members who'd been mistreated, tortured, and killed. Stories flooded in by the thousands. We Charge Genocide members spent days reading and sorting through the stories, identifying common trends during police encounters and gathering data on police violence to include in their report. They spent countless hours reading and rereading what Chicago residents had written and researching other shadow reports in an attempt to understand what would make their report stand out from the rest.

"Anyone can submit a shadow report," Page, a member of the group told me. "And anybody can go to Geneva if they have the means. What's rare is being able to speak." In order to be invited to speak, their report had to be special.

Page told me that most organizations hire lobbyists who try to get their concerns heard. These lobbyists spend the first several days of the gathering trying to convince UN committee members that the groups they represent should be permitted to take the stage. The members of We Charge Genocide wondered how they would fare, going up against so many trained lobbyists. But before members of the organization could cross that bridge they had to deal with a more urgent problem. How would they get to Geneva?

Many members had never traveled outside the United States, much less to Europe. No one had the money to pay for such a trip. Still, they were determined to make the journey a reality. To get there, We Charge Genocide did what I suspect you might have done, William: they started a campaign.

• • •

From reading about the history of your organization, I know that you are no stranger to political campaigns. During the fight to save the Martinsville Seven, your organization produced pamphlets to raise awareness about the impending executions in Virginia. You helped Josephine Grayson organize mass actions in Richmond, Virginia, and when legal appeals on Francis's behalf failed, you helped organize the campaign that led four hundred protestors straight to the door of the governor's office. I can only imagine what you might've done with Twitter!

In this age of social media, members of We Charge Genocide took advantage of online outreach and created a video to raise awareness for their cause. It begins with a close-up of group member Malcolm London's face. After Malcolm speaks, he and Ric Wilson, another group member, begin talking in alternating sentences, seamlessly moving from one to the next, like sprinters in a relay passing the baton.

"We are always unsafe, living in our skin, in this country," Malcolm starts. "It's a permanent condition."

"Our people are stopped," Ric says. "We are frisked. We are criminalized. We are targeted. We are invaded. We are jailed. And we are killed."

Ric's voice plays over a shot of Chicago's skyline. A train runs across the business district known as the Loop. The camera then focuses on Ric standing in front of the Metropolitan Correctional Center, a building whose triangular ugliness is its defining feature.

"The machine grinds on," Malcolm continues. "And we struggle to identify one culprit. One officer. One bad apple. But there isn't just one."

The video cuts to the nighttime. We see a white SUV with the Chicago Police Department logo on its side. The camera pans up toward a blue light surveillance unit and then settles on Page, appearing for the first time.

"So many of us are afraid to speak the word," she says calmly. "We are afraid to lay claim to it. It's too awful to believe." Page shakes her head. She's standing in front of a police cargo van, the kind of vehicle into which, the next year, in 2015, a twenty-five-year-old Black man named Freddie Gray would be disappeared in Baltimore, only to emerge in a coma and die three days later, sparking massive protests that are of a piece with the struggles of your organization, William, and with the struggles of We Charge Genocide—that are, in fact, of a piece with the struggles of oppressed people of color the world over.[10]

"It seems too conspiratorial. Too pessimistic. Too alienating. Too . . . *something*," Malcolm says, searching for the right word.

"Yet there it is," Ric interjects. "On the tip of our tongues."

And then the video reaches its climax, with Page saluting your legacy: "When we are feeling brave and safe among those we love and trust," she says, her voice increasingly more audacious, "we sometimes whisper the words."

"Genocide," Ric says.

"Genocide," Malcolm says.

"Genocide," Page says.

Fade to black as the name We Charge Genocide emerges from the dark, followed by Monica's voice-over: "We are We Charge Genocide and we need your help. This November, we will present a report to the United Nations on Chicago police violence against youth of color. We need to raise $15,000 so that we can send six young people to Geneva, Switzerland."

The video then directs viewers to a website. "Help us get there" is the video's closing line.

An Open Letter to the Late Dominique "Damo" Franklin

I didn't know you, Damo, while you were living. But I do know you in death. You died at twenty-three and were much loved by your friends and family. Nevertheless, as a teenager and as a young adult, you had experienced several run-ins with the Chicago police that had instilled in you a healthy fear of the cops—a fear familiar to many African American youth. I also know that on May 7, 2014, you had stolen a bottle of liquor from a convenience store, and when the police showed up, you ran. The officers chased you down the street and caught you. Once they handcuffed you, they used a Taser on you three different times. The third time, you fell and hit your head on a pole, lapsing into a coma from which you never awoke.

When I think about the circumstances of your death, I can't help but remember the first man to expose police torture in Chicago, Andrew Wilson. I often think of you and Andrew together because his life and your death lead us to question what kinds of police violence we, as Black people living in this country, are willing to accept.

The police electrocuted Andrew with a mysterious device called the black box. Jon Burge supposedly engineered that box for the sole purpose of inflicting pain. The City of Chicago has now apologized to Andrew and the other Black men who were tortured in this way. What Burge did to Andrew Wilson is now considered unacceptable— unlike what the Chicago police did to you.

The police electrocuted you with a weapon we have all become familiar with, a device called the Taser. The Taser Company engineered the device for the sole purpose of incapacitating people who were deemed dangerous. The police tased you in broad daylight as a consequence of your alleged actions. But the City of Chicago has never apologized to you or the other people the police have fatally injured in this way. When it comes to you, our government believes that the police acted within the scope of the law, and therefore, what those officers did to you—how they killed you—has been deemed "reasonable."

I want to tell you, Damo, about the people in Chicago who disagree with this, as well as the efforts of your friends to protest your death. Eight young people from your hometown—some of whom you were extremely close to, others who you knew in passing—formed a group called We Charge Genocide. They made a case, on the international stage, that the forms of police violence that we have come to accept, like tasering someone, can be just as horrifying as the forms that our government regards as intolerable, like planned torture. From the Taser to the black box, all the violence that exists on the use-of-force continuum has at least one thing in common: to some extent or degree, it is indicative of our country's genocidal impulse to deliberately control marginalized groups.

I'm writing you now because your friends at We Charge Genocide have refused to let you be forgotten—they have refused to let the United States dispose of your memory. You deserve to know what they have accomplished in your name. Just seven months after you died, We Charge Genocide left for Switzerland to link your death to conversations about police violence at a global event called the Committee against Torture. The group's goal was to convince the committee to recommend that the US Congress pass a data collection act that would document and monitor police violence—from stop-and-frisk and brutal arrests to torture and death.

The group was giddy at the prospect of international travel but weighed down, too, by the burden of their mission. Before boarding the flight, members took a picture at O'Hare Airport that featured Page, Todd, and Monica holding a sign that read #ChicagoForMarissa. This was meant for Marissa Alexander, a thirty-three-year-old woman who was serving a twenty-year prison sentence for firing a warning shot at her husband after he threatened to kill her. You know your friends, so you must know that cases like these, which are such vivid examples of the disproportionate punishment African Americans face, are always on their minds.[11]

Early the next morning, the We Charge Genocide delegation ar-rived in Geneva. I wish you would've had the opportunity to visit this place with them. As soon as he stepped off the plane, Ric was struck by the differences between the United States and Switzerland. He heard an abundance of languages and accents—many more than in Chicago, where English, Spanish, and Polish are dominant. Geneva's infrastructure also seemed in much better condition than infrastruc-ture was at home. As he made his way around the city later that day, Ric found himself in the unusual position of actually *enjoying* public transportation.

Geneva was immaculately clean and picturesque, the Swiss Alps standing majestically in the distance, but what impressed Ric most was something that would have stuck out to you, too, I presume. During his strolls through the city, he rarely saw police officers. "No one stopped and frisked me when I was walking down the street, or asked me if I had any weed," he said. "I didn't feel like I was targeted at all."

Nevertheless, as exciting as it was for Ric and the other group members to be in a place that seemed so exotic, they knew they were about to engage in a daunting task: lobbying a room full of lawyers and UN officials for the privilege to testify before the Committee against Torture. The entire group had been nervous about this. For-tunately, while they were in Geneva, your friends received help from Crista Noel, a cofounder of a nonprofit called Women's All Points Bulletin and a member of the US Human Rights Network. She be-came an important ally.

"We didn't do all this work so that you can wear $20 T-shirts," Crista told them shortly after they arrived. Yes, she was referring to the black T-shirts the group had planned to wear with your face on them as a way to represent you. But please do not take offense; Crista didn't mean to dismiss you. She just didn't want the group's presence at the UN to merely symbolize your death. She wanted your death to spur change on behalf of the living.

After the group rode the train into downtown Geneva, they met with an eight-person taskforce, a group of lawyers and lobbyists and activists who, like Crista, volunteered for the US Human Rights Network. This group, which came to Geneva whenever it was the United States' turn to present its case, had agreed this year to assist your friends and others who were attending the Committee against Torture for the first time.

As it turned out, Crista's advocacy paid off. Later, on the same day they arrived, UN officials announced that We Charge Genocide would be asked to represent all the organizations from the United States whose reports centered on policing—a significant honor, and entirely unexpected. It is rare for the UN to host a youth-led organization, let alone ask that group to speak on behalf of other organizations. But as thrilled as they were with the opportunity that had been given them, knowing this crew as well as you did, it probably would not surprise you that they kept their excitement at bay with a healthy dose of skepticism.

"Why are they excited that we're here?" Ric asked. "They should be scared."

Ric reasoned that if the UN truly believed in the principles the organization espoused, it would be frightening to listen to a group of young people exposing the fact that a nation as powerful and influential as the United States had broken its treaties time and again, and to hear that young people like him and those who had accompanied him to the hearings were suffering inside US borders. In fact, your friends were deeply suspicious not only of the UN and the US representatives who would be speaking at the conference but also of the Committee against Torture itself. Would the committee really be willing to join them in their indictment of the most powerful nation on earth? Your friends wondered whether their message was going to be taken seriously, or if they were just there to be Black and Brown kids in a photo op. Perhaps it was their skepticism that allowed them to remain steadfast in condemning their native land.

• • •

When it was announced that We Charge Genocide would speak about policing in the United States, group members chose Ethan to represent them. He was picked because of his relationship to you. Ethan was your homeboy, one of your closest friends, the person from We Charge Genocide who was hit hardest by your death.

Sitting in the grand hall, waiting for the speakers' orientation to begin, Ethan was racked with anxiety about the address he was going to give before the committee the next day, a speech that would be broadcast around the world.

In the days following your death, Ethan had been overwhelmed by grief. Yet as tragic as your death was for him, it had led to the formation of We Charge Genocide. Now that he was here, he had the responsibility of telling the world about what had happened to you. He wondered whether he was up to the task. Ethan worried that he wouldn't be able to fully convey the tragedy of your death and how representative it was of what was happening to so many young Black people in Chicago.

He felt your presence, Damo. You had inspired his speech. You were the reason he was even in Geneva. But the pressure not to let you down weighed heavily on him. As he waited in that cavernous room, Ethan commiserated with Martinez Sutton. Martinez was not part of an official organization. He was there to speak on behalf of his sister, Rekia Boyd, a young woman who was killed by an off-duty police officer on Chicago's West Side. The off-duty cop shot Rekia in the back of the head. Her offense: speaking too loudly. Martinez and Ethan met right before the speaker's orientation.

Over the next several hours they would meet other activists. They had all suddenly found themselves in the center of an international debate about the police's use of force. Later on, Ethan and Martinez would meet young activists from Ferguson, Missouri, who had led uprisings in their city after Michael Brown was killed by a police officer leaving a convenience store, just like you. They would also meet Trayvon Martin's parents, Sybrina Fulton and Tracy Martin, who had become symbols of parental grief after a self-appointed "neighborhood watchman" gunned down their son.

As they sat in that capacious room, both Ethan and Martinez were thinking about the talks they would be giving the next day. They both were still coping with grief and anger over their losses. The two young men talked about the uncertainty they felt in being messengers for the dead. Walking that great hall in the Palace of Nations, Martinez and Ethan also discussed how hard it was for them to hide their feelings in public. They understood that they had to control their emotions in order to appeal to "polite society," and they recognized that the burden they had shouldered would be with them for a long time. Having to tell and retell their stories about police violence tormented them to the point that it was difficult for them to hide their pain. Yet that endless voicing of trauma was also therapeutic; it gave meaning and purpose to their suffering.[12]

The fight for recognition was wearing Martinez and Ethan down and saving them at the same time. Speaking to you became one of Ethan's most important outlets. I wonder if you heard him. Later that day Page recorded a video of Ethan reciting a poem he wrote for you. "For Damo" evokes you as a young man "born to live free and wild," a young man whose tasering at the hands of the police and subsequent death is emblematic of the dreadful state of Black life today in the United States. These are from the closing lines:

> The problem is not, and never will be Damo or young men like him.
> But his jailing, and eventual murder has always been America's Final Solution
> To the conundrum of how to keep colored folk in line and obedient.
> His hospital deathbed seemed another stint at an institution.
> The beeping and clicking was drowned out by the sound of Damo's booming laugh

Reverberating in my head.

Reminding me of the glory that exists in this world.

And how little we do to protect it.

The next morning, Ethan and the other seven members of the We Charge Genocide delegation filed into the grand hall where they would testify. Six individuals would speak to the committee before Ethan did. Most of them wore suits and looked important. By contrast, Ethan and his friends were wearing the black T-shirts that honored you. Those who spoke first—lawyers, NGO workers, and other professional advocates—sat behind a long wooden table and cited treaties, conventions, and statistics. But it didn't seem to your friends that any of these professionals were directly affected by the torture allegations they were leveling against the United States. Ethan's presentation, by contrast, would include one crucial element these other presentations lacked: personal experience.

When it was time for Ethan to speak, he intentionally broke UN protocol by standing to deliver his speech, lending gravity to the situation.

"Before Ethan," Page said, "most of the statements that people delivered were very legal, professional, and formal. People read their remarks sitting down.

"When Ethan stood, everyone in the room was caught off guard," Page continued. "They all knew: you're not supposed to *stand*, but Ethan did. And what he stood to deliver wasn't a legalese document. It wasn't a two-minute rant either. It was way more soulful."

Ethan opened by referring to you. "My friend Dominique Franklin is lying dead in a coffin. He was killed by a Chicago police officer who heinously tased him three times as he was handcuffed, leaving him in a coma to die. And my hands are tied. Every day people are being tortured, and people are dying."

For Ethan, this tragedy was compounded by the fact that the police, the very people charged to protect and serve the public, were contributing to the epidemic. "The police kill a Black person every twenty-eight hours," he said, and then repeated that number—

twenty-eight—for emphasis. He urged the committee to advocate
for increased data collection in the United States on the use of force.
This small step toward transparency in policing would go a long way,
Ethan said. His voice growing hoarse, he ended his speech with the
six words that are his group's rallying cry: "We charge torture. We
charge genocide."

. . .

After Ethan finished, and after the committee took a break for lunch,
the delegation representing the US government had their turn. The
members of this group belonged to the UN Human Rights Council;
the Bureau of Democracy, Human Rights, and Labor; the State Department; and the Department of Justice. They were experienced,
senior-level bureaucrats.

When it was time for these seasoned bureaucrats to speak about
the issue of torture, they painted a picture of a fair and just society—a
legal system that members of We Charge Genocide had perhaps read
about in books, or heard about in political speeches, but had never
seen on their own streets. As these young men and women listened
to the testimony of the US delegation, it seemed as though the representatives were simply detached from reality. The absurdity of their
testimony signaled the government's unwillingness to take the Committee against Torture seriously.

The most egregious testimony was given by Deputy Assistant Attorney General David Bitkower, who spoke about the Department of
Justice's prosecution of perpetrators of torture who were members
of the military or the police. Bitkower began by citing prosecutions
of abuses that had taken place overseas, noting that there has been a
spike in incidents of torture by the military since the September 11
attacks, as a consequence, he argued, of the war on terror. One of the
incidents he focused on the longest was that of an US soldier convicted by a military tribunal of raping and killing an Iraqi teenager and
her family. He also spent a substantial amount of time discussing an

incident in which four government contractors shot fourteen civilians in Baghdad.

For Bitkower, these cases were evidence of the Justice Department's commitment to purging "bad apples" from the service. While recognizing that some officers abuse their power, he reiterated that the Justice Department seeks to implement meaningful reform when offenses against human dignity are uncovered. But by framing torture as something that happens only overseas, Bitkower's speech cast a shadow over the more commonplace examples of police violence that occur regularly within the borders of the United States.

To add insult to injury, Bitkower bolstered his remarks with the assertion that the Department's Civil Rights Division had opened more than twenty investigations into law enforcement violations over the previous five years. According to him, those investigations had resulted in fifteen "settlements," although he never specified whether they were civil or criminal suits, or the amount of compensation awarded to victims. They must have been civil cases, because Bitkower began to talk about criminal prosecutions next. In the criminal realm, he added, the Justice Department had prosecuted more than 330 members of law enforcement for misconduct in the same time frame.

What Bitkower did not mention was that during this five-year period, according to the Federal Bureau of Investigation, the number of law enforcement officers working in the United States was slightly more than 954,000. So, 330 was merely 0.03 percent of the total population of officers. We Charge Genocide's group member, Asha, picked up on this discrepancy.

"Three hundred thirty police officers have been prosecuted for police crimes in five years?" Asha later remembered saying to herself. "That number is minuscule compared to all the people who have been violated by the police."

When viewed through the prism of the issues that concerned groups like We Charge Genocide and seen in context of the vast scope of the criminal acts those prosecutions supposedly address, the numbers Bitkower trotted out were so modest as to be offensive. In response to these statistics, your friends laughed in disbelief. But the focus on the small number of prosecutions was only part of what they objected to. They objected to his emotionless voice, as if the acts of torture and death Bitkower addressed were not significant enough to elicit his compassion. They objected to the way he framed extrajudicial force, as if it were purely accidental rather than an inevitable consequence of how the US military and police operate. They objected to what Bitkower did not address, such as the afterlives of torture and death, that is, their lasting impact on the loved ones of people debilitated or killed by the police.

Your friends decided they were no longer willing to subject themselves to what they considered lies and evasions. During Bitkower's speech, in protest, one by one, they stood up and filed out of the room.

· · ·

The next day, the same US delegates who spoke the day before would have questions posed to them by the UN Committee against Torture. The purpose of this hearing was for the UN committee members to ask follow up questions and voice their concerns.

The committee asked questions for nearly two hours. Their inquiries included citizens' claims of mistreatment at the hands of the police, the torture of suspected criminals, police shootings, the protests that had emerged in response to those shootings, and the police's efforts to suppress those protests. They also spoke about the war crimes that military officers committed overseas. For the committee, the ethical and legal wrongdoing of police officers in the United States was to be discussed in tandem with the wrongdoing of the US military. Both kinds of lawlessness were continuous with and inseparable from what it meant for a government to enact torture.

The committee began questioning the US delegation by explicitly requesting that they stop speaking in generalizations about its country's ideals. They took particular exception to Bitkower's use of "freedom" more than twenty times in his testimony the day before.

Instead, the committee asked delegates to focus on the ways those ideals may have been compromised.

Speaking about accountability, for example, committee chair Jens Modvig asked which steps the United States had taken to review police practices following recent events in Ferguson, Missouri. Modvig wanted to know why there was not an independent organization—one with no ties to the police department—whose mission was to oversee the use-of-force continuum.

Moreover, with respect to excessive force, Modvig asked, "How is the oversight and accountability implemented when a police officer uses a Taser gun on someone?" Any doubt about which American city Modvig was referring to was removed when he brought up Jon Burge. He pointed to the paragraphs in the US government's report that gave an account of Burge's conviction in 2011 and asked the United States for an update on what had been done to bring the other officers who had tortured criminal suspects under Burge's supervision to justice. And he was not finished with Chicago.

"What kind of redress is being provided to torture survivors?" he asked.

In mentioning Chicago torture survivors as well as Jon Burge, whose reign of terror began in the 1970s, Modvig implicitly discredited the US timeline, which placed the September 11 attacks as the origin point for torture.

In a similar vein, another committee member, Satyabhoosun Domah, called attention to our country's contradictions: "The US's story seems to be: there was a laudable beginning, and then we strayed for a little while, but we are getting back on track now," Domah said. "However, the fact remains that a number of breaches have occurred in between." Indeed, the Burge torture cases were among these "breaches."

Domah's statement also pointed out the inconsistency between the US representatives' and other politicians' constant reference to national ideals such as freedom and a fundamental respect for individual liberty and human rights along with the amply documented existence of torture. "We all agree that the prohibition of torture is universal and should be practiced everywhere in the US," she said. "But the dark days of democracy show that democratic institutions join forces to frustrate democratic principles."

Domah and the other members of the committee sought to obtain information about the specifics of what the United States was and was not doing to safeguard against torture and to prosecute offenders when it occurred.

As part of the public record, the Committee against Torture's questioning would be vitally important for We Charge Genocide's cause—especially the statements that came from Domah. Her questions, in particular, were directly shaped by your friends' hard work.

"Why haven't police shootings by the Chicago police dropped significantly," she asked, "given that Tasers were supposed to be a nonlethal alternative?" Instead, Tasers had become one more weapon used to administer injury and death to Black Chicagoans. Pointing to metrics she had read from the We Charge Genocide shadow report, Domah noted that between 2001 and 2009, 92 percent of Taser uses involved a Black or Latino target. In the first six months of 2014 alone, there had been 186 uses of Tasers by Chicago police, with 146 of those against Black people.

"Isn't Taser usage an example of how Blacks are being denied basic human rights in the United States?" Domah asked. "What about young people of color who are disproportionately tased, like Dominique Franklin?" There. She said it. Your name had been spoken, not just by one of your friends, but by a UN official, in the Palace of Nations in Geneva.

Page once told me that if delivering a speech before the UN Committee against Torture was the "gold standard" for anti–police torture advocacy, then having a member of the committee mention your report in the official record was the "platinum standard." Domah's words on this international stage elevated the We Charge Genocide report to a level that no one could have ever imagined.

Since arriving in Geneva, your friends had felt like outsiders. Despite their contribution to the committee's proceedings, the group members had thought of themselves more as witnesses than as participants in the hearings. But now, with the sound of your name echoing in their ears, they sensed your energy—and perhaps their own impact. What they appreciated most was that the committee was not asking for statistics; they were asking questions rooted in the personal experiences of people like you.

Domah spoke rapidly in French, but even someone who did not know the language could understand her passion and commitment. She seemed to be speaking from the heart.

"Why aren't Black people guaranteed the same basic rights as the rest of the population?" she wanted to know.

The next day, the United States would have its chance to respond. Once again, members of We Charge Genocide would steel themselves against the cherry-picked stats and fuzzy idealism the US representatives were sure to trot out. But on that day, nothing could diminish the significance of your name being spoken in the Palace of Nations.

. . .

Over the following two days the US delegation would have ample opportunity to address the questions that the committee posed. But throughout the convention none of the responses felt adequate to your friends at We Charge Genocide. Why? Their answers were tainted with the same vacant tone, as if they could not be bothered to express remorse for the violence perpetrated by our government.

One event in particular characterized the inadequate nature of these responses. It was a forum in which the US Department of Homeland Security would take the lead in addressing the Committee against Torture's questions. This forum invoked the legacy of your death as well, but not the way Domah's questions had. Regrettably, members of the US delegation mentioned your death in a way that showcased the deliberate nature of our government's neglect.

Page set the scene: "We heard story after horrific story. One after the other, people testified about rapes, killings, and torture. It was very hard to listen to. . . . We hadn't prepared ourselves emotionally."

What the group members *had* prepared themselves for, however, was a protest. Although they underestimated the emotional impact of the testimonies, they knew the Department of Homeland Security would defend its own interest and attempt to justify the violence that US law enforcement perpetrates against its own citizens.

"The whole event was a charade," Page said. "We knew it would be. But we wanted to participate in the event without participating in the charade."

Before the event, the group had discussed the possibility of a silent protest if representatives of the Department of Homeland Security did not display what We Charge Genocide members deemed to be good faith in answering questions. However, they did not know when the right moment for protest would present itself.

When it came, the moment was obvious. After the testimonies from civil society, the Homeland Security representatives had the chance to respond to what they had just heard. The representatives did so in a way that displayed cold calculation: they opened their briefcases and pulled out statements that had been written before they had even entered the room.

In their response to a litany of abuses that the US government has perpetrated against American citizens, representatives of the Department of Homeland Security said what government representatives had repeatedly said over the previous several days when it came to such matters: "Torture is absolutely prohibited at all times, in all places, no matter what the circumstances." They began and ended their testimony with this statement, and they managed to sprinkle it throughout their testimony, as well. When they were not asserting the abstract values of the United States, they downplayed the concrete reality of police violence in the country, claiming that it wasn't a fundamental problem. And Tasers? "We have conducted studies to show that Tasers aren't lethal," a representative from the Department of Homeland Security said.

This response caused We Charge Genocide to stand and hold their fists in the air with the same Black Power salute that Tommie Smith and John Carlos made famous at the 1968 Olympics. Your friends had planned to hold their fists up for thirty minutes, the amount of time

Rekia Boyd's body lay in the street before police officers took her away. This was group member Malcolm London's idea. Soon, though, maybe three or four minutes into We Charge Genocide's action, a representative from the UN approached Malcolm. "You have to stop right now," she said. "Or we'll have to ask you to leave."

Malcolm said nothing. Undaunted, he and the group continued standing. When their arms grew too tired to hold the Black power salute, they locked hands and held up each other's arms. Now they were making an *X* with their bodies, their legs and arms were fully extended, and they were using each other as bridges for support.

They stood like this because saying that Tasers were not lethal was like saying that We Charge Genocide was not there, or that they had no reason to be present. It was like saying, in effect, that you had not died, Damo.

That's why they stood: so that the United States was forced to acknowledge their presence. With cameras in the room focusing on the linked arms still held aloft, the other young activists from Ferguson, Missouri, raised their own fists in solidarity.

They held their fists throughout the rest of the testimony from Homeland Security, which lasted twenty-three minutes. Fifteen activists joined them in their protest, for a total of twenty-three participants. The number felt especially significant, since you died at the age of twenty-three. Your spirit, it seemed, was in the room.

Only when members of the Committee against Torture began to speak did We Charge Genocide lower their fists and take their seats. When they gave their concluding remarks, the committee members asked the US delegation to address the issue of deadly force. They wanted US delegates to speak about the lack of accountability and punishment for police officers who abuse their power. They wanted the US delegates to explain why the Chicago Police Department had not created a system for documenting, reviewing, investigating, preventing, and providing redress and compensation for offenses. Committee members wanted to know, right then and there, how it was that officers could torture and kill civilians with impunity. And they wanted the US government to address these issues in the future because the delegation they sent had failed to adequately answer all these questions at the present forum.

The forum ended with representatives from Homeland Security reciting more statistics meant to acknowledge that the US government was aware that a problem does exist when it comes to the use of extrajudicial force. But unfortunately, instead of proposing possible solutions to this problem, or even improving the methods for collecting data on the issue, which would at least convey a modicum of concern, the representatives continued to insist that our country is committed to democracy and freedom.

Nevertheless, despite the inadequacy of our government's responses to police violence, shortly after this last event, your friends left Geneva feeling that the Committee against Torture had heard them and intended to hold the United States responsible for answering those questions more fully and responsibly in the future. And they were determined not to let this trip to the UN mark the end of their activism.

All along they felt like you were with them at the United Nations. They felt as though they wouldn't have had the strength to deliver speeches and engage in protests if it weren't for the energizing force of your spirit. They had raised the awareness and necessary funds to show that abuses along the use-of-force continuum were not unique to Chicago, but a problem of US governance more broadly. They had called out the US delegation on their evasion and idealism with regard to how to address the problem. They had made allies and formed partnerships with other groups and organizations that wanted to address police torture and police killings. They accomplished all of this in your name. To this day, they have never taken the memory of your death for granted.

And after learning about your life and death, Damo, neither can I.

An Open Letter to Page May

First and foremost, I must begin by thanking you for helping me with my research project on police torture. I want to express my gratitude to you, especially, for talking to me about your trip to the United Nations as a member of We Charge Genocide. As you know from reading early drafts of my open letters to Josephine Grayson, Francis Grayson, William Patterson, and your friend Dominique "Damo" Franklin, I've been extremely moved by your groups' dedication to addressing the problem of police violence.

I'm grateful for the insights you have given me during our previous exchanges about the mistakes I made when describing your trip. I must thank you, as well, for pointing out the people and topics I neglected to include in my early drafts, such as Mariame Kaba and her selfless vision for bringing We Charge Genocide to the global stage.

But I would be remiss if I didn't express my gratitude for something else, perhaps the greatest gift you have given me, and that is your vulnerability. When I first approached you about this project, I was a stranger. You could not have known what exactly I was going to write about, or how I was going to write about it. I have been an ethnographer for some time now so I know people often approach our inquiries about their lives with skepticism—and rightly so!

Still, I am always surprised and deeply touched when people share things with me that are special to them. I count your letter to Damo among the most precious things that I have received, and so I appreciate your entrusting me with it. That letter put a lot of things in perspective. In preparing to write this book, I have read more letters then I can count. Your correspondence with Damo has easily become one of my favorites, because it is brimming with a sense of urgency, so much so that even your solace comes through with passion.

These are some of my favorite lines:

> You died and we went to the UN. We told them how the police caught you, bound you with their handcuffs, and tased you. We told them how they murdered you. And then they called it justice, no Blacks allowed. Now your story has been covered around the world. You have inspired more people and more organizing. Your tragic, unnecessary, and cruel death is not forgotten. But neither is your life. And this is so important, because often it's implied that our deaths as Black

people mean a lot more than our lives and our living them. But we do this for your life, Damo, and your right to live it. We do this for the living, in order to survive our despair.

I want to thank you for those words because they raised the stakes for my research. You made me see that talking about police violence is not merely about documenting pain or even injustice. It is also about the act of imagining a different world with people who must live through this violence. Along these lines, in your letter to Damo, you said:

> This year, I learned there is nothing natural or easy or instinctive about believing in a better world. About fighting for peace. About reimagining justice, rebuilding community, or transforming relationships. That is the struggle. To fight back and imagine better and carry onward, all while knowing that we were never meant to survive. I keep thinking about that George Jackson quote, "To the slave, revolution is imperative. It is a love-inspired, conscious act of desperation." To me, this is We Charge Genocide. We are desperate. We are conscious. And we loved you. And we love each other. Out of your life + death, Damo, revolution is growing. We must mourn your death. We must celebrate your life. And we must struggle on.

Every time I read the closing lines of your letter, I am moved beyond words. This emotion stems from the fact that I feel implicated in the collective struggle that you are describing to your dear friend. Being so intimately connected to people like you and to people like Damo who have fought and died to expose police violence is daunting. But is also exciting because the possibility of creating a safer world always lingers on the horizon. And, as you told Damo, this struggle is also inspired by love.

After reading your tribute to Damo, I thought long and hard about how his death has served as a focal point for your group, enabling you all to talk about the entire use-of-force continuum—the way mistreatment by the cops, such as being stopped, harassed, and falsely arrested, is connected to police violence, such as being tortured and killed.

I know that on the surface, the number of people who have been tortured and killed is tiny in comparison to the number of people who are mistreated by the Chicago Police Department on a daily basis. And thus, it might seem at first as though torture is relatively unimportant compared to the larger epidemic of police abuse. But as you well know, mistreatment, torture, and death are not separate phenomena.

Most of the Chicagoans I have spoken to cannot understand the impact of torture on their communities without thinking about the prospect of death and the mistreatment that characterizes their daily encounters with the police. For them, torture is a plot point somewhere between mistreatment and death, which is to say that it's inseparable from the wider spectrum of police use of force upon which it resides. Thus, even though the aim of your group was not exclusively to combat police torture, as I read through the shadow report you all created, the existence of torture became more and more apparent; and I learned from you more and more about when and where torture happens.

While studying the forms of police violence you highlighted, these two questions constantly rolled around in my head: How do we stop torture? And what do we do about the use-of-force continuum?

I know now that I was drawn to your work because We Charge Genocide provided multiple answers to these questions at a time when many people, including myself, were at a loss as to what to do. You raised public awareness. You implored institutions to act. You drafted legislation. And these efforts carried you far.

• • •

Buoyed by your newfound local celebrity, I thought you would ride the wave of your success at the United Nations. I must admit that I was almost as surprised as I was impressed that your group got to work almost immediately drafting public policy. Eight months after returning home from the UN, you had created the Stops, Transparency, Oversight, and Protection Act (the STOP Act), which you planned to introduce to Chicago's City Council. As I understand it, the purpose of the STOP Act was to require greater transparency in policing practices. At the top of your list was the practice known as "stop and frisk," which empowers police officers to detain and search individuals at their own discretion.

But as you all pointed out, in Chicago, all that is required to search someone is "reasonable suspicion" of criminal activity. You noted that this phrasing allows police a very large gray area to operate in. After returning to Chicago, you worked diligently to get information and ideas from the communities most subject to unwarranted stops. You wanted to make clear to the public that the overwhelming number of stop-and-frisk cases occur in African American and Latino neighborhoods.[13] But these findings alone are not surprising; the Chicago Police Department admits as much. What the CPD remains silent about, however, is that of the hundreds of thousands of such stops each year, in most cases the police find no evidence of a crime.

I'm sure it wouldn't surprise you in the least that in the summer before your group testified at the UN, Chicago police made more than 250,000 stops that did not lead to arrest. Of those, 72 percent were of Black residents and 17 percent of Latino residents. During that same period, a survey of 1,200 Chicago residents aged sixteen or older found that nearly 70 percent of young Black men had been stopped by police in the previous twelve months.[14]

Your report argued that the potential for abuses of power is inherent in the way Chicago police officers use stop and frisk to racially target people. Along these lines, the testimonials you documented from young Chicagoans were particularly impactful to me. Case in point: Jaden, a twenty-two-year-old man recounted for your group the story of his stop-and-frisk arrest, which resulted in Chicago police officers physically assaulting him and causing permanent physical damage.

Jaden had been walking down the street smoking weed when he saw sirens flashing. He put his hands behind his head, and the officers yelled at him to "get on the ground." Jaden fell to his knees. He remembers a number of police officers descending on his body, after which everything went blank.

"Next thing I know, I wake up in the back of the police station," Jaden said, recalling the events later. "I don't even know what happened to me, to be honest with you. That's how bad they beat me." For the offense of smoking marijuana, Jaden received injuries that included two facial fractures, bruised ribs, an orbital fracture, a nasal fracture, and a tongue so badly cut that it was literally hanging by a thread and required twenty-two stitches to repair.

"I still can't talk right to this day," Jaden said.

Your description of Jaden's ordeal was breathtaking. You noted that his aches have diminished, but like the psychological impact of his beating, they will never be gone completely. Still, what struck me most was that Jaden obeyed the police officers' commands without resistance, yet he was brutalized. "There was no reason to use force like that," Jaden said.

As I see it, your point of recounting this story was to say something like this: although Jaden's case might sound extreme, there's an aspect of it that is quite common. It's representative of the fact that police officers who abuse their power in the course of stop-and-frisk encounters typically go unpunished.

You thought that by collecting more data on police violence, the city could begin to hold the police accountable for using excessive force. This is why the ordinance you drafted would require the Chicago Police Department to collect and share data for all stops of any kind. The data would include demographic information about the people being stopped, the officers involved and their badge numbers, and information about the location, reason, and result of the stop. The Chicago Police Department would be required to provide "arrest receipts" to all people who were stopped. These receipts would include the names and badge numbers of the arresting officers. What I appreciated about these proposed requirements is that they were all built on the value of greater transparency.

With the STOP Act, you moved beyond protest to policy. Your group prided itself on taking the long view of civil rights progress and was committed to a more theoretical and big-picture exploration of what the future could look like. You also wanted your activism to have a practical and immediate impact. But as with many ambitious projects, your entrée into legislative politics presented you with many hurdles, including one from an organization you probably would have never have expected to clash with.

. . .

I was disheartened to learn that just as you were preparing to submit your work, the American Civil Liberties Union (ACLU) of Illinois, an organization you had worked with in the past (and admired), introduced a piece of legislation that also dealt with stop-and-frisk, but in a way that was completely at odds with your own goals. In fact, the ACLU had gone behind your back and negotiated a separate deal with Chicago city government, one that amounted to a watered-down version of the radical revisions to the law that you were proposing. I can only imagine how devastated you felt.

But, as I should've come to expect from you and your spirited friends, you did not take this affront lying down. You wrote an open letter to the Illinois chapter of the ACLU making it clear that you were not interested in garden-variety police reform, which rests on the premise that, most of the time, our criminal justice system works as it should. In your open letter, you wrote:

> Data collection through the STOP Act was the first of many steps in our plan to end stop and frisk in Chicago. You have undermined our movement. You have wasted our time and that of our allies. But, your refusal to acknowledge or take seriously our leadership has neither silenced nor weakened us. We understand freedom will take a while and will not come without a fight. We are proud of what we have accomplished. We are proud of the base-building and power-building we have achieved. We are proud of our young Black leaders and their ongoing work. We are proud of our success. We will continue and build on that strong foundation in the coming weeks, months, and

years. That is how we will win. That is how we will make Black lives matter.

Even though the ACLU betrayed you, the open letter you wrote made clear that you wouldn't compromise your principles to gain favor with political elites. Instead of the concessions the mayor was willing to give, which addressed the problem of police force only superficially, you all held firm that, to achieve effective change in the day-to-day lives of people of color in Chicago, you would have to get beneath the surface.[15] You all believed that police violence was rooted in the "historical anti-Blackness" of the slave trade. Policing, in other words, cannot be disentangled from what Ta-Nehisi Coates once described as the "flaying of backs, the chaining of limbs, the strangling of dissidents; the destruction of families; the rape of mothers; the sale of children; and various other acts meant, first and foremost, to deny African Americans the right to secure and govern their own bodies."[16]

I have come to learn that a major reason you were compelled to question the police's use of force is because you want the bodies of Black youth to be their own, which is to say, free from violation. And so, although I was saddened to hear about the ACLU's attempt to undermine your efforts, I was also encouraged that no breach of trust would compromise the history that grounded you.

After the intensity of your efforts and your determination in the face of unexpected events, it took me by surprise when I heard about the end of We Charge Genocide. Eleven months after you wrote that open letter to the ACLU, your group composed another open letter to the public—this time announcing that your efforts as We Charge Genocide were drawing to a close. At first, I worried that the frustration with trying to work with city government and draft legislation had broken your spirits. But you clarified that We Charge Genocide was more of a political campaign than an activist organization. As a campaign, your course of action was to go to the United Nations, and you had accomplished that goal. Now, all the group members had other kinds of activist projects they wanted to pursue. Group members wanted to return to the agendas and budding careers they were working toward before the magnetic force of Damo's death drew you all together.

Despite ending the campaign, you all insisted that you would continue your activism, but the work would just take on a slightly different shape. "The struggle continues, and WCG members will continue to struggle in multiple spaces across Chicago and beyond." That's what I wanted to talk to you about now, Page, your efforts beyond We Charge Genocide.

• • •

Recently I was excited to see that many of the former We Charge Genocide members are involved in protesting mayor Rahm Emanuel's plan to build a $95 million cop academy. In your collective opposition to the mayor's proposal, I noticed that you took on a leading role in explaining the dangers of the proposed police academy. Instead of investing more resources in emboldening the police, your #NoCopAcademy campaign argues that the $95 million should be invested in communities of color. Your statement of opposition read:

> Chicago already spends $1.5 billion on police every year—that's $4 million every single day. We spend 300% more on the CPD as a city than we do on the Departments of Public Health, family and support services, transportation, and planning and development (which handles affordable housing). This plan is being praised as a development opportunity to help local residents around the proposed site, but when Rahm closed 50 schools in 2013, six were in this neighborhood. The message is clear: Rahm supports schools and resources for cops, not for Black and Brown kids.[17]

You demanded that the $95 million earmarked for the police be redirected into Chicago's low-income communities of color. "Real community safety comes from fully funded schools, mental health centers, robust after-school and job training programs," the opposition also said.

What intrigued me most about this statement, and your role in drafting it, Page, was how your efforts seemed to be a natural extension of your previous activism. You seemed to be cautious of working with well-established organizations, like the ACLU, that had inroads to city government. Instead, you partnered with more than eighty grassroots organizations, all of which agreed to support your statement of opposition. Unlike the ACLU, these organizations were willing to open themselves up to community accountability. This time you teamed up with a host of local groups that had real stakes in dismantling police power.

I was also pleased with this campaign, admittedly, for a more selfish reason: your activism echoed a key argument that I am making in my book. In the book I compare torture in Chicago to a tree—what I call the torture tree. The trunk of this tree is the use-of-force continuum of modern-day policing. The branches are the police officers, the extensions of that continuum. The leaves are the incidents of force that you so devastatingly described in your UN shadow report. But I want to talk about the roots.

The roots are society's investments in fear, which include the public funding that funnels resources to police departments. That's why I am so excited by the #NoCopAcademy campaign. By exposing this fear as racist and flawed, and by trying to cut off the source of police power, you are attacking the very foundation of the torture tree.

• • •

As part of the torture-tree project, I have spoken with youth of color all over Chicago. It wouldn't surprise you to learn that many of them have been deeply affected by police violence. The hardest part of this project has been looking into their eyes when they ask me what they can do to address the problem of police torture, to ensure that their younger brothers and sisters don't have to grow up in the same racist society that they do. Needless to say, I am often at a loss.

I've grown speechless watching the teenagers I've met who do not see themselves reflected in the glossy black-and-white pictures from the civil rights era—that is, they feel somewhat removed from the politics of the past. This does not mean the cops swinging billy clubs at nonviolent protestors in those old photographs don't horrify them. It does not mean that they are not disturbed by the spectacle of unleashed dogs that intimidated and threatened the many protesters who marched for equality a half century ago. It does not mean that the anger bubbling over in the streets isn't familiar to them. But the people being beaten in those photographs are clearly of another era, which leads them to think, perhaps erroneously, that their struggles and the struggles of those fighting for civil rights in the 1960s are far removed.

But when I have shown these teenagers a picture of your group, We Charge Genocide, standing proud in front of the Palace of Nations in Geneva, there is more than a glint of recognition. There is an unabashed acknowledgment that they are seeing themselves not in black and white but in the high definition precision of real life that they are used to.

"I want to go to the UN one day and testify about police violence," a teenager named Kimberly said in an introspective tone. When I asked her why, she mentioned your group before adding: "They were carrying on the legacy of the people who came before them. And I think it's only right that we do the same."

Kimberly's eyes lit up when I told her that you have taken your activism a step further with the #NoCopAcademy campaign. I mention this campaign because, as amazing as it was to see you and your friends travel to Geneva, I'm impressed even more by how you've expanded your activism after you returned. Not only have you organized Chicago's teenagers of color. You've taught them to organize themselves. You've descended on City Hall with hundreds of them to protest the expansion of police power. I've seen the videos of them inside the chambers, chanting the refrain that Assata Shakur made famous, the refrain that We Charge Genocide used to shout in its own protests. This refrain now bellows forth, in unison, from the lungs of Chicago's future leaders:

It is our duty to fight for our freedom.

It is our duty to win.

We must love each other and support each other.

We have nothing to lose but our chains.

Thank you, Page, for planting so many seeds of dissent in the political terrain of this city. May those seeds replace the city's torture tree with many more well-organized campaigns, campaigns that are aimed at transforming our lives.

PART IV Bad Guys

An Open Letter to All the Future Mayors of Chicago

In the last letter I wrote to you—all the future mayors of Chicago—I offered the analogy of the torture tree. I hoped that it would help you visualize the reach of the use-of-force continuum and its often-devastating impact. My intention was to give you a more vivid sense of the terrible ways that police force shapes the lives of many Chicagoans. I told you that the torture tree reinforces a racial caste system that subjects a disproportionate number of Black Chicagoans to injury and death. It erodes the legitimacy of the government, and hence the Office of the Mayor. And by punishing those who are already vulnerable—while ignoring habitual harassment and violence on the part of the police—it makes the city less safe.

But I'm writing now because I want you to know that the everyday ramifications of police torture do not affect only residents of your city, or even just residents of this country. The phenomenon of police torture has an impact on people all across the globe. Knowing this, I hope, will compel you to think of your responsibility as mayor in the broadest possible terms.

How, you may be wondering, is police torture in Chicago a transnational concern? To answer this question, we must reexamine the roots, which is to say, the resources that your city invests in policing. This investment is not derived solely from taxpayers, and it is not just financial—it is also psychological and political. The roots represent the underwriting of fear. Before you take office, it is imperative that you know that your city government has rationalized the need for the torture tree by convincing the public of a lie: that society would descend into chaos without the police—that no one would be safe. This lie is what compels people to invest in fear. The investment in fear—financially, psychologically, and politically—is what allows the torture tree to grow taller and stronger, to sprout ever-more branches.

. . .

When I wrote you before, I referred to the torture tree's branches as the police officers who operate as the human extensions of force. Now I would like to talk about one branch in particular, embodied by a man named Richard Zuley, whose torturous acts have extended from the precincts in your city to the detention center at Guantánamo Bay, Cuba.

Zuley joined the Chicago Police Department in 1977 and served as an officer until 2007. For most of that time he conducted his detective work on the North Side of the city. Toward the end of his career (the last eighteen months of his time on the force, to be exact), Zuley even helped establish a counterterrorism training division within the Chicago Police Department. Zuley's superiors deemed him qualified to head this division because he was also an officer in the US Navy who had been handpicked by decorated military officials to lead counterintelligence missions abroad.

In 2002, five years before Zuley would retire from your police force, Major General Geoffrey Miller, the US Army official in charge of Guantánamo Bay, recruited him to the island. By all accounts, this was regarded as an especially difficult assignment. At the time, the administration at Guantánamo was facing a crisis; the interrogators were overwhelmed. There were only twenty-six interrogators on the base, compared to three hundred detainees, who came from mostly Saudi Arabia, Afghanistan, Pakistan, and Yemen. Only four of the interrogators spoke Arabic. Two spoke Farsi. Zuley wasn't a language expert, but one thing he had going for him was his expressed enthusiasm to work in such a difficult environment. A year after arriving at Guantánamo, Zuley took over the interrogation of a suspected terrorist that the Department of Defense had classified as a "high profile" target. His name was Mohamedou Ould Slahi.[1]

The US government brought Slahi from his home country of Mauritania to Guantánamo because they suspected him of planning terrorist attacks at Los Angeles International Airport as well as the CN Tower in Toronto. These failed terrorist plots took place a short time before the successful September 11 attacks. But after George W. Bush initiated the war on terror, the US government investigated these plots again, as they now believed them to be connected to a larger terrorist network. Because Slahi was thought to be an active member of Al-Qaeda, which the US government blamed for 9/11, they wanted to know: was he the mastermind of other terrorist schemes? Our government wondered whether he was connected to the global network of Islamic terrorism, and they abducted Slahi from his home country to find out.

Before arriving at Guantánamo, Slahi was sent to a black site in Jordan, where he was questioned. It is common for the Central Intelligence Agency to transport terrorist suspects to countries like Jordan, which have less rigorous regulations for the humane treatment of prisoners. After refusing to confess there, Slahi was taken to Guantánamo. To break him, the defense secretary at the time, Donald Rumsfeld, authorized the use of what the US government still blandly and euphemistically refers to as "enhanced interrogation techniques." These methods were put into action after Rumsfeld had signed several memos in 2002 and 2003 arguing that international humanitarian laws, such as the Geneva Conventions, did not apply to the US military while overseas.[2]

The Senate Armed Services Committee has now said that Rumsfeld also bears major responsibility for the abuses committed by US troops at another black site, Abu Ghraib, the camp where the US Army imprisoned Iraqis from 2003 to 2006, during the same time Slahi was imprisoned. That camp became infamous for photographs that US military police took while torturing Iraqi prisoners.[3]

Rumsfeld's "enhanced" methods resulted in a host of human rights violations, including physical and sexual abuse, rape, and sodomy. In Slahi's case, these techniques consisted of being beaten, being subjected to deafening noise, and extreme temperatures, being deprived of food and liquids, having his sleep disrupted, having his medical care withheld, being confined in a coffin-sized box, and being repeatedly slapped. There is more. But I'll get to those details later. For now, I should mention that US Supreme Court decisions, including *Hamdan v. Rumsfeld* (2006), eventually ruled that the Geneva Conventions do, in fact, apply. But by the time that decision was handed down, it was too late to prevent Slahi's torture, which had occurred three years before the decision.

During the period that Zuley oversaw Slahi's interrogation, he eventually made sure Slahi experienced all the torture techniques I just described. But the relationship between the two men did not start out with torture and torment. Zuley befriended Slahi at first. Zuley seemed genuinely interested in Slahi's hobbies and family life, and he used the information Slahi shared to threaten his family members. As if that weren't bad enough, on August 25, 2003, Zuley arranged to have Slahi kidnapped and taken off the island, where he experienced a mock execution at sea.

Slahi's mock execution occurred according to a "special plan," which outlined precisely what would happen to him during that day, and Donald Rumsfeld personally signed off on it. When it came to Rumsfeld's authorization of Zuley's "special plan" for Slahi, nothing was left to chance. The decision to have only four soldiers involved, for example, was carefully considered. Having too many people "in the know" could compromise the mission, and perhaps give Slahi a hint as to what would happen. The use of German shepherds was deliberate as well. The dogs were meant to frighten him, to muffle his screams, and to heighten the sense of chaos during the kidnapping, so that Slahi could be easily transported from his cell onto a boat. In his reports Rumsfeld stated that the purpose of taking Slahi on an hours-long trip on a high-speed boat was to make him think he was being transported off the island, quickly, to a faraway place.

Once they circled back to shore and removed him from the boat, Zuley and the soldiers involved planned to take Slahi to a secluded part of Guantánamo called Camp Echo, where, according to the US Senate Armed Services report, his new cell and interrogation room was to be "modified in such a way as to reduce as much outside stimuli as possible." The doors were sealed so they did not allow even a flicker of light. The room became a literal black box, where the darkness would weigh on Slahi, pressuring him to produce the kind of knowledge that would satisfy our government. And the plan worked: at the end of many months of torture, Slahi did indeed confess—to crimes his interrogators had to tell him about because he had no knowledge of them. He admitted to planning to blow up the CN Tower, for example, despite never having heard of it. Asked if he was telling the truth about his confessions, Slahi answered: "I don't care as long as you are pleased. So if you want to buy, I am selling." Although Zuley was apparently pleased with this, the confession was so clearly the product of torture that the prosecutor at Guantánamo declined to file charges against him. As the ACLU recounted, "The military lawyer originally assigned to prosecute the case against Mr. Slahi in the military commissions, Marine Corps Lieutenant Colonel Stuart Couch, determined that the statements wrung from Mr. Slahi during his interrogations were so tainted by torture that they couldn't ethically be used against him."[4] Ultimately, Couch told his supervisors that he was morally opposed to Slahi's treatment and refused to participate in the prosecution. This is why Slahi was never charged with or convicted of a crime.

Nevertheless, our government held Slahi at Guantánamo for four-teen years. For several of those years, when he was not being interrogated and tortured, when he was alone in his cell, Slahi produced another type of knowledge based on his experience on Guantánamo Bay. He wrote a diary. That is what I want to tell you about now: Slahi's writing. Mohamedou Ould Slahi's diary had a great deal to do with his ultimate release. And that is almost as unimaginable as the torture he endured.

. . .

In 2015, Mohamedou Ould Slahi published *Guantánamo Diary*, the first memoir written by a suspected terrorist while still incarcerated at the detention center at Guantánamo Bay. There are many remarkable things about this book. But the most remarkable is perhaps its very existence. Slahi wrote the 466-page manuscript in English, a language he learned at Guantánamo; and the book went on to become an international best seller for its description of the intimate details of torture.

In addition to the torture that Rumsfeld approved (the "enhanced methods"), Slahi also talks about being force-fed seawater, sexually molested, and kicked and punched across the face. He endured all of this with Zuley telling him that he got permission to detain his mother on Guantánamo. If she came, Zuley said, she would likely be gang-raped.

Still, of all the days Slahi writes about in his diary, the day in which his life is threatened at sea has garnered the most attention. Media and the courts have seized on this day because in checking the veracity of his story, journalists were able to prove that powerful people in the US government, like Donald Rumsfeld, allowed Slahi's torture to happen. They also cross-referenced the information that Slahi wrote about with the public record—this, despite the fact that the US government made the ability to check the veracity of Slahi's claims especially difficult through its use of redaction.[5]

I encourage you to read *Guantánamo Diary*. Once you do, I'm sure you'll be struck by the black-bar redactions on almost every page, over 2,500 in total, which, despite their ubiquity, are unable to mute Slahi's voice. For our purposes, these little black boxes represent the

US government's power to shield its personnel from responsibility for torture through an elaborate censorship process. That process occurred while Slahi was still at Guantánamo and went something like this.

Every time Slahi would finish a section of his manuscript, he would have to surrender his writing to the government for review. Every page of each section, and every word of each page, would be carefully scrutinized. Once Slahi finished writing this manuscript, the government classified it as "secret," which, according to Slahi's editor, is an official designation that "meant that it could cause serious damage to national security if it becomes public." The US government also tagged Slahi's manuscript with the "no forn" designation, which meant that it was not to be shared with any foreign countries or foreign intelligence services.[6]

For several years after Slahi completed the manuscript, his diary was held under lock and key in an unmarked building not far from the White House and the Pentagon. To read his manuscript someone would need full security clearance and an official explanation as to why they needed to see it. Being Slahi's lawyer was not even sufficient reason to have access to the material—this, despite the fact that the information contained in the manuscript could have provided additional evidence that our government had little cause to justify his detention. It would take six years for his lawyers, Nancy Hollander, Theresa Duncan, and Linda Moreno, to carry out the necessary litigation to have the diary cleared for public release.

When Slahi's lawyers finally received the heavily redacted diary in 2011, they gave it to a well-respected writer and investigative journalist, Larry Simes, to edit. By then Mohamedou Ould Slahi was on his way to becoming a well-known public figure. Journalists had reported about his case from information they uncovered through Freedom of Information Act requests, the litigation his lawyers had filed, and Justice Department and US Senate hearings that discussed his detention. Since the information was a part of the public record, Simes decided to introduce annotations and footnotes to Slahi's diary that corresponded to the government's redactions. Simes's annotations made it easier to compare the events that Slahi wrote about with the emerging public record on torture. These annotations also made it possible, in some rare cases, to uncover the identity of military personnel involved in Slahi's torture.

Although Zuley's name was redacted in the body of Slahi's text, the government officials let a separate reference to Zuley slip in the footnotes of the diary. Simes would notice this mistake and comment on it as he edited the book. Those references to Zuley would lead to reporters digging into his forty-year career as a Chicago police officer, where they discovered his history of torture.

• • •

I wrote to you earlier about the use-of-force continuum, which refers to guidelines that establish how much force or outright violence a law enforcement officer is supposed to use on a civilian. But now I want to tell you about another important relationship—that is, the symbiotic relationship between the police and the military.

Scholars of policing have long thought about this relationship. Most often this dynamic is characterized by the phrase "militarization of the police," which refers to the way domestic police departments and their officers draw from, and pattern themselves after, the military. But it is less common in discussions about militarization nowadays to mention the ways that military personnel, in turn, draw from domestic techniques and strategies of policing while working abroad. This second dynamic speaks to the ways that the techniques used by Richard Zuley in Chicago's interrogation rooms were redeployed in the detention camps at Guantánamo Bay. Little did Slahi know that by writing Zuley's name in his diary, he helped illuminate this second dynamic, a dynamic that has recently been referred to as the "policification of military intervention."[7]

And so, when I describe the interaction between domestic police officers and military personnel as a symbiotic relationship, I'm referring to both the militarization of the police and the policification of the military at the very same time.

Since Slahi's diary was published in 2005, several civilian complaints against Richard Zuley have gained renewed attention. One of those, the case of Lathierial Boyd, has been the most prominent, as it was the subject of a widely circulated report in *The Guardian*, written by a leading terrorism journalist, Spencer Ackerman.[8]

According to Ackerman, in 1990, Zuley came to believe that Boyd had shot two men outside Exodus, a Chicago reggae club. Despite the fact that Boyd had an alibi, and despite a lack of evidence suggesting Boyd's guilt, Zuley was determined to connect Boyd to the crime. Initially, when he learned the police were looking for him, Boyd turned himself in, volunteering to participate in a line-up. He stood for two of them. In a 2015 interview with Ackerman, Boyd recalls asking Zuley after the second line-up if anybody had identified him. Zuley said no. To this, Boyd replied: "See, I told you. You've got the wrong guy."

Zuley smiled at him, "We're charging you anyway," he said.

Boyd was then arrested, and shackled to the wall in the precinct station, where Zuley left him for hours. Boyd claims that the police planted evidence in his case. Weeks after the shooting, when there was nothing to connect him to the murder, the police found a piece of paper with his nickname written on it strewn on the floor beside the victim's hospital bed. Without a confession, this was the only hard evidence tying Boyd to the crime.

"That little piece of paper was enough," Boyd said. "Because of that paper, the judge sentenced me to 82 years in prison. 82 years. I remember thinking that the judge had given me a life sentence. But it's not gonna hold up with the jury anyway. They are going to know that I was framed."[9]

"I was wrong," Boyd said. "It held up. It held up. And now half my life is gone. I did 23 years in prison before I was finally exonerated. I was set free in 2013. It still doesn't seem real. It doesn't seem real that I was there and went through all of that, or that I'm free now. I'm still trying to make sense of it."

When Boyd heard about what Richard Zuley had done at Guantánamo, it seemed unbelievable, but the revelation did provide some context for why he was targeted and treated so cruelly.

"Here this guy is, in another country, torturing people, ordering that they be tortured, and so what do you think he'd do to me—a nigger in a Chicago police station."

"I didn't have a chance," Boyd said, "faced off against somebody so sick."

In the same interview with Ackerman, Boyd brought his focus back to Chicago, reflecting on the plight of other victims: "Now I find out that I'm not alone. I've learned that Zuley sent other suspects to prison for crimes they may not have committed. I know who some of them are. The ones who I know, I have to help get them out of there. I have to help them because somebody helped me."

• • •

From studying the history of police torture in your city, I know that your predecessors have listened to victims of police abuse, albeit halt-ingly. Some of your predecessors have then seized on victims' words and emphasized the idea that torturers like Zuley are "sick." Among the police officers, military personnel, and social justice advocates who have commented publicly on Zuley's case, there's a consensus that his actions have undermined the integrity of both the US crimi-nal justice system and the war on terror.

Mark Fallon, the deputy commander of the now-defunct Criminal Investigative Task Force at Guantánamo, said Zuley's interrogation of Slahi "was illegal, it was immoral, it was ineffective and it was un-constitutional."[10]

"I've never seen anyone stoop to those levels," said former Lieu-tenant Colonel Stuart Couch. "It's unconscionable, from a perspec-tive of a criminal prosecution—or an interrogation, for that matter."

The problem with these expressions of contempt is that, while ac-knowledging that the policing strategies Zuley used to interrogate Slahi were "unconstitutional" and "unconscionable," they also char-acterize Zuley as a 'bad apple,' which of course makes him easy to scapegoat.

"There have been a number of really bad apples in the Chicago Police Department who unquestionably have railroaded unknown numbers of innocent people into prison," Rob Warden of Northwestern University's Center on Wrongful Convictions said to the *Guardian*. "[But] Zuley may be unique in being a police officer who graduated from Chicago to Guantánamo."

Instead of making Zuley out to be an exception, future mayors, I hope it has become clear that Richard Zuley rose to prominence within the Chicago Police Department and the US military—not in spite of the fact that he did horrible things to other human beings, but *because* he did these horrible things.

What do we make of the fact that, when Zuley showed up at Guantánamo Bay, military commanders "touted him as the hero they had been looking for"? What does it mean that Zuley's reputation for "closing case after case" in Chicago and his "knack for getting confessions" made him an attractive recruit for the war on terror?[11]

I would like you to think about these questions instead of focusing on the idea that Zuley was a disturbed individual. To be clear, there is no doubt that Zuley was a sinister human being who seemed to delight in causing physical and psychological pain. Most police officers, I do not believe, harbor such sadistic desires. However, the insistence on Zuley as uniquely awful is also a way to focus our attention on individuals rather than the conditions that allow torturers to excel in the profession of law enforcement. Doing so effectively absolves you and your city of any responsibility. Instead I challenge you, future mayors, to focus on your role in overseeing the department that has put people like Zuley in a position to extort and coerce Black Chicagoans like Lathierial Boyd. And I challenge you to think about how the nearly four decades Zuley spent as a Chicago police officer qualified him to torture terrorism suspects at the behest of our federal government.

This is why I have written you: to tell you that the damaging effects of the torture tree do not stop at Chicago's borders. The torture tree makes the entire world less safe.

An Open Letter to the Boy and Girl with Matching Airbrushed Book Bags on the Corner of Lawndale Avenue and Cermak Road

When I think about the two of you, I think about how police encounters can change the course of our lives in an instant. If we are lucky, the police show up when we need them the most and help us. But for so many Black Chicagoans, that is not the case; the police show up and the result is mistreatment or violence. And that encounter leaves something with us.

I've thought about the two of you again and again while conducting research for this project. You have come to mind as I've conducted interviews with Black Chicagoans because they've grown up in your city and experienced so many run-ins with the police that resemble your own. From harassment and mistreatment to torture and death, throughout the course of my research, hundreds of incidents like yours have flittered down and accumulated all around me like fallen leaves. If every fallen leaf represents a new incident of police violence, then for every year I have studied this problem, countless fresh green leaves sprout up and grow and fall at my feet again.

Surrounded by these leaves as I have been for so long, I have come to believe that each and every one tells us a story. And since you two have come to embody the ever-present danger of policing for me, I would like to share a story with you. This story is about the all-pervasive and far-reaching impact of Chicago's legacy of police torture. It centers on a man from a foreign country who found himself targeted by the United States and taken to a detention camp at Guantánamo Bay. The primary reasons for his detention were where he was from and what he believed.

• • •

I became aware of Mohamedou Ould Slahi's detention after learning that he was interrogated and tortured by a former Chicago police officer. After hearing this, I wrote him an open letter. Imagine my surprise when I found out that a colleague of mine actually knew him! It would be as if, upon reading my letter to you, someone that I knew recalled the same scene of your stop and frisk encounter and gave me your contact information.

When I first wrote to Mohamedou, I never thought that he would actually read my letter or that we would exchange emails and eventually talk. But much to my surprise, we did. I remember so vividly our first Skype interview—me at my office in Cambridge, Massachusetts, and him in his office in Bir Moghrein, Mauritania. The colorful world map posted behind his right shoulder reminded me of the expanse between us. Despite this distance, however, his experience at Guantánamo gave me many useful examples of how the open secret of police torture in Chicago is tied to our country's ideas about guilt and innocence.

Discussing how torture could be so boldly hidden in plain sight led us to a conversation about how people write about the traumatic experiences that they have lived through. Writing is what kept Mohamedou sane. From reading about his case, I knew that our government had confiscated his diary. But I had no clue that he had written four other books while incarcerated. I was blown away by what he was able to accomplish at Guantánamo Bay, while being tortured intermittently, for fourteen years.

One thing I learned quickly from the scope of his writing projects—a self-help book, a comedic book about the English language, and two novels—is that he did not want to be defined for the rest of his life by what happened to him at Guantánamo Bay. He had gotten that out in the *Diary*, and he had other things he wanted to think about and write about. During our discussion, he also said that writing was just a hobby of his. He had gone to school to become an engineer. Then he told me what led him to his professional field of choice.

"When I was in high school," he said, "my Arabic teacher told me that I should consider going into literature. But I didn't want to because I wanted something that has rules. Literature has no rules. But mathematics is very clear. And I grew up very poor. I was obsessed with being in a place where there are rules that I could predict. Outcomes. If I do well, I know that I will be rewarded accordingly. But in literature—in writing—it's different: if the teacher is happy with it, you get an A. If the teacher is unhappy, you get an F. And no student can argue about this. You can argue, but there is nothing that can be done. But mathematics—for you, for me, for the Chinese man, for the German man—it's the same.

"This is very ironic," Mohamedou continued, "because my whole life has been ruled by lawlessness. No rules whatsoever."

As I reflected on the lawlessness that has shaped his life for so many years, and the longing for predictable "outcomes" and "rules" that informed his decision to study engineering as a young man, I could not help but be reminded of the concept of the black box, especially since I had spent so much time writing about the way police torture gets concealed.

• • •

Concealment is at the root of all social interactions, says the sociologist Georg Simmel. I take this to mean that what we want to keep secret has an impact on our every decision; the things we have to hide shape which things we decide to share. Since reading his *Diary*, I have been in awe of Mohamedou for what he's decided to share. Part of the reason I'm even telling you about him is because he wanted to share his suffering with you. He wanted US citizens to read his book and become allies in exposing the injustice he faced. Mohamedou was confident that this could happen, that he could win over American men and women because many of the US citizens he met during his detention were sympathetic to his plight.

Throughout his ordeal, in fact, Mohamedou remained perplexed by the contradiction between the US citizens he would come to know and their country, which held him in captivity. Remarkably, when we talked, Mohamedou reiterated numerous times that he had feelings of friendship toward the United States.

He explained: US lawyers had fought for him over the course of eleven years. A US legal team worked for seven years to convince the government to allow him to publish his book, and an American editor worked for nearly two years on the manuscript that eventually allowed him to write his way free. He even said that some of his guards expressed more happiness than he did when they found out about his release. They knew that he should never have been detained in the first place because he was never proven guilty, much less charged with a crime.

Mohamedou told me that the concern that some US citizens expressed to him made it all the more difficult to understand the philosophy of guilt in our country. "I actually believe that Americans are very good people," he said. "They are generous. They are caring. I see a lot of attributes in them that I also see in myself. But I did not know the United States of America: my biggest problem was ignorance."

Mohamedou explained that he grew up under a military regime in Africa. After high school he moved to Germany, a democracy. For him, "the difference was like night and day." He explained that in a military dictatorship, your freedom depends on whether or not the military is happy with you. But in a democracy, where there is rule of law, you are not supposed to have to be in the good graces of a government official in order to be safe. Safety is supposed to be a right. He enjoyed the privilege such a structure of government afforded and presumed the United States abided by the same democratic principles he had become accustomed to in Germany. This presumption, he now believes, was a mistake.

"In America, it's very hard to decipher. I don't believe America is a military dictatorship. But is it a democracy? I don't know. But I do know that certain strata of society, especially outside the United States, are not treated democratically. That is very clear," he explained.

Mohamedou considers himself to have been oblivious to the ways of the United States. "I didn't understand the concepts of guilt and innocence as they seem to exist in the US," he told me. "My understanding was that if you didn't do anything wrong, then you don't have to be afraid of anyone. You don't need to cooperate. You don't need to smile at your interrogator. You don't need to do anything. You can say, 'Screw you, I'm going home!' You can do whatever you want to do. I learned that attitude in Germany. This attitude is very bad in America," Mohamedou said.

"In America the philosophy is that you should be a good boy. And a good boy should be very good with the FBI and with the police. And guilt? I thought *guilty* meant that you did it, or didn't do it. But guilt—the philosophy of guilt—in my experience with the US is not like that."

During our interview, Mohamedou told me that, knowing what he knows now, he would not have turned himself in. He thought that by making himself available to the police in his country, he could clear up any suspicion. But doing so led only to his rendition and detention.

While being interrogated, he remained determined to prove his innocence; or rather, he felt that the United States should have to at least tell him what he was being charged with. "I kept telling them, 'You tell me why you brought me to this place, and I will talk to you. If this question is not answered, I will not cooperate.'"

"That kind of talk does not work when there is no rule of law," Mohamedou eventually realized.

While talking to Mohamedou, I reflected on the fact that one of the awful powers of torture is that it takes away the rules. We all have some kind of basic understanding of how we are supposed to be treated. And then one day a person in power walks into your life and changes the rules. Even after he left Guantánamo, Mohamedou's right to be a citizen of any country at all quite literally disappeared.

"Ever since my release," Mohamedou told me, "I've lived in Mauritania. I was given two options: Germany accepted me because Germany is the country where I went to study after high school. I lived in that country until my kidnapping in January 2000."

Mohamedou told me that United States did not want him to go to Germany, even though that was his preference. Our government decided that he would be sent back to Mauritania instead. According to Mohamedou, the United States "did not want me to go anywhere I could assert my rights, or where I could seek any relief."

Chuckling to himself, Mohamedou said that he was well aware of these "shenanigans," so he wasn't surprised when US officials told him, "We'll send you back to Africa." What struck him as ironic, though, was that two months before his release, the State Department had issued a statement urging Mauritania to abide by the Geneva Conventions, the protocols of international law that establish basic rights for wartime prisoners.

The irony was almost too much to bear. For fourteen years, the United States had treated him like a prisoner of war. They were about to send him to a country, ruled by a dictator, that the United States had recently condemned for the inhumane treatment of its citizens—all so the United States could deny his human rights.

"I live here now," he said, "but I don't have my rights yet. I'm still denied my papers. I'm still denied my ID cards. I'm denied everything," he said, before launching into a list of what he can now not do: "I cannot pay taxes—which is good, I guess." He laughed. "I cannot open a bank account. I cannot have a membership at a health club. I cannot travel anywhere."

Mohamedou explained: "I went to the places where you get that stuff. They said that the US government asked them not to give me anything. I said, 'Is there a law to govern this?' They said, 'No.' I said, 'Did I violate any law in my country?' They said, 'No, absolutely nothing. But the US government said so.'"

As Mohamedou spoke, I realized that such denials serve a purpose: through them, the dynamics of the war on terror remain mysterious even to those closest to it. What I mean is that the law enforcement official who denied Mohamedou's papers in his native land, whether apologetic or indifferent to his plight, does not have to think about the consequences of that denial for a man who lived in a detention camp for a decade and a half of his life. He does not have to wonder whether Mohamedou's inability to fully participate in society will last a few months or a lifetime. All that matters to him, the law enforcement official behind the desk, is what his superiors say the US government has demanded that Mohamedou cannot do.

From our country's continued harassment of Mohamedou Ould Slahi, from his detention through his torture at a US-operated black

site, our government has consistently worked to render him powerless; and all those evasions and layers of denial used to justify his
torture make it difficult to hold anyone to account.

In some ways, the whole apparatus resembles an elaborate Rus-
sian doll: layer within layer within layer, an evil tucked inside a lie,
tucked inside an evasion, tucked inside feigned ignorance, seemingly
ad infinitum. Our government protects those who participate in law
enforcement from having full knowledge of what they are doing and
grants plausible deniability to those who know it's happening but do
not actually witness it.

This is how talking to Mohamedou served to confirm my thinking about police violence and torture. I became more certain than
ever before that what I have really been writing is an exegesis of my
country's greatest open secret—a secret long buried in a black box.
The symbiotic relationship between police and military that connects
your harassment—you two teenagers in Chicago—to Mohamedou's
torture is, and has always been, foundational to the US rule of law.

Mohamedou now believes that the rule of law in the United States
does not apply to people who are marginalized. It was this—his
marginalization—that made Mohamedou feel a connection between
himself and the torture survivors from Chicago. This connection, he
assured me, was not merely because they had been tormented by the
same person. It was because of the same philosophy of guilt that they
had all been subjected to.

"One of the people who spent many years in Guantánamo around
the same time as me," he said, "was also interrogated and tortured by
Richard Zuley. Zuley told him the same thing he was telling me—the
same thing he was telling people in Chicago, apparently. Zuley said
it did not matter to him whether this man was innocent or guilty. It
didn't matter because to Zuley, this was a bad guy."

"It seems to me," he went on "that in the US, *guilty* means that you
are a bad person. But is it supposed to mean that? In a democratic
country, I thought that *guilty* is supposed to mean that you did this
or that crime. Does it matter from a legal perspective whether you

were a good or bad guy? I don't think so. But this 'bad guy' mentality is brought up over and over in interrogations."

Mohamedou explained that Zuley mentioned the figure of this "bad guy" during his interrogation. It was at a time when he knew Mohamedou's confession was erroneous and might not hold up in court. But instead of trying to pursue the truth, Zuley decided to fish for more bad guys.

"Zuley told me, 'I need you to talk about the other people that were involved.' I said, 'Look, I can write down the names of people, but they didn't do anything.' Then his sergeant said, 'We know these guys are bad, so it doesn't matter whether or not you lie about them.'"

When Mohamedou refused, Zuley took his file. He approached another detainee at Guantánamo and told him that if he testified against Mohamedou, then the US government would offer the man a deal. After discussing this aspect of his run-in with Zuley, Mohamedou said: "This is the kind of lawlessness that is reigning in the United States. If you don't have a very strong tribe backing you up, you're screwed."

"By 'tribe' do you mean wealthy people, and lawyers?" I asked.

"Yes," Mohamedou explained. "We call that a tribe in Guantánamo: people who have money, who have power, and who can threaten people in government. You need a tribe in order to survive."

· · ·

I've given you so much detail about my interview with Mohamedou Ould Slahi because I believe that the terrorism suspects who have been tortured by the US military at Guantánamo Bay, and victims of injustice in Chicago who have been framed and tortured in police custody, the teenagers who are mistreated and harassed by the police on a daily basis, and even people like me, who wish to rethink the role of the police in our society—we all belong to the same tribe.

We may not have the money and resources of the US government. But we do have the power to bring about a massive change. One thing we must change is our country's de facto philosophy of guilt, which, as Mohamedou explained, is not about what you did but rather who you are. I realize that by now, fourteen years after I witnessed your encounter with the police, you might have been stopped and frisked many more times, or you might have experienced far worse than that. You probably have your own way of making sense of your encounters with the police.

But if I could rewind and go back to the moment that you two were released, I would beg your forgiveness for bothering you and ask your permission to say a few words. It was not your fault that you were stopped by the police, I would say. I know they probably suggested it was. They probably said they thought you were guilty of some crime or that you fit the description of a criminal suspect. Yet, as I would explain, there's something that members of our tribe know to be true. Those accusations are just a way of concealing the open secret: this kind of police harassment inevitably grows into torture and can even result in death, because, to the detriment of humankind, the police's use of force is rooted in their fear.

An Open Letter to Mohamedou Ould Slahi

During our Skype conversation I got caught up in the stories you were telling me—so caught up, in fact, that I didn't get a chance to speak to you about an idea that I've been wrestling with. For so long I've been searching for a concept to help me explain what nourishes torture and allows it to grow, to explain how and why the legacy of torture is firmly planted in the US soil, and to explain how the branches of torture become transnational, connecting you, a citizen of Mauritania to a detention camp on Guantánamo Bay. As imperfect as the analogy may be, my idea, simply put, is that torture is like an enormous, deformed tree—a torture tree, I call it.

I'm writing you now to get your perspective on this concept, and I'm also writing you today for another, related reason. Race is crucial to how I think of torture and all the other forms of police force, from mistreatment and harassment to brutality and even death. This is because a person's race increases the likelihood that they will be tortured; and at the same time, a person's perspective on torture is informed by the racism they have faced. Yet after corresponding with you, I'm not certain that you would agree. In fact, I have reason to believe that you would not.

I know that race and racism didn't explicitly come up as a topic when we spoke, but it did in the very first email you wrote me. Do you remember that? You started by thanking me for sharing my work with you and agreeing to my interview request. You said you had just finished reading some of my writing on police torture in Chicago and that it was "shocking indeed," even to you. Then you mentioned that you love reading about history, especially the parts that people do not mention so often. I was struck by the examples you gave—examples that emphasized the hypocrisy in the way supposedly powerful Western nations have operated in the world: "When the US was freeing Europe from the Nazis, back home, Black people were treated as second-class citizens, at best." You also wrote, "During the Belgian ethnic cleansing in the Congo, the biggest news in Brussels was the king's new wife."

You linked these historical episodes to my government's hypocritical stance on human rights. While you were at Guantánamo you were caught off guard by a statement made by Hillary Clinton, then secretary of state, about the Chinese dissident Chen Guangcheng: "As part of our dialogue, the United States raises the importance of human rights and fundamental freedoms. We believe all governments have to answer to our citizens' aspirations for dignity and the rule of law and that no nation can or should deny those rights."[12] You were sitting in your cell in Camp V, while watching this news conference. It was like "a bad comedy scene," you said; you were "called to cry" but decided to laugh instead.

You couldn't help but wonder, "How could someone be so blind to his or her own shortcomings?"

But of all the things you wrote me in that email, perhaps the most surprising to me were the last several sentences, in which you cautioned me against highlighting your religion and the race of people in Chicago as a way to contextualize torture.

"Such practices are human nature more than anything else. I wouldn't emphasize race or religious background. I think we humans can't handle having power as well as one might think," you told me.

I want you to know, Mohamedou, that I understand your perspective. From World War II, to colonial-era Belgium, to modern-day Guantánamo Bay, I appreciate your alerting me to a common historical tendency in which powerful Western nations assert the moral high ground while exploiting the marginalized people of the world. The drive to conquer—to create social difference as a way to exploit others—you seemed to be saying, is part of human nature and has little to do with race.

I want you to know that I have considered your ideas carefully and have allowed them to challenge my thinking, and yet I feel that I must be honest with you. The concept of race remains fundamental to my understanding of torture. I do not believe that it is a coincidence, for instance, that even in the examples of injustice you gave me, the people who were being exploited were Black and Brown.

I'm not mentioning our different viewpoints on this matter because I want to prove you wrong. I agree with you that torture does exist because of some deeply held human trait, an instinct to want to make ourselves feel powerful and an instinct to attack the things that we are afraid of. Furthermore, your all-too-intimate experience with torture means that you understand the visceral reality of torture in a way I never will. I am in no way diminishing your understanding. I'm writing because, despite our different perspectives, we have the opportunity to be allies—and I don't want to squander it.

I've experienced your generous spirit firsthand, so I know that it is not your intention to suggest that African Americans should downplay our identities, censor the way we see ourselves in the world, or ignore how we are seen. In the United States, living a life in which one ignores the social fact of race is possible only if someone is extremely privileged, and even then, it is very difficult to do. And thus, to build a bridge across our differences, the solidarity we forge together cannot be based on muting those differences. I certainly would not want you to suppress your beliefs, passions, and values—the sense of who you are—so as not to offend or threaten me.

I've spent more than a decade trying to imagine a world in which everyone invested in eradicating torture is able to amplify the most radical aspects of themselves as a beacon of hope for surviving US imperialism. I want to know, Mohamedou, can you imagine that world, too?

I believe that your answer to this question is yes, and I believe that there is something that we can build together. And that collective project is to form an alliance that will work toward uprooting the torture tree.

• • •

Living trees nourish us. They absorb carbon dioxide, our waste product, and transform it into the oxygen we need. The torture tree takes something that we do not need and then creates something even more pernicious: it absorbs society's fears and manufactures divisions and hierarchies that are harmful to us all. When it comes to how people in the United States think about terrorism, it is clear that such divisive hierarchies are at work.[13]

Your diary, Mohamedou, implicitly asked whether US citizens would be outraged and demand change if they knew what was happening to men like you at Guantánamo Bay. As a US citizen I'm embarrassed to admit this, but you displayed a more nuanced understanding of the US Constitution than many people living in my country. (Trust me, Mohamedou, as a college professor, I know.)

But even beyond your knowledge of our laws, you made convincing ethical arguments in your book. So much so that reading your diary reminded me of the words of one of our most gifted writers, James Baldwin, who in 1965 made an observation I think you would agree with. Baldwin said that a person's perspective on the American dream has to do with "where you find yourself in the world" and is dependent on our most fundamental assumptions, those beliefs "which we hold so deeply as to be scarcely aware of them."[14]

One of the many things that struck me about your diary, Mohamedou, was its impassioned appeal to my fellow Americans, its attempt to bring us *into* awareness, to introduce us to troubling realities that most of us would find hard to believe. This is part of the aim of my book as well. We both, in our own way, want to make people aware that the US government's immoral engagement of the use-of-force continuum is about preserving our most powerful citizens' way of life. It is not primarily about keeping Americans safe. But in the United States, many believe the opposite is true.

As I have talked to people from all walks of life in Chicago, I have heard many people make troubling excuses for torture. The most extreme perspective came from a forty-four-year-old Black man named Todd. I want to tell you about him because his perspective exemplifies a deeply ingrained struggle that many Chicagoans face: striking a balance between one's own vulnerability to crime and one's simultaneous vulnerability to police victimization.

• • •

Even though, over the course of a lifetime, Todd had been mistreated by the police many times, he has still internalized the "bad guy" mentality that you were telling me about—the mentality that your interrogators used to justify your torture.

When I interviewed him for my research project, Todd said that there could, indeed, be circumstances where the police would be justified in using torture. Then he gave me this example: Once there was a "gangbanger," he called him, who shot and killed a sixty-five-year-old grandmother because her grandson owed him money. According to Todd, this guy was the epitome of a menace, someone who he felt no remorse for.

"Just go ahead and kill him," Todd said, as if granting permission to the police. "Don't give him no jail time. He deserves death."

I mentioned early on in this letter that experiencing racism can shape people's understanding of police violence, and that point is especially relevant here. After my interview with Todd, I spent a fair amount of time trying to understand his perspective on policing in light of what he said about his past. For example, Todd's first encounter with the police occurred when he was eleven years old. The police department had enforced a curfew law, and he and his cousin were trying to make it home before they violated curfew. They had lost track of time, and they didn't want to get in trouble with their parents or the cops. But that was not to be.

A police officer stopped them and asked where they were going. The cop said he needed to call their parents because they were underage. Upon hearing this, eleven-year-old Todd flailed his arms in exasperation. He never told me exactly why. Perhaps it was because he feared the repercussions of having his mother and father pick him up from the precinct. Perhaps it was because he wished he had run fast enough to beat curfew. Whatever the reason, Todd learned a crucial lesson that day: Black people shouldn't make sudden movements in the presence of the police.

When Todd moved his hands like that, the cop took it as an indication that Todd was armed. The officer pulled out a gun and pointed it toward his chest. At the time, Todd couldn't fathom that the cop actually thought he had a weapon. The only thing he was armed with was a pocket full of crayons.

Todd went on to explain that a lifetime of being victimized had made him anticipate police violence; he learned to sensitize himself to the force of a police presence, developing an ability to metabolize police abuse. Still, he insisted that our conversation needed to be "balanced." He wanted to end our interview by describing a positive encounter with the police. One day, Todd said, he was walking downtown when he felt a sting on his leg. He looked down and saw that a spider had bitten him. Todd swatted the insect away. Several hours later, Todd's leg began hurting so he went to the park to relax. He was in the affluent neighborhood of the Gold Coast. As Todd was sitting on the bench he saw that his leg was swelling up. "I just had a reaction out of nowhere," he said.

Todd decided to make his way to the hospital, but within an hour, his leg had swollen to the point that he could barely walk.

Todd didn't have the twenty-five dollars he needed to catch a cab, so he decided to take the train. If he could get to the Blue Line, he would be in good shape because the Cook County Hospital had its own stop. Todd limped on. But as soon as he reached the Museum of Contemporary Art, he fell down and could not move.

Eventually a policeman approached him. The cop thought Todd was a drug addict, or a vagrant, or a stubborn, drunken bum.

The cop yelled at him "aggressively" and demanded that he leave. When Todd told him he couldn't move, the cop picked him up and began to "manhandle" him.

"But he realized I wasn't bullshitting," Todd said, "when he saw the size of my leg."

The police officer eventually took Todd to the hospital. And Todd was surprised that he actually stuck around. After a nurse confirmed Todd's story by saying, "Looks like you might have gotten bitten by something," the cop even apologized.

He told Todd he was sorry about coming at him "a little bit aggressive" before explaining that they have "a lot of riffraff in the neighborhood." Then he wished him a speedy recovery. The two men shook hands as the cop walked away.

"That showed me that they're very human, because he didn't have to stick around. He wasn't trying to make an arrest."

"I found that very noble, because he was white," Todd continued. "I was like, 'Wow. That was incredible.' He really went the extra mile."

· · ·

My guess is that you would appreciate the sense of balance that Todd was attempting to interject into our interview; after all, you're such a positive, levelheaded person. You might also be pleased to know that there was one basic element of Todd's story that reminded me of you, in particular. His ability to find gratefulness in a situation associated with fear. This aspect made me think of your concept of portable happiness.

You told me about this concept when discussing the self-help book you were planning to write. I remember it well. You said that the book was based on an epiphany you had while you were locked up.

"One time I was very scared," you told me. "But the interrogators and guards in the room with me weren't anxious. They weren't afraid of anything. They were laughing and joking. I was the only one in the room who was scared."

You said that you couldn't understand why you should be scared because you weren't being beaten. You weren't being hurt. You weren't even being threatened at that particular moment in time.

"I deduced that I was the one who was terrorizing myself," you said, before discussing how you changed your way of thinking.

From that moment on, you stopped anticipating what could happen next. Instead, you tried to master the capacity to be content wherever you are. When you told me about developing the skill to dwell in any moment and find happiness there, my first thought was, "This man is redefining what it means to be grateful." I was in awe of how you found your humanity against a backdrop of terror. Had I been in your situation, I'm quite sure that I would have been lost for a long time in a murky fog of fear.

It was because of what you told me in our interview and what I read in your book about finding a glimmer of inspiration in the darkest circumstance that my ears perked up when Todd said he wanted to share a positive encounter with the police.

I hoped that he, too, might talk about finding a moment of gratitude in an atmosphere of hostility. Yet there was a major difference between the gratitude that Todd exhibited and the appreciation that you displayed during your captivity. Todd's happiness in the positive encounter he described depended on an external factor: a police officer's benevolence. But your sense of happiness was derived from within.

The reason I have compared your time in detention with Todd's encounter with the police is because I have been looking for a way

forward. I once had a hunch that building on people's positive experiences with law enforcement could provide a model for transforming
the criminal justice system. But the more I explored this possibility,
the more I realized that I was wrong. After speaking with one hundred Chicago residents about police torture, I still had not found a
viable model.

The reason I don't think Todd's approach will work is because I do
not believe we can count on the kindness of an individual police officer to keep us safe—especially when the laws, policies, and political
climate that an officer is beholden to depend on him locking up a disproportionate number of Black people. In such a context, suspicion,
mistreatment, and coercion will be the norm, and individual acts of
kindness will be the exception to the rule.

But I must admit I had a problem with your approach as well, albeit
for a different reason.

First, let me say that I admire your ability to enter into a meditative
space and find happiness while being surrounded by danger. As I understood it, you were speaking about a concept that was precious and
valuable—something that I want to develop within myself. But as a
collective strategy for everyone who will be unduly subjected to police
force, from the war on drugs to the war on terror, I don't think we can
realistically expect marginalized people all across the globe to achieve
individual contentment in time to avoid being debilitated or killed.

I also think that marginalized people should not have to find a solution to their own subjugation from within themselves. When we do
that, it absolves law enforcement of their role in perpetuating violence. In short, I fear that your approach would let my government
off the hook too easily.

Perhaps our alliance should instead be premised on the collective
action you took while at Guantánamo Bay, the way you and the other
detainees shared knowledge to retain what was important to you as
humans.

While the Central Intelligence Agency met the claim that you no
longer had ties to Al-Qaeda with disbelief, the fact that you were a
devout Muslim when you arrived at Guantánamo Bay was never in

doubt. You were among the 1.8 billion followers of this monotheistic religion who believe that there is only one God (Allah) and that the prophet Muhammad is his messenger. What this means, in practical terms, is that you adhere to The Pillars of Islam, or the five basic religious acts that are considered obligatory for all believers of the faith. There is the shahadah, a testimony that must be recited in prayer, which affirms that Muhammad is the messenger of God; there is the salat, ritual prayers intended to focus a believers mind on God, which are recited in the direction of Mecca, Muhammad's birthplace; there is zakat, or charity, which entails gifting a portion of your accumulated wealth to the poor or needy; there is Sawm, or fasting, the purpose of which is to facilitate closeness to God; and there is the hajj, the obligatory religious pilgrimage to the city of Mecca that every follower who is able must take at least once in his life. Of those Pillars, the ones that you used to sustain yourself on Camp Echo were shahadah (testimony), salat (prayer), and sawm (fasting), though your Guantánamo diary makes clear that the US military intelligence anticipated that you would use your pillars as a resource, and thus part of their strategy for interrogating you was to make you betray your beliefs. Nevertheless, you would depend on your religious faith to live in the moment, and by so doing, gain knowledge of your surroundings.

This is one of the most impressive things about your diary: the way you acquired knowledge while being detained. Your captors tried to strip you of your humanity by limiting what you knew about the world. They did not want you to know which day of the week it was or hour of the day or anything about them as your interrogators. But you and the other detainees would find ways to obtain this knowledge just as you stole moments of prayer, even when the US military prevented you from practicing your faith. You would steal time by glimpsing interrogators' watches during interviews. You would steal names by eavesdropping on your interrogators' conversations. You would trade this knowledge with fellow detainees like contraband so that you could know who was tormenting you or what time to turn toward Mecca during salat. You hid these kernels of knowledge because, as a detainee, you never knew when these pieces of intelligence would come in handy (like when you found out the name of your interrogator and were able to expose him in your diary). You always knew more than your captors thought you did. At the same time, you were able to use that knowledge to build bridges of solidary with other detainees.

The reason I appreciate this approach is because you did not stop anticipating the harm that could befall you at any given moment. That is important, because many marginalized people cannot afford to do that. Rather you used your fellow detainees as resources to rebel against your dehumanization. That kind of rebellion is essential because we cannot assume that my government's stance on torture will become more humane over time. The current political climate makes that all the more clear.

. . .

In his 2017 inaugural address, the president of the United States Donald Trump said the following: "We will unite the civilized world against radical Islamic terrorism, which we will eradicate completely from the face of the Earth."

Sound familiar? Many Americans feel that Trump's Islamophobia is heinous. But fewer of us grapple with how easy it is to make Islamophobia seem necessary in the American mainstream. In the spring of 2016, while I was in the throes of this research project, I watched one of the Republican Party presidential primary debates. In it, candidate Marco Rubio said that then president Barack Obama "should be putting people into Guantánamo, not emptying it out." He added, "We shouldn't be releasing these killers, who are rejoining the battlefield against the United States."[15]

As if this troubling stance weren't enough, since becoming president, Trump appointed Gina Haspel as director of the CIA. During the same year you were imprisoned at Guantánamo, Haspel was serving as chief of a CIA black site in Thailand where prisoners were subjected to the same "enhanced interrogation techniques" as you were in Camp V. Her role in torturing terrorism suspects and then destroying evidence of torture did not rule her out for this position. Nor did it block her Senate confirmation. This speaks to how acceptable torture in my country actually is.

My president's remarks about torture being a necessary evil to deal with a "dangerous" population speaks to one of the central arguments of my book: the assumption of guilt is used to justify extrajudicial force. The president promises to refill detention facilities like Guantánamo Bay. He will consider creating even more black sites. His rhetoric differs from that of previous administrations positions because he has stripped away the veneer of progress and allowed torture to seem acceptable—even necessary. But aside from this brash rhetoric, how much have the policies on torture in the United States actually changed? The answer to the question is "not all that much," especially when it comes to punishing torturers.

What I'm saying is that Trump should not take all the blame for the US government's current embrace of torture. As president, Trump can reinstate torture without fear of repercussion in part because in the past, by appealing to the so-called state-secrets privilege, the US government has successfully blocked the release of information that would implicate law enforcement personnel who engage in torture. Both the Bush and Obama administrations used claims of secrecy to dismiss lawsuits by survivors of torture, arguing that such information needed to be kept secret as a matter of national security.[16]

As a result, despite numerous lawsuits against the "architects and perpetrators of the CIA torture program" during the time Bush and Obama held office, US courts "did not consider the claims of a single torture victim," as Dror Ladin, attorney for the ACLU National Security Project, has recently noted.[17] The US government has repeatedly argued that torture cases cannot be litigated without disclosing "state secrets," claiming that the litigation itself would undermine national security interests. This has allowed the government to end entire legal proceedings before they even start. Without judicial accountability, the US government has used executive orders—consensus-based decisions by particular administrations—to shut down black sites or release detainees like you from places like Guantánamo.

The problem with this approach is that it does nothing to prevent future administrations from reopening black sites or extolling the merits of torture. Had President Obama sought to hold high-level Bush officials accountable, for example, legal precedent for the kind of punishment a torturer could expect to face would at least exist. Unfortunately, it now does not. Therefore, we have no reason to expect that government officials who perpetuate torture will not be shielded by the rule of law as they have been in the past.

I know you would agree that this is a crucial mistake. By not holding torturers accountable, my country is actually inviting troubled men to live out their sadistic fantasies with the backing of the US military.

Your torturer, Richard Zuley, is a prime example of the urgent problem this poses. The world now knows Zuley's true identity because of the sloppiness of government redactors, and also because his name had earlier appeared in the footnotes of the Senate Armed Services Committee's 2008 investigation into military torture. But did you know that Zuley himself revealed something about his identity in—of all things—a signed review on the Amazon website for a novel entitled *Killing Sharks*?[18]

According to the cover copy, *Killing Sharks* invites readers to "dive into the explosive world of terrorism and those fearless enough to fight it." It centers on Lieutenant Commander Grant Chisholm, who "is on a mission to thwart jihadists. His latest assignment as a liaison officer to Guantánamo brings him face to face with the Taliban and Al-Qaeda, and their hatred of the United States." In his review of the book, Zuley wrote the following:

> Wentz's ability to generate excitement and the desire to keep reading because you need to find out what happens next is right there with Vince Flynn. . . . The author doesn't give up classified material but, like Clancy, he certainly flirts with it while describing what could be a very real scenario in a fictional setting. *Killing Sharks: De Profundis* is fiction that could easily be fact. The enemy is real, the plot not only plausible but one we prepared for, and the characters are people

we all knew. I thoroughly enjoyed *Killing Sharks* and look forward to Dr. Wentz's next book and hopefully a continuation of the exploits of LCDR Grant Chisholm!

LCDR Richard Zuley, USN (Ret.)

Former EUCOM LNO, senior interrogator and Special Projects Team Chief, Joint Task Force—Guantánamo (2002–2004)

This review stands out for what it reveals about the military imagination. The way Zuley signs his comment suggests pride in his position as "senior interrogator," and one can only wonder what "special projects" he headed up. What's more, the enjoyment he seems to derive from the book conveys how exciting he finds the hunt for terrorists to be, and also his belief that the terrorists it portrays are "people we all knew." He clearly means for his title as lieutenant commander and his position as a senior interrogator to give credibility to his assertion that the people and events in the book are based in reality.

I'm calling this review out to clarify the way that books like *Killing Sharks* work alongside the popular news media, official reports, and even scholarly treatises to anticipate terrorist events before they happen, creating a mythic "terrorist" in the popular consciousness. Such leaps of the imagination amplify violence and turn people whom the US government suspects of being enemies into "sharks," until the war on terror becomes a self-fulfilling prophecy.[19] By recruiting people who already believe that terrorists are dangerous (menaces who, it must be said, are invariably of a darker skin color than they are) and need to be hunted, and constantly rewarding those recruits with opportunity, the US government protects torturers as a smokescreen for its own crimes.

That, Mohamedou, is how an overeager cop, with grandiose ideas about "the enemy"—based as much in popular thrillers as in his own experience—eventually comes to be your interrogator. And that is how the same man who tortured you—and who knows how many others—was employed by the City of Chicago for decades. Here's another example of a "bad comedy scene," as you put it, something that's so sad that you almost have to laugh in order to hold back the tears: For three years and seven months, after he retired from the police department, Richard Zuley worked as a senior emergency management coordinator at the same Department of Public Health that is currently funding the Chicago Torture Justice Center. And, even though he recently retired, it's important to note that when the Chicago Torture Justice Center first opened its doors, Zuley was still a projects administrator for the City of Chicago.

As you can see, protecting torturers from sanction fertilizes the seeds of the torture tree, allowing it to grow from US cities like Chicago all the way to the detention center in Guantánamo Bay and back to the Windy City, where Zuley's forty-year career as a government employee undermines the city's efforts to make amends for the police crimes of the past. The erosion of moral standards in my country's actions overseas also has a trickle-down effect, altering moral standards of citizens and authorities alike, creating a crisis of oversight back home.

As for Guantánamo, as I'm sure you know, Mohamedou, our current president, vice president, and attorney general are all for keeping it open and—as our president has said—filling it with "bad dudes."[20] The institutionalization of torture in our legal system will persist until citizens rise up and demand that it cease—and this point brings me back to our alliance.

. . .

It is due time to add to the foundation you built, Mohamedou. A major part of the despair your diary invokes is that you were incarcerated and tortured by the US government while deprived of due process and never charged with a crime. That gives your voice authority, because—like African Americans who were denied citizenship while the US fought the Nazis during World War II—your story contradicts the tenets my country is supposed to hold dear.

I know that it has been extremely important for you to assert your innocence, and no one can fault you for that. In forging our alliance, though, let us take an even more radical step forward. We must insist that no one ever deserves to be tortured, no matter what a person may have done. That principle must supplant the "bad guy" mentality, which is currently more popular than ever in the United States. It must become our compass and point us toward collaboration and change.

May our alliance consist of everyone, across the globe, who is negatively affected by the use-of-force continuum that justifies escalating violence against marginalized groups. May it also include the symbiotic relationship between the police and the military that extends the military's reach into spaces like Guantánamo that transcend the rule of law in the name of the public good. Once our alliance is forged, we can model our mode of collaboration after your relationship with the detainees at Guantánamo Bay. We will share moments of gratitude with each other as collective resources, and those moments will be the ones we have stolen from the fear-inducing spaces we've been brought to against our will. We will use gratitude wrought from fear as a way to bridge our vulnerabilities. Perching ourselves on the bridge we've built, we will engage in a dialogue that is committed to truth, that is willing to struggle, and that is defiantly hopeful for recovery.

My dear Mohamedou, it is my sincerest hope that you are on board with this vision.

Conclusion

An Open Letter to the Late Andrew Wilson

Andrew, you passed away on November 19, 2007, in a prison hospital, while serving out your life sentence in Menard Correctional Center. But I am writing you because in Chicago—and, I suspect, in worn-out neighborhoods and overburdened cities all across the United States—your memory is very much alive. I don't know where your soul or spirit resides, but in this world, your name will be forever linked to that of Jon Burge. I have to imagine that this connection is a painful one for you, given that your relevance is tied to the horrors you endured and the man who created them. So I want to shift the narrative in which Burge is the villain and you are the victim. Instead of focusing solely on you as a victim, I want to emphasize another aspect of your life: you were the first person to have the courage to act decisively against him. You filed the civil suit that marked the beginning of the end of his reign of terror in Chicago's Area 2. It's equally important to note what you were not. You were not merely a symbol of what to avoid. You were not merely a criminal. You were someone who displayed great courage and bravery, even if that courage is remembered by only a few.

In contrast, Burge's name has become widely known, at least in

Black communities across Chicago, a symbol of all that is wrong with the police force. Some even use it as a derogative verb, saying that someone they know was "Burged"—tortured or brutalized by the police or another vigilante. Everyone in Chicago's Black neighborhoods, it seems, knows what the term means.

Many of the details about Burge's horrific crimes have become public. And yet even though you endured the worst of those crimes, I still don't know how much you knew about their extent. I don't know what information you had access to in Menard. I don't know if you read the newspaper or talked to other prisoners about Burge. Did you ever realize the scope of your tormentor's torture operation? Your lawyer, John Stainthorp, stayed in touch with you until just before you died, so you must have been aware, to some extent, of the evolving mass of evidence that was becoming part of the public record. Even so, and although it might be difficult to hear, I think you deserve to know what has happened since you died. I want you to understand the magnitude of the evil you helped to thwart, at great personal cost to yourself, considering you suffered that torment all over again each time you took the witness stand.

Likewise, I think people all across the United States deserve to know what happened to you and people like you—so-called Black menaces—under Jon Burge's regime.

I'll admit that when I first read about your case, I had a hard time separating the fact that you were a confessed cop killer from the violence Jon Burge inflicted on you. Like those white jurors in your first and second civil trials, I let myself believe that because you had confessed to killing two of Burge's fellow police officers, he and his A-Team had tortured you out of rage, a terrible but understandable emotional outburst. But Flint Taylor made me see the issue differently; your lawyer, as overworked as he was underpaid, revolutionized my understanding of police torture. The legitimacy of torture is separate from the question of guilt, because even the guilty have the right not to be electrocuted. Even the guilty have the right not to be suffocated and beaten within an inch of their lives.

That belief—that every human being has the right *not* to be tortured—has changed my life, animated the past decade of my professional career, and convinced me to write to you. That belief, though, is not easy to come by. Those jurors could not accept this belief. Judge Duff could not accept it either. Even the most liberal of Chicagoans had a hard time, during those weeks of relentless press coverage of your first civil trial, of actually looking at what happened to you—and of actually seeing the black box as a violation of your most basic human rights.

And then you had to endure all that disbelief again, years later, in your second civil trial. Presented with overwhelming evidence that Jon Burge and officers in his charge tortured you, the jurors in that trial also concluded, just as I once had, that the abuse you suffered amounted to a temper tantrum on the part of the police. As far as those jurors were concerned, the fact that you had been convicted of murdering two cops justified that abuse.

Now, many people in Chicago have come to understand how false this justification was. In the end, your trials set the stage for an airing of the truth that would never have happened without you. People at virtually every level of Chicago city government spent decades trying to cover up the truth of Burge's torture ring, and despite the impressive number of investigations that confirmed its existence, it persisted, sometimes abetted by the same people who were supposed to be investigating it.

I don't know if it would sadden you or bring you relief to know that your brother, Jackie, who was arrested with you in 1982, was recently released from prison after thirty-six years. He was finally granted a new trial on the basis that he had been tortured. Jackie is now part of the ever-expanding community of torture survivors.

As the history of police torture illustrates, it doesn't matter what a given criminal suspect did or did not do: for the rule of law to have any meaning, no suspect—whether innocent or guilty—should have to suffer what you suffered. That's why your case led to a profound transformation in my thinking about torture. Your story taught me the unlikeliest of lessons: finding empathy for you, and others who've endured torture, was a test of my own humanity. In the process I stopped thinking of you as merely a cop killer or merely a victim. I began to think of you as a survivor.

. . .

I recently reread the famous letter that Martin Luther King Jr. wrote to his fellow clergy from a jail cell in Birmingham, Alabama. I thought of it because it was quoted in a court ruling that I came across in an archive years ago. The ruling described the scene of a Black boy's torture.

In 1991, that boy, Marcus Wiggins, then thirteen-years-old and only sixty-five pounds, was one of a group of children brought into Area 2 for questioning about a murder. A few hours later, Wiggins was electrocuted with a silver device, the size of a toaster that had wires coming out of it, akin to the black box: "They started—my hands started burning, feeling like it was being burned. I was—I was shaking and my—and my jaws got tight and my eyes felt like they went black. . . . It felt like I was spinning. . . . It felt like my jaws was like—they was—I can't say the word. It felt like my jaws was sucking in. . . . I felt like I was going to die."[1]

After the torture, Wiggins confessed. Several years later, his case was dismissed in juvenile court. He subsequently sued Burge, a number of his detectives, and the City of Chicago. In 1996, Wiggins's lawsuit was settled for $95,000.[2]

After the trial, the police lawyers wanted evidence related to the Wiggins case kept confidential. They maintained that "the police officers' privacy interest is a factor weighing against disclosure." Judge Ruben Castillo disagreed; he ordered the public release of numerous police disciplinary files containing allegations of torture. His rationale was that the files "must be exposed to the light of human conscience and the air of natural opinion."

In making his case, Judge Castillo referenced King's letter: "Like a boil that can never be cured as long as it is covered up but must be opened with all its pus-flowing ugliness to the natural medicines of air and light, injustice must likewise be exposed, with all of the tension its exposing creates, to the light of human conscience and the air of national opinion before it can be cured."

I could not agree more with King's sentiment, or with Castillo's application of it. And yet comparing the torture of a thirteen-year-old to a boil does not do justice to the suffering that people like Wiggins experience. A boil can be "cured" relatively easily. The mental and physical scars left by torture—and by the racism that justifies and enables that torture—can last a lifetime. Moreover, because torture is so deeply rooted in the culture of the Chicago police force, and in the legal, judicial, and political system that have allowed it to thrive, we require another, more apt metaphor. Police torture is a tree—a hideous and disfigured tree, a tree that blooms death rather than life, a tree that casts a long and dark shadow.

• • •

As I was finishing this letter, I found out Jon Burge had died, and his death prompted me to think about all that has happened as a result of the torture he inflicted and oversaw. As a consequence of the four inmates on death row being pardoned by Illinois's former governor George Ryan, who concluded that Burge had tortured them, a moratorium on capital punishment was declared in Illinois in 2003. Six years later, in 2009, the state established the first Torture Inquiry and Relief Commission in the United States. Two years after that, in 2011, Illinois became one of twenty US states to abolish the death penalty, partly because of the way torture has been tied to forced confessions. After all of my research, I'm convinced that none of these legal milestones would have occurred without the political activism that sought to hold Burge accountable for torture.

Upon hearing about Burge's death, John Conroy, the first reporter to write extensively about torture in Chicago, said, "Greater transparency has resulted from the abuse here." Likewise, when speaking about the landmark reparations judgment for victims of police abuse, the outgoing mayor of Chicago, Rahm Emanuel, referred to Burge's tenure on the police force as a "dark chapter" in the city's history.[3]

For me, these reflections on police torture, occasioned by Burge's death, suggest that a diseased limb of the torture tree has fallen. That limb was so massive that, upon its falling, it shook the earth beneath it, injuring countless people who were in the vicinity, bringing attention to the tree from which the limb once sprouted. We are now aware of the torture tree unlike ever before. But the fact that we now know about its existence does not mean that the tree has stopped growing. To the contrary, it is still firmly planted in Chicago's soil.

I want you to know that it is because of this—the way that torture is still so deeply entrenched in your city—that I did not write Jon Burge a letter like the one I've written you. All of my open letters are written to people who have expressed a genuine interest in addressing the legacy of police torture. Burge remained defiant and unremorseful until his death. In the last interview he granted to Martin Preib, a representative of the police union, he exclaimed: "I find it hard to believe that the city's political leadership could even contemplate giving 'reparations' to human vermin." Burge might be gone. But his ideology of hate persists, and it's always in danger of further infecting the police.[4]

Speaking of the racial violence in the United States that spreads like a disease, Black Power activist Stokely Carmichael once said: "If a white man wants to lynch me, that's *his* problem. If he's got the power to lynch me, that's *my* problem. Racism is not a question of attitude, it's a question of power."

In telling the world about your torture, I want everyone to know that if a person holds an unfavorable attitude toward someone who has committed a crime or has been suspected of committing a crime, that is that person's prerogative. But if that person wears a badge and has the power to torture a criminal suspect, then that is everyone's problem.

Perhaps the greatest testament to your legacy, Andrew, is that many people now recognize that what you endured is their problem, too.

Epilogue
A Model for Justice

An Open Letter to You, the Reader

You may be a curious reader who has stumbled on this title in a local bookstore, or a college student who has been assigned this book for a class; you may be a police or prison abolitionist who is drawn to critical books about law enforcement, or a civil rights lawyer interested in fighting for racial equality; you may be a social scientist like myself; a victim of police violence or the loved one of such a victim. Whatever your background is and however you've come to read this book, if you believe that torture is not a necessary evil but should be eradicated, and that torturers should be held accountable for their crimes, then the message of this letter is especially for you.

I realize I haven't addressed you, reader, directly until now. But part of the reason I've made my letters "open" is so that you can read them as well. If you've read my other open letters, then you know that alongside the torture tree, a central metaphor herein is that of the black box. But there is one kind of black box that I've only mentioned in passing until now. And that is the black box as a recovery tool. Let me explain.

When investigators arrive at the scene of an airplane crash, the first thing they search for—after survivors, of course—is the black box.

In this instance, the phrase refers to a device that records the audio from the cockpit and flight data; a typical model can record more than one hundred hours of information. The box also includes a flight transponder that sends information back to air-traffic controllers. Insulated by armored steel that protects it from impact, fire, and seawater, the black box is designed to provide an accurate record of the flight from takeoff to landing—or, more important, to crash landing.

It is tempting for us scholars to envision the research process as something like a black-box recovery mission. Part of me would like to imagine myself as a crime scene investigator, finding the black box of torture deep in the sea of denials, evasions, and lies. Ever since I learned that Jon Burge is rumored to actually have thrown his torture device in Lake Michigan from his boat, named *Vigilante*, I wanted to be the one to find it. Perhaps not literally, but I have been searching for evidence that would tell me how torture happened in the past and why it continues to happen now.

Civil rights lawyers probably dream about finding the incredibly persuasive witness or the incontrovertible piece of evidence—that thing that stops a trial in its tracks, the thing that proves your client was the victim of, for example, a hate crime, that proves the presence of injustice. Well, for anthropologists like me, the desire to "discover" a supposedly hidden reality dates back to the founding of our discipline—in the 1800s, when ethnographers made contact with people in remote parts of the world. What we "find," however, is not like evidence in a trial. Instead, we often "find" aspects of social life that are so banal most people don't deem them worthy of close study, because everyone already believes them to be true. They only strike us ethnographers as interesting because the world in which we "found" or "discovered" these things is different from our own.

In Chicago, the belief that the police hate Black people and mistreat them, brutalize them, torture them, and kill them is so commonplace as to be banal. It's only surprising to the person who is unfamiliar with those communities of color, the person who lives somewhere else, or who simply does not care about what happens in these communities. Likewise, the idea that a social scientist could "discover" an aspect of police violence that Black Chicagoans didn't already know would be more than laughable. It would be insulting. The implication being that you were attempting to take credit for "finding" a struggle against police abuse that has been going on for over a century. Black Chicagoans have been protesting police violence at least since the Second Great Migration in the 1890s, when Black people first moved to the city in vast numbers.

I mentioned at the outset of this book that the reality of researching something that people already know had implications for how I conceived of this project. This is why, instead of trying to piece together the scene of an accident, I began from the premise that I would take what my interlocutors told me seriously; I would use their words and their thoughts to guide my project. And what they told me, again and again and again, was clear: police torture is nothing like a plane crash. Police torture is not an accident at all. It is intentional, predictable, and expected.

Most Chicagoans I talked to for this research project already understood my subject better than I did: they knew that police torture has existed for a long time and that the city government has historically done little to stop it. I did not "discover" this phenomenon—far from it. What I have done, I hope, is clarify the shape and structure of police torture as a way to amplify the concerns of the people who have lived it.

The torture tree is a concept that can help you visualize the range of police force, which we have called the use-of-force continuum. I have shown that the torture tree has profound implications for how Chicagoans of color live. This is because it reinforces a racial caste system that subjects a disproportionate number of them to debilitation and death. It erodes the city government's legitimacy. And it makes not only Chicago, but the world, less safe.

Through my open letters in this book I have also made clear that our country bears responsibility for the torture tree. This is because our collective investment in fear is what allows the tree to grow.

• • •

If you've taken the time to read my letters, you've put yourself in the shoes of future mayors of Chicago, youth of color in this city, the current superintendent of the police department, former police officers, civil rights activists, social justice advocates, victims of police violence, and torture survivors. You've imagined what it is like to be them and have grappled with their concerns. The purpose of writing open letters to the range of people whom I've written to in this book is so that none of us can claim ignorance; my hope is that, once you read this book, it will be impossible to ignore the use-of-force continuum and its detrimental effects. I've also made clear how various people have been complicit in police torture. In addressing all these people—all somehow connected to the scandal of police torture—it has not been my intent to make anyone feel alienated or defensive, angry or inadequate. I want them to feel inspired and inventive, curious and empowered by what they know. In reading my open letters to them, I hope you feel the same way.

For social scientists interested in social justice, in particular, I want them to feel hopeful because of what I have to ask: join me in reimagining the role of the police in our society. I've mentioned the activist efforts in Chicago to divest public funds from excess policing and toward community development. Along these lines, a concrete step we can take is to divest our intellectual resources from reproducing a world based in fear to reproducing ways of doing research based on collaboration and trust.

Might we use our training to develop and advance and realize community-oriented approaches that enhance the quality of life of vulnerable people? We can also use our significant resources to advance such approaches toward making society more equitable and fair.

I have a suggestion to make in this regard: As opposed to seeing the black box as a torture device that inflicts pain, or a concept to illustrate how knowledge is concealed, or a revealing trove of information, perhaps we can use the black box to represent something else. Maybe the black box can usefully serve as a repository that we fill with the fruits of our efforts to expose the open secrets among all of us that maintain social inequality. If so, we all would do well to learn from the torture survivors.

• • •

Eight years ago, around the time that activists in Chicago began to host teach-ins, lectures, and other public events about the history of police torture, when reparations for the torture survivors were still just a seed beginning to grow, I attended a roundtable discussion in Chicago, hosted by survivors of torture, at which they spoke about the political activism that might emerge from their suffering. Anthony Holmes, a man who spent thirty years in prison after having been tortured by Burge, was asked what sort of public memorial would honor the victims of Jon Burge's wrath. Holmes replied that Burge's black box should serve as a memorial: "If you set that black box on a panel—on a plateau—that's a memorial because that represents all of us. Because we're the ones that went through that. We're the ones that were suffocated, and shocked until we passed out and almost died from it. We're the ones that were pronged, shotgun stuck in the mouth, the whole nine yards."

Holmes took a breath before continuing: "The bottom line is: that Box is the key. That's what got Burge—that box. That box is everything."

If you truly care about change, you must take heed of Holmes's words, especially the last one—*everything.* By discussing *everything* that the black box has meant to people of color in Chicago, I'm not trying to sensationalize their predicament or make it seem that they alone bear the brunt of an exceptional horror. My hope is that you, my reader, can learn from this city's tumultuous relationship with political corruption and police torture—even if it can (and no doubt will) be argued that what happens in Chicago is not entirely representative of the way police officers across the nation conduct themselves. Precisely because of the reality of Chicago's streets—because of what has happened in them and what can happen again if that reality remains secret—the torture survivors insist that much can be learned from their experiences. They insist, in other words, that we must speak the secrets out loud. We must give voice to this painful reality. This is the lesson of the torture survivors. They are helping, as James Baldwin once said, to "reveal more about America to Americans than Americans wish to know."

This is a model for social justice that we all must follow. Let us make the black box our repository of truth. Not a box that is closed and guarded, but a box that we as a community have pried open. A box whose insides are now on display for all to see. By exposing the internal components of the machine, let us finally see where all the wires are connected: the wires connected to Black criminal suspects have led to the police department and to the legal apparatus of Cook County. Let us see how all of these wires are connected to the larger engine of fear. Much like the motion on the handle of Burge's fiendish machine, cranking electricity into his victims, fear catalyzes police power and military might, causing people at the top and the bottom of their respective chains of command to ignore their colleagues' crimes and to maintain silence about what they knew. Fear of "the other" made it possible for torture to become a routine part of interrogating criminal suspects in certain Chicago precincts. That same fear allowed the tentacles of torture to reach the shores of Guantánamo Bay.

With this contraption splayed wide open, let us all finally see how understanding police torture—and taking concrete steps to prevent it—requires us to dismantle the fear at the root of this pernicious American practice.

Appendix
Letters on Method

Sometime in the spring of 2015, just before I started my focus groups, I drafted an open letter to students of color in Chicago. It began like this:

Dear Chicago Public School Students:

The category denoting the life stage you're currently in—that is, "public school student"—acquired a troubling dimension during my time living in your city in the early 2000s. I first encountered the label in the papers and on local news. Journalists and anchorpersons, reporting the various daily violence in Chicago, tended far too often to punctuate their reports with statistics like this: "A 14-year-old Hazel Crest boy shot Friday night in the Morgan Park neighborhood became the 28th Chicago Public School student killed this school year."[1] What they meant by "public school student" was not merely that the deceased had attended a state-funded educational facility, but rather that the student—number twenty-eight, thirty, or thirty-six—was poor and Black, and the community in which he or she lived was violent.

Writing this book has been tremendously humbling. When I drafted my first letter, to Chicago public school students, I sent it to a friend who had taught in Chicago Public Schools for years. Her feedback was unvarnished. My prose would be incomprehensible, she chided. She urged me to simplify my vocabulary. We talked for an hour about the ethics of writing to an audience in a language that they may feel alienated from. The experience was humbling, to say the least. Part of me felt defeated and intimidated by the task. But through that intimidation I eventually found ways to stretch myself as a writer and as a researcher, which was ultimately very rewarding.

As a result of the conversation with my friend and many others, with both educators and otherwise, I have been experimenting with a method that I refer to as *ethnographic lettering*. As a methodology, ethnographic lettering includes three ways of layering field research. First, it transforms research "subjects" into "interlocutors" during the research process by focusing on the projects they are already invested in as a way to explore broader social problems; second, it includes exchanges with interlocutors in the research and writing phases of the project; and third, it positions one's interlocutors and the communities they want to address as the primary audience for the ethnographic material that will ultimately be produced.

I have found that the merits of ethnographic lettering are manifold. One benefit is that the approach includes interlocutors in the process of analyzing data and determining which data should be written about. In this way, it ensures that the stakes of the research are relevant to the community members being written to. Another benefit is that, in placing many different community members in conversation with one another, this method develops a nuanced portrait of a given social problem.

In this appendix, I start with a slightly less obvious benefit: this approach differs from the ways cultural anthropologists have thought about the ethnographic significance of the letter. Of course many people from many fields have studied letters. But the way cultural anthropologists have approached this form of writing is particularly relevant for my book's concerns.

Cultural anthropologists are interested in how people experience certain social problems and the way they make sense of those experiences. In doing so, they center the point of view of the people they study, as opposed to merely bringing their own theories and philosophies to bear on the social problem at hand. Letters are interesting from an anthropological perspective because they are windows into the worldview of the subjects of the study. Traditionally, when it comes to letters, among cultural anthropologists, two modes of thinking predominate. Let's explore both.[2]

The Archival Approach

The first way that cultural anthropologists tend to see letters is rooted in the historical tradition of empiricism. To understand how liberal democratic states develop and wield power, historians have asked, how do government agencies produce knowledge that shapes a particular vision of "subjects"? But because anthropologists are primarily interested in the perspective of the socially marginalized, it is more common for them to flip this question on its head. They ask, how do subjects produce knowledge that shapes a particular vision of governance? In answering this question, they have gravitated toward nontraditional archives.

In a moving article about three generations of a family in New Mexico who had struggled with heroin addiction, Angela Garcia (2016) describes the endeavor of creating a prison archive and the connections between women that this prison archive facilitates.[3] The central figures in Garcia's article are Bernadette, imprisoned on drug-related charges, and her mother, Eugenia, herself a former addict. The artifacts of the prison archive are the letters written from Bernadette to Eugenia.

In a letter dated April 7, 2006, Bernadette writes:

I feel like I'm shouting and no one hears. It's hard to write because it hurts. I have to be honest with you. It bothers me my cellmate gets more visits from her family even though they live in Window Rock. I think that is further away. That's what she said but maybe she's just trying to get me. She seems pretty nice though. She reminds me of Piñon because she is so short and round. Why don't you come? You can ask Laura to give you a ride. Her sister is in Level 3 and I heard from Brenda who is here too that she comes at least once a month. You are in my prayers. Please keep me in your prayers. Please don't forget me.

In this quote, Garcia shows the "material traces" of the relationship between Bernadette and her mother. The letters she references represent familial connections but also the social marginalization indicative of both life on this particular Native reservation and life in prison. They also represent feelings of isolation and dislocation, shaping a narrative of love, loss, and regret. Furthermore, by highlighting documents that are not cataloged and maintained by agents of the state, but "wards" of it, Garcia's gripping article reminds us that letters are an essential way to convey the texture of someone's life.

Indeed, ordinary people, the world over, have been writing and receiving letters for centuries. A crucial element of letter writing has always been to tell stories, to contribute to an ongoing dialogue, and to open up questions about social life in a particular time and place. Garcia's approach expands on these enduring elements of letter writing, using them to question unequal power relations. In the process of exploring power relations, the ethnographer becomes an archivist, finding and caring for forgotten things, focusing on the forms of knowledge contained in the object of the letter, and thereby including in the ethnographic writing or other social science text a perspective on social life "from below."[4]

My approach similarly draws on what I learn from examining nontraditional archives. The difference is that I use this knowledge to participate in an "unfinished" and ever-evolving dialogue with the people and groups implicated in the social problems I study, as a way to better understand these problems.[5]

Letter as Event

The other dominant view of the letter is as an event. Unlike the archival approach, with letter as event, letters are not primarily used
to address the personal histories of one's interlocutors and amplify
hidden voices. Instead, the letter begs the reader to reflect on the ethnographer's subject position, by which I mean a researcher's identity
and role in the community he or she studies vis-à-vis one's research
"subjects."

Here, the multiple dialogues and voices entailed in the letter allow
the anthropologist to demonstrate that there is no one "native" voice.
Analyzing the letter thus affords the opportunity to set the voices
of multiple interlocutors in argument with one another, such that
what the ethnographer ultimately writes about is not "the community view" in a strict sense, but the constellation of arguments that
comprises an internal discourse.

This way of thinking is characterized by James Ferguson's classic
article "Of Mimicry and Membership," in which he tells the story of
two African youths who were found dead in the undercarriage of a
plane headed to Brussels.[6] The article centers on the letter found on
the bodies of the teenagers, Yaguine Koita (age fourteen) and Fode
Tounkara (age fifteen), who had smuggled themselves onto the plane:

> Members and officials of Europe, we are appealing to your gracious-
> ness and solidarity to come to our rescue. Please, help us. We are suf-
> fering enormously in Africa. Help us, we have problems, and those
> problems include the lack of children's rights. . . . As for children's
> rights, in Africa, and especially in Guinea, we have plenty of schools
> but a great lack of education and teaching. Only in the private schools
> can one get good education and good teaching, but it requires quite a
> lot of money and our parents are poor, they must feed us. . . . There-
> fore, we Africans, especially we, the African children and youth, are
> asking you to set up a great, effective organization for Africa so that

it might make progress. And if you find that we have sacrificed our lives, it is because we suffer too much in Africa. We need your help to struggle against poverty and to put an end to war in Africa. Our greatest wish, though, is to study, and we ask that you help us to study to become like you in Africa. Finally, we beseech you to forgive us for daring to write such a letter to you important people whom we truly respect. Do not forget that it is to you that we must plead the weakness of our strength in Africa.

Written by two Guinean children,
Yaguine Koita and Fode Tounkara

In Ferguson's analysis, which regards the letter as an event, the letter operates as a rhetorical device that occasions the anthropologist to reflect on the role of ethnography and the history of the discipline. This letter is not used to delve into the biographical contours of Yaguine and Fode's lives in Guinea, as Garcia does with Bernadette and Eugenia. Instead, the letter begs the reader to reflect on his or her own subject position in relation to the research being conducted. "There is a specific sort of embarrassment, as well as a stark horror, in reading this letter," Ferguson writes. "It is the embarrassment of encountering Africans—in this ostensibly postcolonial era—who humbly beg Europeans to come to their aid and who bluntly ask for help 'to become like you.'"

In this case, the "embarrassment" provoked by the letter is connected to the broader discomfort felt by ethnographers conducting fieldwork in Africa. In response to this letter, for example, Ferguson asks, how does the ethnographer respond to Africans with "passionate appeals for salvation" when the ethnographer in question is there precisely to develop his anticolonial convictions into a strident scholarly critique?[7]

Like Ferguson, I address the discomforts that are part of the research process. But my approach differs in that I incorporate the subjects of the study into this process. Even when people are deceased like Yaguine and Fode, I use what I know about their lives to pose questions to them and speculate about how they might have responded. I also interview and conduct focus groups with people in similar circumstances. This allows me to make meaning out of their lives, even in death.

In this way, my work highlights the "socially produced nature of the 'field' itself," as I seek to unsettle common conceptions of the role of the ethnographer and the practice of ethnography.[8] The people whom I address in my letters always emerge from the context of my research; thus, as I convey key findings and insights that bear some relationship to their identity, social status, and their occupation, I also demonstrate the stakes they have in the problem of police violence. In the process, I cannot help but reveal the stakes I have in this issue as well.

Throughout the book, I advocate for the end of police torture. Letter writing forced me out of the typical, discipline-imposed shell of objectivity, making me account for myself as a speaking person, a person who helped fashion and develop a set of ideas that sometimes demanded a reply.[9]

A Third Way

I would like to suggest a third way of using the power of the letter ethnographically that differs from these two dominant approaches. But first let me say that I share a lot in common with these two modes of thinking and practice. Scholars who have adopted both the archival approach (which illuminates ethnographic evidence) and the letter-as-event approach (which illuminates ethnographic events) would likely agree (as I do) with philosophers like Roland Barthes that the sentimental value of the letter resides in its capacity to "prick" and "bruise" a person's senses; and with Jacques Derrida, that letters, as a type of correspondence, raise basic questions about the author of the letter, about the addressee, about the message being sent, and about where that message will ultimately be delivered.[10] Yet in these traditions, letters serve primarily as objects of analysis. What letters are not, in these two traditions, are embodiments of exchange that place the onus of analysis on the ethnographer as well as research participants. In this book, this onus of analysis is imperative from the beginning to the end of my work with Chicago residents.

Because the archival tradition often depends on the academic's status as an insider, and because the tradition of regarding the letter as an event highlights one's outsider status, the two sides of this ethnographic coin often conflict with one another. The method that I describe, however, cracks open this opposition. I have done so by viewing the letter in another way: as a mode of ethnographic writing and research methodology that sheds light on the perspectives of both the insider and the outsider.

Although I have lived in Chicago in the past, I do not live there now—nor was I born or raised there. Despite my long-standing relationships with people who live there and my intimate knowledge of certain neighborhoods, I am unequivocally an outsider. Yet the content of each of my letters is the result of interviews and group discussions with insiders, specifically Chicago residents who have stakes in addressing the problem of police violence. In my exchanges with them, we discussed who these letters should address, the information that should be contained in them, and how their own experiences play a role in shaping the message that was ultimately conveyed. As a result, my outsider perspective became more nuanced through and by the research process.

My methodology is indebted to, but differs slightly from, a lesser-known approach to letter writing, which focuses on purposeful exchanges with interlocutors in the field. Here I am referring to James Smith and Ngeti Mwadime's experimental venture in ethnography, *Email from Ngeti*.[11] Reading this book, which is largely told through email between Smith and Mwadime, the reader is struck by how the co-constructed narrative highlights the different life trajectories of the two authors. For Smith, Ngeti Mwadime is an exemplar of a young generation of Africans navigating the multiplicity of contemporary life on the continent—a process that is affected by the globalized reach of Hollywood, international demand for natural resources like coltan, and the internet. Keenly aware of the world outside Kenya,

"Ngeti dreams big," Smith tells us, "with endless plans for striking it rich." Depicting Mwadime's struggles to free himself from a constricting environment, *Email from Negeti* uses letter writing to think through the co-constitutive nature of ethnographic fieldwork and illustrates how exchanging forms of writing with research collaborators can produce new possibilities both for methodological practices and for the research that results.

Although my approach is influenced by Smith and Mwadime's work, there are some important distinctions to make. This approach takes the idea of exchange quite literally. Exchange refers almost exclusively to the act of sending and receiving email. As I have written to a host of dead people, others who had no interest in responding to me, and to another group who did respond but whose responses are not included in this book, my idea of exchange is much more expansive than Smith and Mwadime's approach.

For me, the exchange process refers to sharing information from the archive (such as historical records, documents, and reports) with my interlocutors. They, in turn, shared their personal experiences with the police and their thoughts about what it would take for society to change.

This brings me to another key distinction between my own and Smith and Mwadime's approach. Their work together depends on the intimate relationship they developed over many years. By contrast, my research scales up the exchange process, allowing many more people into the dialogue.

The method I have developed could be used for any topic. But two factors are crucial to its success: first, there must be a body of people invested in the social problem at hand; second, they must have some idea of an institution, organization, or person they want to reach out to. They may not ever actually reach out, the organization may be defunct, and the institution might not yet exist. Nevertheless, having a clear sense of purpose is an important aspect of letter writing.

Indeed, a letter of any kind—whether a Roman epistle or a contemporary email—shares two qualities: a sense of voice and a sense of purpose. Every letter contains a felt sense of who the author is and what the author wants—whether to declare love for another, to justify the invasion of a foreign country, or to solicit a donation for a political campaign. Thus, any use of the epistolary form, whether in a work of fiction or nonfiction, must follow these essential attributes.

My training as an ethnographer let me highlight the voices of my interlocutors as well as hone in on the sense of purpose they had in wanting to address particular people and groups. As ethnographers, we are uniquely positioned to mediate the concerns of research participants by placing those concerns within a broader conversation and situating them within a social and historical context. In my case, the conversation I facilitated with Chicago residents centered on local ideas concerning social justice. Ultimately, I decided to focus on this theme because, in adopting a stance that found solidarity with groups addressing documented and proven injustice, I also started to think of the purpose of my own research differently. I began to see my research interlocutors as theory makers in a multidimensional conversation that came out of the lettering process.

By intentionally creating circumstances that invite my interlocutors to analyze research material and to build theory with one another, I draw from various efforts at collaboration in the ethnographic tradition. This tradition is epitomized by Harvard's Chiapas Project and invoked in Rouch's notion of shared anthropology.[12] Though distinct, the Chiapas Project and Rouch's approach share a common origin: they both push back against the dominant Malinowskian ideal of the ethnographer. This popular trope is characterized by the "Euro-American, white, middle-class male" who embarks upon a heroic "journey into Otherness."[13]

In this project, I deconstruct the self-other divide to which Malinowski's paradigm is indebted, borrowing instead from a Boasian tradition that offers a radically different understanding of fieldwork. As Bunzl has written, Franz Boas's understanding of fieldwork "does not rest on a distinction between ethnographic Self and native Other but, instead, draws its analytic leverage from a rigorous historicity that refigures the question of Otherness in terms of temporal rather than cultural alterity."[14] Like Zora Neale Hurston and Ella Deloria, who also follow in the tradition that Bunzl cites, my own understanding of fieldwork is different from Malinowski's model in that I try to break down the barrier between my interlocutors and myself by thinking through social problems with them. We tried together to situate the use-of-force continuum within the contemporary moment to examine whether change is possible and to imagine what change would look like. In sum, we grapple with "temporal alterity" by exploring new possibilities against a backdrop in which police violence has long been a prominent feature of everyday life.

More specifically, by anchoring my project in an examination of how people live with police mistreatment, harassment, torture, and death—that is, the use-of-force continuum—we think together about what it would mean to address Chicago's youth of color who might face similar circumstances, or police officers who may actively ignore this violence, or police superintendents who oversee the perpetrators of this violence, or the future mayor of Chicago who plays a key role in funding the police department, or activists who are developing solutions to make their communities safer. By using my research to craft messages to people complicit in police violence and those fighting for redress, I explore the ways my interlocutors grapple with the history of police violence as my point of departure.[15]

Research Design

For this project I conducted ethnographic fieldwork in two stages: the research phase and the writing-as-research phase.

Phase 1: Research

The purpose of phase 1 was to document the history of the police torture cases. The initial phase of this study was typical of ethnographic fieldwork methods used in anthropology and sociology. Over the course of several years, I attended rallies and marches on police violence and community forums on the Chicago Police Department torture cases, conducting participant observation at such events. I reviewed the case files of known torture survivors, some of whom I had listened to at public rallies. I also scanned the city newspapers from 1982 to the present for articles mentioning police torture. I found approximately five hundred articles that were especially relevant to my study. Another large data set came from the Chicago Torture Archive at the University of Chicago. This was a nontraditional archive in the sense that it was maintained online, with links to thousands of legal documents pertaining to the Chicago torture cases that the People's Law Office had donated to the archive. I conducted discourse and content analysis of case files and affidavits, which were also contained in the Chicago Torture Archive. Additionally, I analyzed semistructured interviews, newspaper articles, and media reports contained in this archive. This amounted to coding and searching for thematic patterns in more than one thousand unique documents.

After I coded this material and had a sense of which documents were important to uncovering the scandal of police torture, I used these primary sources to structure interviews and group discussions with Chicago residents. (More on this to come).

As I began to sift through my interviews, newspaper articles, and media reports for quotes and other contextual information, I realized that the concerns expressed by Chicago residents addressed the multiple audiences whom they felt were responsible for maintaining the open secret of police torture, or alternatively, the people and groups they wanted to thank for exposing it. Sometimes these residents wanted to critique politicians; sometimes they wanted to express their gratitude to the survivors of police torture; other times they wanted to appeal to the activist community to learn how to more effectively organize.

Unlike my previous research on gang violence, in which Black Chicagoans expressed disdain about the way they had been portrayed in scholarly books, no one I spoke to mentioned scholars among the people they wanted to address. When I asked them about the role of scholarship, they told me that police torture was not an issue they needed help understanding. Evidencing their own expertise, many of them turned the question around, transforming me into the interviewee: "Now that you know about the open secret of police torture," they asked me in various ways, "what are you going to do about it?"

It was then that I decided that my research would not be aimed at an exclusively academic audience. Instead, I would address the multiple constituencies my research collaborators cared about and the issues that they identified as important for their community.

Phase 2: Writing-as-research

The purpose of Phase 2 was to explore the ways that Chicago residents were making sense of the history of police torture. To assess the impact of this history on everyday Chicagoans, as previously mentioned, I conducted both focus groups and interviews with three groups of interest: youth of color in Chicago, survivors of police torture and police violence, and other Chicago residents. The combination of focus groups and in-depth interviews allowed me to speak to more than one hundred residents in total (I discuss how I arrived at this number later on).

As opposed to interviews, focus groups had the added benefit of increased topic coverage as respondents in the group cued others about relevant concepts and reactions that made for a richer qualitative data set. Meanwhile, in-depth interviews allowed me to explore a narrower set of concepts and reactions in more depth with a select number of respondents.

To expand this experimental methodology, I began each interview and focus group by presenting participants with archival material. This material included, but was not limited to, court testimony from civil trials on police torture, letters from whistle-blowers contained in case files, police reports describing the interrogation of torture survivors, newspaper reports about the police torture scandal, activist testimony from UN proceedings on torture, and diary entries from torture survivors. My aim was to use this material to gauge my interlocutors' understanding of the scope of the problem. But I also wanted to gain a nuanced understanding of the impressions of the material that my interlocutors had. I was especially concerned with whether those impressions differed depending on the group to which they belonged.

. . .

To guide our discussion of archival material, as well as the broader conversation about police violence that blossomed out of this material, I developed a discussion protocol for each focus group. I created several different protocols, which changed depending on the focus group. The reason for this was that I had to be sensitive to different issues while discussing police violence with different populations. For example, with youth of color I discussed what their parents had told them about police violence and what they had learned in school about the topic.

What remained constant regardless of the population was that, through the protocols, I steered the conversation outward from the archival material to their own experiences and perspectives on police violence. The protocols were not rigid scripts. I allowed the conversation to flow naturally from the main points articulated in the archival material, then made sure that I followed up with additional probes to flesh out ideas that arose during the discussions.

I did not conduct focus groups with survivors of police violence and police torture. To do so, I decided, risked reviving trauma in a group setting that might still be affecting their daily lives. I preferred to talk to them one-on-one, so that I could constantly check in and see if they wanted to continue. I also wanted their personal experience of police violence to be the center of our discussion and not overshadowed by anyone else's story.

As with the focus group protocols, I created a separate in-depth interview protocol for each of the groups of interest. My interviews with the other groups followed up on focus group discussions. I interviewed different people than those who participated in the focus groups to ensure that the themes and conversations that had arisen were not unique to that particular group dynamic. I wanted to be sure that what we discussed during these sessions was an accurate reflection of the perceptions and experiences of people who belonged to a given group.

Recruitment

Recruitment for phase 2 of the research chiefly relied on recruiting in public spaces in Chicago. For each of the groups of interest, recruitment ended when I reached the point of saturation. In qualitative social science, *saturation* refers to the principle that further data collection is unnecessary because the ideas and themes have become so repetitive that they can be taken as an accurate reflection of a group's perspective as a whole. The question of when saturation is reached depends on the nature of the research being collected and the questions being asked. For example, in their study of data saturation, Greg Guest, Arwen Bruce, and Laura Johnson found that even though they conducted sixty interviews, they had reached saturation after twelve interviews, with most of the themes emergent after just six interviews.[16]

I analyzed data as I collected it for each group to determine the point of saturation. For each of the youth-of-color and citizen populations of interest, I conducted two focus groups, with each group having approximately eight to ten members. When I analyzed the data, the themes overlapped so much that I found a third focus group in either case to be unnecessary. I conducted in-depth interviews with members of each group, as well as with survivors of police torture and police violence. For all these groups, I was conservative in determining the point of saturation. Once I had felt that I reached saturation, I conducted two or three more interviews to be sure that the themes I had identified were truly consistent.

With that said, I recruited approximately thirty-five Chicago youth of color (between the ages of fourteen and eighteen years old) through a threefold approach. First, I placed posters in public places in Chicago that Black and Latino teens frequent, including Boys and Girls Club bulletin boards and recreation facilities in the city. I explored the possibility of recruiting directly from Chicago high schools, but significant administrative hurdles served as barriers to entry into Chicago Public Schools facilities. Additionally, I advertised on social media such as Craigslist. Finally, I used a snowball technique, asking participants if they had friends or others in their social networks who might want to participate in the research. If the participant did have friends who might be interested, I asked him or her to contact other potential participants on my behalf. During my recruitment I made sure that roughly half of the recruited participants were young men and the other half were young women.

I recruited twenty-six survivors of Chicago police violence and torture. To accomplish this, I relied on social media and flyers in locations that survivors of police violence and torture were known to visit. These included bulletin boards near legal-aid services and other social service agencies. Additionally, I relied on snowball recruiting to see whether participants knew other survivors who might be interested in participating in the research project. After eight months, I confirmed ten survivors of police torture who were willing to participate and ten survivors of police violence. I interviewed three more from each category to determine whether the themes they discussed were consistent enough for me to group them together for the purposes of this study as "survivors of police torture *and* police violence" rather than two separate groups. As it turns out, analyzing together the findings of these torture survivors and survivors of other kinds of police violence allowed me to see torture as my participants did: as a part of a broader, use-of-force continuum.

To recruit thirty-six Chicago residents from various backgrounds and professions, I likewise relied on social media and flyers placed in locations throughout the city. I also took advantage of events like City Council and ward meetings to recruit civically engaged Chicago residents to participate. The goal of my recruitment was to get a cross section of Chicago residents from different areas of the city with regard to age, race, and gender. Half the residents in this group were men and half were women. Their ages ranged from eighteen to fifty-one years old. As mentioned, they came from diverse racial and ethnic backgrounds. They also resided in a variety of geographical areas in the city.

Deepening the Method

In addition to using letters to center my discussions with Chicago residents, I ended each focus group session by sharing two excerpts from letters I had written. One excerpt was from my letter to the future superintendent of the Chicago Police Department. The other was from the letter I had written to Chicago youth of color. A focus group session in the summer of 2017 exemplifies how the craft of lettering can deepen traditional social scientific methods.

During this session, one of the people who consistently voiced his opinion was Will, a librarian. He suggested that I change the scope of my address from "Chicago Public School students" to "African American high-school-aged youth in Chicago" because my message seemed to be especially targeted to them and because he regarded the "public school" designation as limiting. He told me that he encountered a number of high school dropouts in the library who were brilliant but had a difficult time with formal education.

"They would also welcome such a letter and should not be excluded," he said.

Likewise, during my first focus group with Black youth, they insisted that I needed to include Latino teenagers because they were "in the same boat." I expanded my focus group and interview pool to include them, which ultimately led me to address my letter to "Chicago youth of color."

What's more, after one focus group session, several Black and Latino youth pointed to a passage that Will had also said was confusing and unclear. Here it is:

I know that many well-intentioned adults have told you to avoid the people on the so-called wrong path out of fear that, by virtue of any association with them, you might commit some hideous and irreversible act (or be the victim of such an act). I know that adults in your life have made it seem like your success in life, perhaps even your life itself, depends on your completely turning your back on certain peers and shutting your ears to them. But I am here to say that the experiences of the very same people that your teachers and your parents are telling you to shun can offer you valuable lessons—lessons that are no less valuable just because these people have landed in trouble. In fact, their lessons quite possibly couldn't have been formed without the trouble they've encountered.

In response to this passage, one teenage girl named Patrice wrote the word *vague* in the margins of her copy of the letter. "Aren't you just saying that we have more to learn from our 'bad' friends than 'do not emulate' them?" she asked in the context of a focus group. As it turned out, that was precisely what I had wanted to convey.

However, the feedback on the letters in the context of focus groups should not be mistaken for simple editorial suggestions. Rather, such commentary was a key component of theory making, helping me refine my arguments and analysis. As academics, we seldom talk about the substantial feedback we receive from others, usually while teaching or sharing our work in public lectures, as we rarely consider our teaching or public presentations part of our methodology. Yet these opportunities to present and share ideas teach academics which examples work best in relationship to their arguments and urge them to develop the theories most pertinent to their analyses.

While conducting research for this project, I shared the same versions of my letters with academic audiences that I did with focus group participants. No one in the academic settings where I presented my work took issue with the ethical implications of my prose, or expressed concern that I was not getting to the point quickly enough, or that my categories of analysis were too narrow. I have no doubt that without thinking about writing as part and parcel of the research process I would have produced a text that satisfied an academic audience. But I am equally confident that the people I was writing about would have found that text problematic on many fronts.

One reason academic research is commonly criticized in Chicago has to do with the city's status as a hub for research on urban poverty. Black Chicagoans are especially weary of how they are represented in academic texts. In my experience, Black people living in the city recognize the potential benefit of research in its ability to create interventions that can improve their communities, yet they dislike how their city has historically been portrayed as pathological. The issue has to do with voyeurism, how an audience outside of Chicago may interpret low-income communities as exotic and "dangerous." Ethnographic lettering works to displace the gaze of the voyeur by addressing people and groups that are implicated in the problem of police violence. This shift in audience and voice addressed many of the concerns around exoticism that my interlocutors originally had. In this regard, my project extends the work of feminists of color like Faye Harrison and Linda Tuhiwai Smith who have advanced "decolonizing methodologies," which expose the ways academic research has been implicated in imperialist projects.[17]

Drawing from critical ethnographic methodologies, my approach opened up a space to think about ethnography as a series of purposeful exchanges in writing. It is not "of and about peoples," but "with and for the people who are its subjects," a future in ethnography that Michael Fischer pushes us toward.[18] Ethnographic lettering thus has the potential to galvanize people into action in ways that other approaches to letter writing do not because the anthropologist, out of necessity, becomes part of the material he or she is writing about, and also because the form invites a response. I also suspect that by flattening the distinction between the anthropologist and the subject he or she is studying, this approach has the potential to be more fundamentally egalitarian than other modes of inquiry and discourse in the discipline. But I am still in the early stages of this experiment. Only time will tell.

Acknowledgments

I want to express my sincerest gratitude to everyone in Chicago who was gracious enough to spend time with me and share their thoughts. I learned countless lessons from you all; and hopefully I have successfully conveyed at least some of them to the wider public. I especially want to thank those who have experienced police violence and those who have been tortured by the police for being willing to revisit those harrowing experiences in the hopes that you could contribute to addressing this problem. I am also grateful to those who have never experienced police violence, but nevertheless had ideas about how this issue impacted their lives and communities. I would also like to thank NORC at the University of Chicago for providing space and resources for me to conduct interviews and focus groups. I owe a debt of gratitude, in this regard, to Vince Welch, Nella Coleman, and Erin Fordyce for your support and dedication to this project.

During the research process I thought long and hard about how to represent the experience of torture. Some key representations were borrowed from popular culture. Given this, I would like to thank the Edward B. Marks Music Company (BMI) and Hal Leonard LLC for allowing me to reprint the lyrics to the song Billie Holiday made famous, "Strange Fruit."[1]

1. Strange Fruit. Words and Music By Lewis Allan. Copyright ©1939 (Renewed) by Music Sales Corporation. All Rights outside the United States Controlled by Edward B. Marks

Much of this research was conducted during my time at Harvard University from 2011 to 2018. I would like to thank my former colleagues in the Department of Anthropology for your support. I owe a great deal of thanks to Anya Bernstein, Ted Bestor, Davíd Carrasco, Steve Caton, Rowan Flad, Byron Good, Nicholas Harkness, Ieva Jusionyte, Arthur Kleinman, Matthew Liebmann, George Paul Meiu, Ajantha Subramanian, Jason Ur, and Gary Urton. A special thanks is due to Jean and John Comaroff who read sections of this book early on, when I was still struggling with how to theorize the concept of ethnographic lettering. You have given me unwavering support from the time I first met you as a graduate student at the University of Chicago, until this day. I am very grateful to have you both as mentors.

I would also like to thank my former colleagues in the Department of African and African Americans Studies at Harvard, especially Vincent Brown, Marla Frederick, Alejandro de la Fuente, Claudine Gay, Evelyn Higginbotham, Elizabeth Hinton, Jamaica Kincaid, Michèle Lamont, Sarah Lewis, Ingrid Monson, Marcyliena Morgan, John Mugane, Jacob Olopona, Tommie Shelby, Kay Shelemay, James Sidanius, Doris Sommer, Brandon Terry, Cornel West, David Williams, and William Julius Wilson, who was a great mentor during my time at Harvard. I owe a special thanks to Larry Bobo and Henry Louis Gates Jr. for all of the sage advice you have given me throughout the years.

A number of fellowships allowed me to carry out this research and afforded me the time and space to develop this project. While I was at Harvard, the Edmond J. Safra Center for Ethics and its tireless director, Danielle Allen, provided material support for my policing research. I cannot thank you enough, Danielle. In 2015, I also received the Andrew Carnegie Fellowship from the Carnegie Corporation of New York. It was an honor to be among the inaugural class of recipients. Thank you. Finally, a research fellowship at the Radcliffe Institute for Advanced Study from 2015 to 2016 was instrumental in bringing this project to completion. While at the Radcliffe Institute,

I met a wonderful group of scholars. I am grateful to now call them my friends. Thank you Joyce Bell, Ayesha Chaudhry, Ross Gay, Kris Manjapra, Alyssa Mt. Pleasant, Lesley Sharp, and Reiko Yamada. I am especially grateful to Kristiana Kahakauwila for reading an early draft of this book and providing a wonderful set of comments.

To my friends—Kerry Chance, Eve Ewing, Peniel Joseph, Amy Moran-Thomas, and Karla Slocum—thank you for investing time and energy into engaging my work and offering your thoughts, conversations, and critical feedback. I am especially grateful for Lucas Bessire, who has probably seen more versions of this book than anyone else. The arguments of this book were also strengthened from giving invited lectures at a host of different universities. I am grateful for invitations to participate in seminars and colloquia where chapters or sections of the book were first drafted and critiqued, including anthropology colloquia at Cornell University in August of 2016, the University of North Carolina in September of 2016, New York University in October of 2016, Columbia University in December of 2016, Northwestern University in October of 2017, and Bard College in November of 2017.

I have been most fortunate to work with Priya Nelson at the University of Chicago Press, and I am thankful for her support. I am grateful to the book's anonymous reviewers for their comments and suggestions, which helped immensely. I also want to thank Thomas Andes, David Lobenstine, and Beth Rashaum for reading my work and offering careful and generous feedback.

As I was finishing this book project, I relocated from Harvard to Princeton University. I am thankful for the conviviality and intellectual community of Princeton's Department of Anthropology. I thank my colleagues John Borneman, Elizabeth Davis, Julia Elyachar, Carol Greenhouse, Rena Lederman, Ryo Morimoto, Serguei Oushakine, Lauren Coyle Rosen, and Carolyn Rouse. I especially want to thank João Biehl for being an enthusiastic supporter of my work ever since we first met at the Institute for Advanced Study in 2012.

I would be remiss if I didn't thank my family for being my biggest group of supporters. Thank you, Michael Ralph Sr., Lynette Ralph,

Wolé Ralph, and especially Michael Ralph Jr. for always being there to listen and encourage my ideas as this project developed. My family expanded over the course of writing this book. I got married in 2017, and we had a child—my two greatest achievements in life so far. To the love of my life, Aisha Beliso–De Jesus, thank you for understanding the sense of urgency I needed to cling to while writing this book. Thank you, as well, for your emotional support, for your encouragement, and most of all, for your love. And finally, to Amina De Jesus–Ralph, thank you for expanding your daddy's heart beyond the bounds of possibility.

Notes

1. In this book, when I refer to the number of torture survivors, I use the estimate of approximately 125, which is clearly conservative, as it refers only to documented and proven Burge-related cases. Nevertheless, by restricting myself to the cases from Area 2 between the years I mention, I hope to shed light on the epidemic as a whole.

2. Area 2 is both the name of a detective headquarters (a building) and a geographical location that covers a certain number of neighborhoods on the South Side of Chicago. In the 1980s, when most of the events I describe take place, the city of Chicago was broken down into six detective "Areas." However, when I refer to "Area 2" in this book I am most often referencing the detective headquarters (the building) rather than the boundaries of a district. Although Chicago's police stations are referenced as "districts," this parlance is unique to Chicago. So in this book I often refer to Chicago's "districts" and "areas" as "precincts" or "police stations" for the sake of clarity.

3. For more information on the Illinois Torture Inquiry and Relief Commission and its expanded role in recent years, see Duaa Eldeib's "Torture Claims No Longer Limited to Burge, Chicago Police," *Chicago Tribune*, October 6, 2016, http://www.chicagotribune.com/news/ct-illinois-torture-commission-beyond-burge-met-20161006-story.html.

4. Women have also been tortured. Although Flint Taylor, the lawyer who tried most of the cases involving police torture, has hard evidence of only a single case involving a woman named Doris Miller, over the years, he believes that other women were victimized. At one point he received a series of calls from an anonymous cop who told him the following: "I thought it was OK to torture guilty guys. I thought

it just had to be done. But when we started torturing innocent people and *women*, that's when I realized we were doing something really, really wrong."

5. To understand the nature of the open secret, it is helpful to examine the role of secrecy in society, more generally. In his groundbreaking *The Secret and the Secret Society*, Georg Simmel (1950, 312) tells us that secrecy is linked to the lies people tell. It is grounded in concealment, which is at the root of all social interactions, affecting individuals' decisions to share knowledge and receive it back in return. In the context of the secret societies that Simmel studied, he found that people wanted to conceal information. Doing so allowed for them to retain power, to boast about misconduct while evading sanction. Ultimately, secrecy worked to ensure group cohesion and to enable certain groups and organizations to maintain power and control in society.

The paradoxical nature of all secrets is that they depend on the members of society's ability to keep information confidential, but the open secret differs in that it can be widely known but is not articulated. Although I refer to the "widely known" character of these secrets as "open" (because that's how people in Chicago describe them), within the scholarly literature these kind of secrets are most often referred to as "public secrets." Most of the academic literature on the public secret is rooted in Elias Canetti's (1984, 295) work, which notes that "a large part of the prestige of dictatorships is due to the fact that they are credited with the concentrated power of secrecy." The anthropologist Michael Taussig (1997) famously extends Canetti's argument, noting that the act of revealing a familiar public secret is often accompanied by a fall from grace, because such revelations are not considered socially acceptable. As a result, people develop elaborate ways of pretending not to know what they do know. Consider, for example, a staffer who is aware that her boss, a politician, is involved in a scandal that could cost him the election. Many of the other staffers may also be aware of the scandal, but they all know that to reveal the scandal would cost them their jobs. Anthropologists who study public secrecy are often interested in the ways people are expected to live and work in situations that obligate them to maintain secrets. The obligatory nature of the secret makes it such that, in this example, staffers' life and work begins to revolve around the information they know, do not want to know, and are actively avoiding acquiring any more knowledge of. It is important to note that a scholar of public secrecy who is studying the campaign in this example may not be interested merely in the nature of the scandal and whether it causes the politician to lose the election. More interesting is how the scandal shapes the culture of this campaign and sustains and exacerbates some of the power relations among the staff (see Geissler 2013). In this way, public secrecy revolves around power and dominance. As a consequence, people in vulnerable positions protect those who provide them with material resources, which is another way of saying that public secrecy involves substantial risks. For this reason, scholarship on public secrecy raises questions such as "How do people come to live with impunity?" and "How [do] people 'remoralize' their social worlds following lengthy periods of intimate violence?" (Theidon 2006, 98). This is also why, as Jones (2014) notes, public secrecy has been of interest to scholars studying violence and historical injustices (Geissler 2013; Mookherjee 2006; Penglase 2009; Roy 2008; Theidon 2006; Thomas 2017).

6. For more on the link between Blackness and criminality, see Muhammad (2011); Hinton (2016); and Alexander (2012).

7. An example of this kind of thinking is evident in torture survivor Madison Hobley's case. After his wife and infant son died in a fire, the police held Hobley responsible. Despite a paucity of evidence and a coerced confession after being tortured, Hobley was convicted and sentenced to death in 1987. He served sixteen years until, after many hearings, on January 9, 2003, he received a pardon from then governor of Illinois George Ryan. During the investigation into the death of Hobley's wife and child, the police officer interrogating him, Robert Dwyer, admitted that he had doubts about Hobley's guilt. "Between you and me," Dwyer told Hobley, "I don't know if you're the one we're looking for." But that fact mattered little to the detective: "We have you in custody, so I guess you'll be the nigger that did it today." For more information on Hobley's arrest and the testimony of police officers in his conviction, see *People v. Hobley*, 637 N.E.2d 992 (Ill. 1994).

8. Later in the book I discuss the context in which millions of dollars have been given to victims of police violence in recent years.

9. On the debilitating effects of state violence, see Puar (2017).

10. For the full context of Judge Joan Lefkow's statement about how torture damages the criminal justice system, see *United States v. Burge*, No. 08 CR 846 (Ill. 2011).

11. For more on the history of lynching, see Mitchell (2011).

12. See Sánchez-Eppler (1993).

13. See the Chicago Police Department's 2017 Use of Force Policy, available at http://home.chicagopolice.org/wp-content/uploads/2017/05/G03-02_Use-of-Force_TBD.pdf. As of December 2018, the 2017 Use of Force Policy is the latest the department has on record.

14. For the full quotation on deadly force, see the Chicago Police Department's Use of Force Policy. In addition, for an in-depth analysis of use-of-force policies across the United States, see DeRay McKesson, Samuel Sinyangwe, Johnetta Elzie, and Brittany Packnett, "Police Use of Force Policy Analysis," *Campaign Zero*, September 20, 2016, https://static1.squarespace.com/static/56996151cbced68b170389f4/t/57e1b5cc2994ca4ac1d97700/1474409936835/Police+Use+of+Force+Report.pdf.

INTRODUCTION

1. See Andrew Schroedter's article "Fatal Shootings by Chicago Police: Tops among Biggest U.S. Cities," Better *Government Association*, July 26, 2015, https://www.bettergov.org/news/fatal-shootings-by-chicago-police-tops-among-biggest-us-cities.

2. See Crimesider Staff, "How Chicago Racked Up a $662 Million Police Misconduct Bill," *CBS News*, March 21, 2016, https://www.cbsnews.com/news/how-chicago -racked-up-a-662-million-police-misconduct-bill/.

3. Hamaji et al. (2017, 60).

4. On restricted versus discretionary funds, every city and county has multiple individual funds within its budget, each of which generates revenue from specific sources and most of which have restrictions on use. Individual funds are created by laws, grant requirements, or decisions made by the governing body. A restricted fund is often limited for specific uses and must be reported separately to demonstrate compliance. All funds that are not restricted are accounted for in the "general fund." The general fund is primarily funded by property taxes and is the most flexible, discretionary fund. Whether restricted by legislation or allocated through the discretion of city council, each fund reflects city priorities and commitments.

5. Hamaji et al. (2017).

6. Fisher and Reese (2011); and Daly (2002).

7. Hamaji et al. (2017), 25.

8. These figures are projected from a 2007 City Council Finance Committee hearing at which several aldermen requested that a statistical expert project the range of exposure in attorney's fees, costs, and judgments for which the city could be liable in the five pending torture cases. Upon release of the report, on September 25, 2007, the *Chicago Sun-Times* ran an editorial titled "Stop the Financial Torture: Settle the Burge Lawsuits Now."

9. For the symbiotic relationship between police and military, see Balko (2013); Brodeur (2010); Kraska (2007); and Rahr et al. (2015)

10. In this study I use pseudonyms to protect the identities of participants in focus groups and interviews. The statements and the contexts described, however, are real.

PART ONE

1. For an important scholarly discussion of reparations that inspired Coates's work, see William Darity Jr., "Forty Acres and a Mule in the 21st Century," *Social Science Quarterly* 89, no. 3 (2008): 656–64.

2. The complaints about the dragnet are documented in the 1990 Office of Professional Standards report. See also Sanders (1990).

3. For details of Wilson's arrest and interrogation, see Conroy (2000) and Sanders (1990). See also *State of Illinois v. Andrew and Jackie Wilson,* Indictment No. 82-1211, Charge: Murder, etc. (November 12, 1982).

4. For the long-term effects of Wilson's torture, see John Conroy, "The Persistence of Andrew Wilson," *Chicago Reader*, November 29, 2007.

5. In preparing this letter, I investigated Burge's military career, finding that he

enlisted in the army in 1966 and quickly rose through the ranks to attain the position of staff sergeant. Immediately hailed as a promising cadet, Burge served time as a drill instructor and attended military police school at Fort Benning. His superiors, impressed with his performance, sent him to Korea and then Vietnam, and he served as military police in both places. Burge was twice awarded the army commendation for valor, both times for leaving a bunker to drag wounded men to safety in the midst of incoming fire. He was also given the Bronze Star for meritorious service, the Vietnamese Cross of Gallantry, and a Purple Heart. In 1969, Burge took an honorable discharge after suffering an injury on the battlefield. A year later, at the age of twenty-two, he joined the Chicago Police Department. Soon after, he subsequently became a lieutenant in charge of the Violent Crimes Unit at Area 2, where he would introduce to detectives devices that "helped along" confessions. For more information on Burge's biography and military career, see Conroy (2000).

6. On the role of John Yucaitis, see *State of Illinois v. Andrew and Jackie Wilson* (November 12, 1982).

7. The details of Wilson's hospital visit, including testimony from hospital workers and doctors, are detailed in Sanders (1990).

8. Here I am referencing Hortense Spillers's concept of hieroglyphics of the flesh, those hidden messages that obscure social inequality because of society's collective preoccupation with Western man. While the Italian philosopher Giorgio Agamben distinguishes a legally recognized life from a disposable, "bare life," Spillers distinguishes a legally recognized personhood (which she calls a "body") from someone who is considered not quite human. Because the state does not recognize this being as belonging to a political body, what justifies the being's deprivation is the nature of his or her "flesh." If the body represents legal personhood, the flesh designates a deprived social being upon which state violence is enacted. Yet the flesh is different from Agamben's idea of bare life because "racializing assemblages" are inscribed on the skin. These assemblages consist of state institutions that produce social and political differences that masquerade as biological and thus natural distinctions. For more on Spillers's notion of the flesh, see Spillers (1987).

9. For more on the concept of the black box, see Bateson (2012): 313.

10. *Merriam-Webster's 11th Collegiate Dictionary*, s.v. "black box," http://unabridged .merriam-webster.com/collegiate/black%20box.

11. For more details on the Gettleman ruling and Burge's firing, see Conroy (2001, 235).

PART TWO

1. For the present-day corruption in the criminal court system, see Van Cleve (2016).

2. It is important to note that Jon Burge referred to his elite unit by other names in addition to "the A-Team," such as the "Mission Team" or the "Midnight Shift."

3. For this quote, see Joan Lefkow's ruling in *United States v. Burge*, No. 08 CR 846 (Ill. 2011).

4. See Mary Ann Ahern, "Former Chicago Police Supt.: Code of Silence 'Has Always Existed,'" *NBC Chicago*, March 3, 2016, https://www.nbcchicago.com /blogs/ward-room/Former-Chicago-Police-Supt-Code-of-Silence-Has-Always -Existed--370994101.html.

5. The events and descriptions detailed in this section are from a letter William Parker submitted to Flint Taylor, the lead attorney on many of the torture cases. Statement of William Parker on Oct. 12, 2004, *Patterson v. Burge*, 328 F. Supp. 2d 878 (N.D. Ill. 2004) (No. 03 C 4433).

6. Statement of William Parker, 7–16.

7. Statement of William Parker, 7–12, 16–17.

8. Before I decided to make all the letters in this book open letters, I did attempt to send some of the letters to the people they were addressed to. But even in those rare cases where people received and read the letters I had written to them, no one has read the final version of these open letters as they are written now. For more on the letter-writing process, see the appendix.

9. A postconviction case refers to a legal process that takes place after someone has been convicted of a crime. In this case, Aaron Patterson challenged his murder conviction on the grounds that he was tortured, arguing that John Byrne was among the police officers involved in his unlawful detention. For more on the deposition of John Byrne in *People v. Patterson* (March 1, 2001), see Report on the Failure of Special Prosecutors Edward J. Egan and Robert D. Boyle to Fairly Investigate Systemic Police Torture in Chicago (April 24, 2007).

10. On the racism Lacey faced, see Statement of Sammy Lacey on October 12, 2004, *Patterson v. Burge*, 328 F. Supp. 2d 878 (N.D. Ill. 2004) (No. 03 C 4433).

11. Jodi Rudoren, "Report on Chicago Police Torture Is Released," *New York Times*, July, 19, 2006.

13. It is important to note that Biebel has denied that Egan ever informed him that his nephew worked under Burge. This conflict of interest gained attention after the special prosecutors' report was issued, when the *Chicago Sun-Times* broke the story on August 6, 2006. The news outlet informed the public that Egan was the uncle of a violent crimes detective, William Egan, who had worked under Burge at Area 2 from 1982 to 1986. The *Sun-Times* also wrote about the long history of Edward Egan's family on the police force. More important, for our purposes, the paper wrote that Area 2 Detective Egan had participated with Burge and another officer in the 1983 arrest of torture victim Gregory Banks. The major conflict of interest came from the fact that the special prosecutors investigated this case, with no criminal charges being pursued.

13. Opinion and Order of Judge Joan H. Lefkow, *United States v. Jon Burge* (N.D. Ill. 2011) (No. 08 CR 846).

PART THREE

1. This event was also recorded and can be seen on YouTube: "We Charge Genocide Reports on Chicago Police-Part 1," video, 11:19, posted by Kevin Gosztola on October 22, 2014, http:// https://www.youtube.com/watch?v=qn-bMbNaWX0.

2. See Nixon (2011).

3. For more information on the interview, see Frank Green, "A Year of History: Martinsville Seven Executions Remain 'A Raw Wound' for Many," *Richmond (VA) Times Dispatch*, February 6, 2011.

4. Mariame Kaba, "We Do This for Damo . . . ," *Prison Culture* (blog), May 20, 2015, http://www.usprisonculture.com/blog/2015/05/20/we-do-this-for-damo/.

5. Mariame Kaba, "We Do This for Damo," *Prison Culture* (blog), May 20, 2015, http://www.usprisonculture.com/blog/2015/05/20/we-do-this-for-damo/.

6. See also Simpson (2007).

7. Patterson was ordered to surrender his passport at the US embassy in France. When he refused, US agents said they would seize it at his hotel room. Patterson fled to Budapest, where through the newspaper *Szabad Nép,* he accused the US government of attempting to stifle his voice by prohibiting his travel and hence his ability to engage in international activism. The US government ordered Patterson to be detained when he passed through Britain and seized his passport when he returned to the United States. "W. L. Patterson Says U.S. Bars Him at U.N.," *New York Times,* January 1, 1952, 10; and "U.S. 'Muzzle' on Genocide Charge Alleged," *Washington Post*, January 1, 1952, 2.

8. I am referring to what happened after the verdicts of the Black men accused of rape. All the families of the Martinsville Seven, except for the Graysons, retained attorneys from the National Association for the Advancement of Colored People (NAACP) to adjudicate the appeals process. Even though most agreed that the NAACP was the right choice, the Graysons had faith in William Patterson and the Civil Rights Congress. But because the lawyers from the NAACP feared that involvement by the Civil Rights Congress could endanger the defendants, they pressured Francis Grayson to abandon Patterson because the organization had heavy communist leanings. Thurgood Marshall, chief counsel for the NAACP, personally informed Francis Grayson that unless the Civil Rights Congress relinquished the retainer the Grayson family gave them, the NAACP would completely withdraw from all cases. The Civil Rights Congress returned the money, stating that they did so in "the interests of the other men whose lives would be jeopardized" by their presence. For more information on what happened, see "NAACP Leaders Are Asked for Joint Drive by CRC to Save 'Martinsville 7,'" *Arkansas State Press* (Little Rock), June 16, 1950.

9. The Convention against Torture reads: "Under article 19 of the Convention against Torture, the Committee against Torture (CAT) is mandated to examine reports on the measures that State parties are taking to implement the provisions of the Convention" (in Schulberg 2014).

10. On April 12, 2015, Baltimore police officers arrested Freddie Gray and placed him in a police van. Gray emerged from the van severely injured and in a coma. He died three days later. Gray's death was followed by a series of peaceful protests, but on the day of his funeral, April 27, the city erupted in what the national media called "riots," with Maryland's governor declaring a state of emergency, installing a curfew, and calling in the National Guard. All six police officers involved in Gray's arrest were eventually acquitted of all charges.

11. On May 2012, thirty-one-year-old Marissa Alexander was prosecuted for aggravated assault with a deadly weapon and received a twenty-year prison sentence for firing a warning shot in her own home. Alexander said that she fired the shot after her husband attacked her and threatened to kill her. The case has gained some public recognition because of comparisons made to the widely covered case of George Zimmerman, who was prosecuted for fatally shooting Trayvon Martin. Both cases were prosecuted by the same Florida state prosecutor, Angela Corey. Alexander, a Black woman, was sentenced to decades in prison for firing a warning shot; Zimmerman, a white man, was acquitted for pursuing and then killing an unarmed Black teenager. Many argued that the sentencing revealed the disproportionate forms of punishment African Americans face today. In part because of the protests surrounding Alexander's story, she was eventually granted a new trial. She was released from prison on January 27, 2015, under a plea deal that capped her sentence at the three years she had already served.

12. For more on Black maternal grief, see Ralph (2015) and Smith (2016).

13. I mean to point out that, as justification for stop-and-frisks, it is common for police officers to claim that someone told them they were doing something illegal; that is, someone says to the officer, "I have weed in my pocket." Incriminating oneself in this way justifies a search. However, many Black Chicagoans claim that the police have been known to lie, and that when they do not incriminate themselves, police still search them and claim they have done so. In a court of law, they lose this argument every time because the judge always takes the police officer's word over a criminal suspect's.

14. Police Accountability Task Force, "What Is the Task Force," https://chicagopatf .org/about/what-is-police-accountability-task-force/.

15. In tracing the history of police formation to legacies of colonialism and slavery, Seigel (2017) argues that "state racism leaves no hope for successful reform," but demands a commitment to police abolition. However, in Chicago I find a practical and thoughtful commitment to police abolition that also grapples with strategic reform to make everyday life tolerable for people who have to navigate the city under the persistent threat of police violence. Former members of We Charge Genocide, for example, are among the most vocal leaders of the police and prison abolition movement in the city. Improving the conditions that make life livable all while attempting to imagine a world that does not yet exist is a key challenge for police and prison abolitionists, as Angela Davis and Dylan Rodriguez (2000) point out.

16. For more information, see Coates (2015).

17. For the full transcript of the opposition, see the No Cop Academy website, at http://www.nocopacademy.com. See also Laura Rodriguez, "Chicago Youth Stage 'Die-In' at City Hall to Demand Defunding of $95 Mil Cop Academy, More Community Resources," *Chicago Tribune*, March 28, 2018.

PART FOUR

1. For Zuley's recruitment to Guantánamo, see Ackerman (2015); and Linnemann (2018).

2. For more on Rumsfeld and "enhanced interrogation," see Gallagher (2009); Johnson (2016, 121); and Smeulers and Van Niekerk (2009).

3. For more on this scandal, see Lewis (2005); and Danner and Fay (2004).

4. For the quote, see American Civil Liberties Union, "*Slahi v. Obama*—Habeas Challenge to Guantánamo Detention," October 25, 2016, http://www.aclu.org/cases/slahi-v-obama-habeas-challenge-guantanamo-detention.

5. Slahi (2015). For more on the nature of the redactions themselves, see Goyal (2017); Trapp (2016); and Moore (2016).

6. Slahi (2015).

7. Rasmussen (2009).

8. Ackerman (2015).

9. The quotes here from Boyd are from Spencer Ackerman's (2015) article.

10. The quotes mentioned here referring to Zuley as a "bad apple" also frame the discussion of Slahi's torture in Spencer Ackerman's (2015) article.

11. Ackerman (2015).

12. I was unable to find the exact broadcast that Mohamedou referenced in his letter to me. But his account of Clinton's stance on Chen Guangcheng is compatible with various media reports. See, for example, the BBC article from October 18, 2003, titled "Hillary Clinton: Chen Guangcheng Crisis 'Touch-and-Go,'" at http://www.bbc.com/news/world-asia-china-24577038.

13. See Sidanius and Pratto (2001).

14. This Baldwin quote is from the historic debate between James Baldwin and William F. Buckley Jr. at Cambridge University on this question: "Is the American dream at the expense of the American Negro?" Video of the debate is available at https://www.youtube.com/watch?v=oFeoS41xe7w&t=1621s. Published on October 27, 2012 by The Riverbends Channel, 58:57.

15. For coverage of the Republican endorsement of torture during the Republican Party primary debate, see Zack Beauchamp's February 10, 2016, article in Vox, "Why Republicans Are Debating Bringing Back Torture," at http://www.vox.com/2016/2/10/10961760/trump-rubio-torture. See also Tessa Berenson, "Donald Trump Defends Torture at Republican Debate," *Time*, March 4, 2016, http://www.time.com/4247397/donald-trump-waterboarding-torture/.

16. On the states secrets privilege, see Zagel (1965, 875); Frost (2006, 1931); and Lyons (2007, 99).

17. More specifically, Ladin notes that "both the Bush and Obama administrations . . . sought to use claims of secrecy to completely shut down lawsuits by survivors of torture, claiming that even *considering* their claims would harm national security." This is why claims in the past have not been adjudicated in American courts. This could have changed recently with *Salim v. Mitchell* in March 2017. But an undisclosed settlement was reached, and the suit against psychologists who designed torture techniques for the government never went to trial. Dror Ladin, "In a First, the Trump Administration Moves to Invoke Secrecy Claims in Torture Lawsuit," *ACLU*, March 9, 2017, http://www.aclu.org/blog/national-security/torture/first -trump-administration-moves-invoke-secrecy-claims-torture/.

18. For the initial exposé of Zuley's book review on Amazon, see Ackerman (2015).

19. Masco (2014); Douglas and Zulaica (2010).

20. For more on Trump's pledge to "load [Guantánamo Bay] up with bad dudes," see Carlo Muñoz, "10 Years After Taking in Its Last Detainee, Gitmo Is Ready and Waiting for Trump's 'Bad Dudes,'" *Washington Times*, March 13, 2018, http:// wwww.washingtontimes.com /news /2018 /mar /13 /Guantanamo-bay-waits -donald-trumps-bad-dudes/.

CONCLUSION

1. *Wiggins v. Burge,* Sworn Statement of Marcus Wiggins (Chicago, IL, 1993).

2. Liliana Segura, "Families of the Victims Tortured by Chicago Detectives Rejoice at First Arrest," *AlterNet*, October 27, 2008, https://www.alternet.org/2008 /10/families_of_the_victims_tortured_by_chicago_detectives_rejoice_at_first _arrest/.

3. Sam Roberts, "Jon Burge, 70, Ex-Commander in Chicago Police Torture Cases, Dies," *New York Times*, September 21, 2018, B13.

4. On the systematic way misconduct spreads within the Chicago police force, see Rob Arthur's article in The Intercept, "Bad Chicago Cops Spread Their Misconduct Like a Disease," August 16, 2018: https://theintercept.com /2018/08/16 /chicago-police-misconduct-social-network/.

APPENDIX

1. Mike Thomas and Monifa Thomas, "28th Chicago Public School Student Killed this Year: Gregory Robinson, 14, Died Shielding Kids from Bullet," *Chicago Sun-Times*, May 25, 2011.

2. There are other approaches to letter writing in cultural anthropology, of course. Another lesser-known approach to letter writing that I do not explicitly address in this book is the tradition established by Margret Mead. In *Letters from the Field,*

1925–1975, Mead writes correspondences to friends and family about her time in conducting research in different countries. The many letters that span fifty years are largely a day-to-day account of her life in places she regards as "remote." So much so that the text as a whole takes on the feel of a travel book. My approach in this book differs from Mead's in that the letters I write are not meant to reinscribe the distinction between field and home. My work highlights the social production of the "field," as I seek to unsettle common conceptions of the role of the ethnographer and the practice of ethnography. See Mead (1977).

3. Garcia (2016).
4. See Dunbar-Ortiz (2014).
5. On the "unfinished" nature of ethnographic fieldwork, see Biehl and Locke (2017).
6. Ferguson (2002).
7. See Piot (1999, 43–44).
8. Middleton and Cons (2014).
9. Fortun (2009).
10. Barthes (1981); and Derrida (1987, 5).
11. Smith and Mwadime (2014). Smith and Mwadime's approach is just one prominent example of the anthropological examination of letter writing as a form of exchange. See also Parikh (2016).
12. Kemper and Peterson Royce (2002); and Rouch (2003).
13. Gupta and Ferguson (1997, 12, 16).
14. Bunzl (2004, 435–42).
15. Trouillot (1995).
16. Guest, Bunce, and Johnson (2006)
17. Harrison (1991).
18. Fischer (2018).

Bibliography

Alexander, Michelle. *The New Jim Crow: Mass Incarceration in the Age of Colorblindness*. New York: New Press, 2012.

American Civil Liberties Union. "Slahi v. Obama—Habeas Challenge to Guantánamo Detention." October 25, 2016. www.aclu.org/cases/slahi-v-obama-habeas-challenge-guantanamo-detention.

Balko, Radley. *Rise of the Warrior Cop: The Militarization of America's Police Forces*. New York: PublicAffairs, 2013.

Barthes, Roland. *Camera Lucida: Reflections on Photography*. Translated by Richard Howard. New York: Hill and Wang, 1981.

Bateson, Gregory. "Metalogue: What Is an Instinct?" *Readings in Zoosemiotics* 8 (2012): 313.

Biehl, João, and Peter Locke, eds. *Unfinished: The Anthropology of Becoming*. Durham, NC: Duke University Press, 2017.

Brodeur, Jean-Paul. *The Policing Web*. New York: Oxford University Press, 2010.

Bunzl, Matti. "Boas, Foucault, and the 'Native Anthropologist': Notes toward a Neo-Boasian Anthropology." *American Anthropologist* 106, no. 3 (2004): 435–42.

Canetti, Elias. *Crowds and Power*. New York: Macmillan, 1984.

Coates, Ta-Nehisi. *Between the World and Me*. New York: Spiegel & Grau, 2015.

Conroy, John. *Unspeakable Acts, Ordinary People: The Dynamics of Torture*. Berkeley: University of California Press, 2000.

Daly, Kathleen. "Restorative Justice: The Real Story." *Punishment & Society* 4, no. 1 (2002): 55–79.

Danner, Mark, and George R. Fay. *Torture and Truth: America, Abu Ghraib, and the War on Terror*. Vol. 2. New York: New York Review Books, 2004.

Davis, Angela Y., and Dylan Rodriguez. "The Challenge of Prison Abolition: A Conversation." *Social Justice* 27, no. 3 (2000): 212–18.

Derrida, Jacques. *The Post Card: From Socrates to Freud and Beyond.* Translated by Alan Bass. Chicago: University of Chicago Press, 1987.

Douglas, William, and J. Zulaica. *Terror and Taboo: The Follies, Fables and Faces of Terrorism.* New York: Routledge, 1996.

Dunbar-Ortiz, Roxanne. *An Indigenous Peoples' History of the United States.* Boston: Beacon Press, 2014.

Fassin, Didier, ed. *Writing the World of Policing.* Chicago: University of Chicago Press, 2017.

Ferguson, James G. "Of Mimicry and Membership: Africans and the 'New World Society.'" *Cultural Anthropology* 17, no. 4 (2002): 551–69.

Fischer, Michael. *Anthropology in the Meantime: Experimental Ethnography, Theory, and Method for the Twenty-First Century.* Durham, NC: Duke University Press, 2018.

Fisher, Tracy, and Ellen Reese. "The Punitive Turn in Social Policies: Critical Race Feminist Reflections on the USA, Great Britain, and Beyond." *Critical Sociology* 37, no. 2 (2011): 225–36.

Fortun, Kim. *Advocacy after Bhopal: Environmentalism, Disaster, New Global Orders.* Chicago: University of Chicago Press, 2009.

Frost, Amanda. "The State Secrets Privilege and Separation of Powers." *Fordham Law Review* 75 (2006): 1931.

Gallagher, Katherine. "Universal Jurisdiction in Practice: Efforts to Hold Donald Rumsfeld and Other High-Level United States Officials Accountable for Torture." *Journal of International Criminal Justice* 7, no. 5 (2009): 1087–1116.

Garcia, Angela. "The Blue Years: An Ethnography of a Prison Archive." *Cultural Anthropology* 31, no. 4 (2016): 571–94.

Geissler, P. Wenzel. "Public Secrets in Public Health: Knowing Not to Know While Making Scientific Knowledge." *American Ethnologist* 40, no. 1 (2013): 13–34.

Goyal, Yogita. "The Genres of Guantánamo Diary: Postcolonial Reading and the War on Terror." *Cambridge Journal of Postcolonial Literary Inquiry* 4, no. 1 (2017): 69–87.

Guest, Greg, Arwen Bunce, and Laura Johnson. "How Many Interviews Are Enough? An Experiment with Data Saturation and Variability." *Field Methods* 18, no. 1 (2006): 59–82.

Gusterson, Hugh. "The Cultural Turn in the War on Terror." *Anthropology and Global Counterinsurgency* (2010): 279–96.

Hamaji, Kate, Kumar Rao, Marbre Stahly-Butts, Janaé Bonsu, Charlene Carruthers, Roselyn Berry, and Denzel McCampbell. *Freedom to Thrive: Reimagining Safety & Security in Our Communities.* New York: Center for Popular Democracy, 2017.

Harrison, Faye. *Decolonizing Anthropology.* Washington, DC: American Anthropological Association, 1991.

Hinton, Elizabeth. *From the War on Poverty to the War on Crime.* Cambridge, MA: Harvard University Press, 2016.

Johnson, Douglas A., Alberto Mora, and Averell Schmidt. "The Strategic Costs of Torture: How Enhanced Interrogation Hurt America." *Foreign Affairs* 95 (2016): 121–32.

Jones v. City of Chicago. 856 F.3d 985 (7th Cir. 1988).

Jones, Graham M. "Secrecy." *Annual Review of Anthropology* 43 (2014): 53–69.

Kemper, Robert V., and Anya Peterson Royce, eds. *Chronicling Cultures: Long-Term Field Research in Anthropology.* New York: Rowman Altamira, 2002.

Kraska, Peter B. "Militarization and Policing—Its Relevance to 21st Century Police." *Policing: A Journal of Policy and Practice* 1, no. 4 (2007): 501–13.

Latour, Bruno. *Science in Action: How to Follow Scientists and Engineers through Society.* Cambridge, MA: Harvard University Press, 1987.

Lewis, Anthony. *The Torture Papers: The Road to Abu Ghraib.* Cambridge, MA: Cambridge University Press, 2005.

Linnemann, Travis, and Corina Medley. "Black Sites, 'Dark Sides': War Power, Police Power, and the Violence of the (Un)known." *Crime, Media, Culture* (2018): 1–18.

Lyons, Carrie Newton. "The State Secrets Privilege: Expanding Its Scope Through Government Misuse." *Lewis & Clark Law Review* 11 (2007): 99–132.

Masco, Joseph. *Theater of Operations: National Security Affect from the Cold War to the War on Terror.* Durham, NC: Duke University Press, 2014.

Mead, Margaret, and Ruth Nanda Anshen. *Letters from the Field, 1925–1975.* New York: Harper & Row, 1977.

Middleton, Townsend, and Jason Cons. "Fieldwork(ers): Research Assistants, Researchers, and the Production of Ethnographic Knowledge." *Ethnography* 15, no. 3 (2014): 279–90.

Mitchell, Koritha. *Living with Lynching: African American Lynching Plays, Performance, and Citizenship, 1890–1930.* Urbana: University of Illinois Press, 2011.

Mookherjee, Nayanika. "'Remembering to Forget': Public Secrecy and Memory of Sexual Violence in the Bangladesh War of 1971." *Journal of the Royal Anthropological Institute* 12, no. 2 (2006): 433–50.

Moore, Alexandra Schultheis. "Teaching Mohamedou Ould Slahi's Guantánamo Diary in the Human Rights and Literature Classroom." *Radical Teacher* 104 (2016): 27–37.

Muhammad, Khalil Gibran. *The Condemnation of Blackness.* Cambridge, MA: Harvard University Press, 2011.

Nixon, Rob. *Slow Violence and the Environmentalism of the Poor.* Cambridge, MA: Harvard University Press, 2011.

Parikh, Shanti. *Regulating Romance: Youth Love Letters, Moral Anxiety, and Intervention in Uganda's Time of AIDS.* Nashville, TN: Vanderbilt University Press, 2015.

Penglase, Ben. "States of Insecurity: Everyday Emergencies, Public Secrets, and Drug Trafficker Power in a Brazilian Favela." *PoLAR: Political and Legal Anthropology Review* 32, no. 1 (2009): 47–63.

People v. Hobley. 637 N.E.2d 992 (Ill. 1994).

Piot, Charles. *Remotely Global: Village Modernity in West Africa*. Chicago: University of Chicago Press, 1999.

Povinelli, Elizabeth A. "The Woman on the Other Side of the Wall: Archiving the Otherwise in Postcolonial Digital Archives." *Differences* 22, no. 1 (2014): 146–71.

Puar, Jasbir K. *The Right to Maim: Debility, Capacity, Disability*. Durham, NC: Duke University Press, 2017.

Rahr, S., Rice, Stephen K., and John F. Kennedy School of Government. *From Warriors to Guardians: Recommitting American Police Culture to Democratic Ideals*. Washington, DC: US Department of Justice, Office of Justice Programs, National Institute of Justice, 2015.

Ralph, Laurence. Becoming Aggrieved: An Alternative Framework of Care in Black Chicago. *RSF: The Russell Sage Foundation Journal of the Social Sciences* 1, no. 2 (2015): 31–41.

Rasmussen, Maria. *Ronald Crelinsten: Counterterrorism*. Cambridge, UK: Polity Press, 2009.

Rouch, Jean. *Ciné Ethnography*. Vol. 13. Minneapolis: University of Minnesota Press, 2003.

Roy, Srila. "The Grey Zone: The 'Ordinary' Violence of Extraordinary Times." *Journal of the Royal Anthropological Institute* 14, no. 2 (2008): 316–33.

Sánchez-Eppler, Karen. *Touching Liberty: Abolition, Feminism, and the Politics of the Body*. Berkeley: University of California Press, 1993.

Sanders, Francine. *Special Projective Investigative Summary Report*. Chicago: Office of Professional Standards, 1990.

Schulberg, Jessica. "U.S. Violates U.N. Convention against Torture Signed 20 Years Ago." *New Republic*, October 21, 2014.

Segura, Liliana. "Families of the Victims Tortured by Chicago Detectives Rejoice at First Arrest." *Alternet*, October 26, 2008.

Seigel, Micol. "The Dilemma of 'Racial Profiling': An Abolitionist Police History." *Contemporary Justice Review* 20, no. 4 (2017): 474–90.

Sidanius, Jim, and Felicia Pratto. *Social Dominance: An Intergroup Theory of Social Hierarchy and Oppression*. Cambridge: Cambridge University Press, 2001.

Simmel, Georg. 1950. *The Sociology of Georg Simmel*. Translated and edited by K. Wolff. London: Free Press.

Simpson, Audra. "On Ethnographic Refusal: Indigeneity, 'Voice' and Colonial Citizenship." *Junctures: The Journal for Thematic Dialogue* 9 (2007): 67–80.

Slahi, Mohamedou Ould. *Guantánamo Diary*. New York: Little, Brown, 2015.

Smeulers, Alette, and Sander Van Niekerk. "Abu Ghraib and the War on Terror—A Case against Donald Rumsfeld?" *Crime, Law and Social Change* 51, nos. 3–4 (2009): 327–49.

Smith, Christen A. "Facing the Dragon: Black Mothering, Sequelae, and Gendered Necropolitics in the Americas." *Transforming Anthropology* 24, no. 1 (2016): 31–48.

Smith, James H., and Ngeti Mwadime. *Email from Ngeti*. Berkeley: University of California Press, 2014.

Spillers, Hortense J. "Mama's Baby, Papa's Maybe: An American Grammar Book." *Diacritics* 17, no. 2 (1987): 65–81.

Statement of Doris Byrd on November 9, 2004. *Patterson v. Burge*, 328 F. Supp. 2d 878 (N.D. Ill. 2004) (No. 03 C 4433).

Statement of Sammy Lacey on October 12, 2004. *Patterson v. Burge*, 328 F. Supp. 2d 878 (N.D. Ill. 2004) (No. 03 C 4433).

Statement of William Parker on October 12, 2004. *Patterson v. Burge*, 328 F. Supp. 2d 878 (N.D. Ill. 2004) (No. 03 C 4433).

State of Illinois v. Andrew and Jackie Wilson. Indictment No. 82-1211. Charge: Murder, etc. (November 12, 1982). In *United States v. Burge*. No. 08 CR 846 (Ill. 2011).

Taussig, Michael T. *Defacement: Public Secrecy and the Labor of the Negative*. Stanford, CA: Stanford University Press, 1999.

Taylor, Flint. *The Torture Machine: Racism and Police Violence in Chicago*. Chicago, IL: Haymarket Books, 2019.

Theidon, Kimberly. "The Mask and the Mirror: Facing Up to the Past in Postwar Peru." *Anthropologica* (2006): 87–100.

Thomas, Deborah A. "Public Secrets, Militarization, and the Cultivation of Doubt: Kingston 2010." In *Caribbean Military Encounters*, edited by Shalini Puri and Lara Putnam, 289–309. New York: Palgrave Macmillan, 2017.

Thompson, E. P. *The Making of the English Working Class*. New York: Vantage, 1966.

Trapp, Erin. "Redacted Tears, Aesthetics of Alterity: Mohamedou Ould Slahi's Guantánamo Diary." In *Terror in Global Narrative*, edited by George Fragopoulous and Liliana Naydan, 55–76. Cham, Switzerland: Palgrave Macmillan, 2016.

Trouillot, Michel-Rolph. *Silencing the Past: Power and the Production of History*. Boston: Beacon Press, 1995.

Van Cleve, Nicole Gonzalez. *Crook County: Racism and Injustice in America's Largest Criminal Court*. Stanford, CA: Stanford University Press, 2016.

Wiggins v. Burge. 173 F.R.D. 226 (N.D. Ill. 1997).

Zagel, James. "The State Secrets Privilege." *Minnesota Law Review* 50 (1965): 875–910.

Index